PUBLIC SECTOR RECORDS MANAGEMENT

For Nicola, Jennifer and Karen

PUBLIC SECTOR RECORDS MANAGEMENT

A Practical Guide

Kelvin Smith

ASHGATE

Published by
Ashgate Publishing Limited
Gower House
Croft Road
Aldershot
Hants GU11 3HR
England

Ashgate Publishing Company
Suite 420
101 Cherry Street
Burlington, VT 05401-4405
USA

Ashgate website: http://www.ashgate.com

British Library Cataloguing in Publication Data
Smith, Kelvin (Kelvin John)
   Public sector records management : a practical guide
   1. Public records – Management
   I. Title
   352.3'87

Library of Congress Cataloging-in-Publication Data
Smith, Kelvin (Kelvin John)
   Public sector records management : a practical guide by Kelvin Smith.
      p. cm.
   Includes bibliographical references and index.
  1. Public records--Handbooks, manuals, etc. 2. Records--Management--Handbooks, manuals, etc. I. Title.
   JF1521.S44 2007
   352.3'87--dc22

ISBN: 978-0-7546-4987-8

2007014531

Typeset by IML Typographers, Birkenhead, Merseyside.
Printed and bound in Great Britain by MPG Books Ltd, Bodmin, Cornwall.

Contents

Acknowledgements

I have spent all my working life in records management and archives administration. I have enjoyed (almost!) every minute of it but that would not have been possible without the help and support of so many people. In many ways this book is an acknowledgement of that support, particularly from The National Archives and its staff over the past forty years.

In putting the following chapters together I have called upon much of the work that I have undertaken over the past few years as part of my official duties. I am grateful to The National Archives for their permission to take my work forward into this book. In addition I have been able to develop many of the ideas in practical situations through working with some excellent organisations – not least Liverpool University Centre for Archive Studies (superbly run by Caroline Williams and Margaret Procter), the International Records Management Trust (driven by the indefatigable Dr Anne Thurston), and the Records Management Society, whose large membership has regularly been a source of lively debate. My thanks to them all.

I am grateful to the following organisations for permission to use relevant documents:

- University of Newcastle upon Tyne – Survey questionnaire.
- Office of Government Commerce – PRINCE 2 methodology.
- Bedfordshire and Luton Records and Archives Services – collection policy.
- Norfolk Record Office – archive collecting policy.
- Westway Development Trust – file plan.

Kelvin Smith
Thame
March 2007

Introduction

Records management is a subject that has become more interesting over the last few years. It has always been an asset for efficient and effective business and it may seem strange that this highly significant driver of business efficiency has received so little attention over the years. Organisations, however, concentrated on their core functions and were reluctant to commit scarce resources to what was viewed as a support function. From 1997 a significant driver in the United Kingdom in the shape of proposed Freedom of Information legislation brought records management sharply into focus. This was soon joined by another important driver, initially in the government sector but soon to spread further – electronic business and the need to manage electronic records effectively.

AIMS

The aim of this book is for it to be *practical*. It is intended for people who know little or nothing about the subject, or who have read the theory and now want to know how to put it into practice. While recognising different theories, it does not dwell on the academic arguments but puts forward basic principles and procedures, drawing on best practice from many sources. There seems little point in dwelling on 'what is a record?', 'what is the difference between records management and archives administration?' and similar questions. If you accept the aim stated here, this should not worry you. You know the answers to such questions and will want to get on and undertake records management.

There is also an attempt to include an international flavour to the book, particularly bearing in mind the countries of the Commonwealth, which are familiar with British official practices and procedures. The effective management of records and archives throughout their life cycle is a key component of national development. Unorganised or poorly managed records mean that government does not have ready access to authoritative sources of administrative, financial and legal information to support sound decision making or the delivery of programmes and services. Nor does it have the means of holding itself accountable for what it does or upholding the rights of its citizens.

FRAMEWORK

It will come as no surprise that the framework that follows is based very much on the information life cycle. After some basic discussion of *The records management function* and *Compliance and regulation* (chapters 1 and 2) it follows the pattern of *Record creation and classification, Records maintenance, Records appraisal* and *Archiving* (chapters 3 to 6). The next three chapters (7 to 9) examine some of the underpinning issues – *Access to records, Roles and responsibilities* and *Training and development*. It finishes with some suggestions for *Developing an integrated programme* for developing records management in your organisation (chapter 10).

BACKGROUND

Much of the guidance and advice that follows has its origins in The National Archives (where the author has spent all his working life). Nearly all of this is aimed at central government but it nonetheless has great significance and relevance to other parts of the public sector.

It should always be remembered that the main driver for good records management is business efficiency. In this respect the international standard ISO 15489 is a most important document. It was developed in response to a consensus within the international records management community to standardise international best practice using the Australian Standard AS 4390, Records management, as its starting point. It focuses particularly on the business asset that records provide to an organisation and emphasises that a good records management system will result in a source of information about business activities that can support subsequent activities and business decisions and can ensure accountability to stakeholders.

Another crucial and pivotal document for records management in the United Kingdom is the Lord Chancellor's Code of Practice on the Management of Records under section 46 of the Freedom of Information Act 2000. See Appendix 1 for a full copy. This is referred to at several points in the text and is itself written in the context of the information life cycle. Shortly after the Code was published (November 2002), model action plans were developed on behalf of UK public authorities. Experience with the development of these model action plans has formed the basis of much of what follows. The framework of the chapters is closely aligned to the nine steps that are advocated by the action plans. It seems worthwhile, therefore, to describe each of those steps.

1 THE RECORDS MANAGEMENT FUNCTION

Records management should be a function that is recognised as a specific corporate programme. It should have clearly defined responsibilities and objectives, and have the organisational support to ensure effectiveness. It ought to be on the same level as other generic functions – such as finance, human resources, health and safety, etc. A champion at Board level should oversee the function, ensuring top-level support and encouragement.

2 ROLES AND RESPONSIBILITIES OF RECORDS MANAGERS

An organisation should appoint a member of staff of appropriate seniority to have lead responsibility for records management – for all records of the authority (in whatever format) from the moment that they are created to their ultimate disposal (whether by destruction or permanent transfer to an archive). The person must have enough authority to be able to ensure implementation of accepted records management policies and procedures.

3 RECORDS MANAGEMENT POLICY STATEMENT

Organisations should have in place a records management policy statement that is endorsed by top management and made known to all staff. It is the manifestation of the authority's commitment to records management and a mandate for all related actions. It should be a clear and concise statement, able to be read and easily understood by everyone in the organisation.

4 TRAINING AND AWARENESS

Staff directly engaged in the records management function should receive the appropriate training. All other staff should be aware of their record keeping responsibilities. The immediacy of freedom of information legislation means that staff at the records creation stage have to be careful with their filing and be more aware of file plans, retrieval and disposal, and all those other records management functions that are likely to affect the handling of requests for information.

5 RECORDS CREATION AND MANAGEMENT

Organisations should have in place an adequate system for documenting their activities – otherwise known as a records classification scheme or file referencing system or file plan. Their records should be part of a standard, authority-wide system so that everyone in the organisation can find what information they need, when they need it, and if there are regular staff movements, individuals do not have to learn a different system.

6 RECORD MAINTENANCE

Storage accommodation for the records – active and closed – should be clean and tidy and handling procedures should be in place that will minimise damage to the records.

7 RECORD DISPOSAL

When information is no longer required, its destruction should be documented. This will enable organisations to meet any requests regarding information that has been so dealt with – to assure the public that official information is being destroyed in accordance with proper procedure and practice. The most effective method of documentation is by the use of disposal schedules.

8 ACCESS

A more accurate description of this step might be 'Tracking' – freedom of information requests have to be logged and tracked. This has three main purposes: 1) giving the organisation the required information to handle appeals against non-disclosure; 2) monitoring the twenty working day deadline (in the UK Freedom of Information Act); and 3) promoting consistency across particular parts of the public sector.

9 PERFORMANCE MEASUREMENT

The last step in developing good record keeping is to ensure that, when a records management system is in place, it is operating effectively. The system's performance should be monitored, or measured. A series of performance indicators ought to be agreed between the records manager and business managers to enable this to be done.

I hope you find this book useful. Its intention is to be very practical and it is aimed at those in public sectors (in the United Kingdom as well as other countries) who want to get on and undertake records management. It is also for those who have records management problems and want to do something about them.

1 The records management function

AIMS

This chapter takes an overall look at the function of records management. It examines its organisational context and the key principles such as the life-cycle concept and policy development.

Inevitably, we have to start with a little theory...

RECORDS AND INFORMATION

There have been many debates – academic and otherwise – on the definition of a record, and on how records differ from information and knowledge. For you, the practitioner, the most important distinction is probably between documents and records. The difference between these two is a matter of context. A document can stand alone; it does not depend on other relationships; it can be identified and interpreted without having to see it in the context of its relationship with other documents. Thus, documents are records without context and records are documents with context.

Records are essential to the business of all organisations. They document the work of public authorities and private companies, support their operations and form the basis for the many services that are provided by them. They are essential to effective operations in several respects:

- *Supporting the delivery of services* – you will want to document how policies and statutes are carried out, what services were provided, who carried out the work and how much it cost, and, in the longer term, your organisation's accomplishments.
- *Supporting administration* – by providing information for the direction, control, decision-making and coordination of business.

1

- *Documenting rights and responsibilities* – your organisation needs to provide evidence of the scope of its terms of reference, evidence of what it owns and evidence of its obligations. Records are important also in documenting the rights of corporate bodies and individuals in matters such as ownership, legacy, etc.
- *Legal documentation* – many records comprise formal legal documents – regulations, local orders, etc. – or formal documentation of the relationship between governments and people or institutions. They may, in this respect, be used in legal undertakings or be required for evidence in a court of law.
- *Evidence of the work of public authorities* – your organisation needs to document the decisions, actions and obligations that it undertakes, and in this way provide accountability measures.
- *Future research* – some of the records your organisation creates and uses will be preserved and will form the contents of archival establishments, providing important historical information on political, social, economic and other issues.

Records are therefore created or received in the conduct of business activities and provide evidence and information about those activities. They come in all kinds of format and media. A formal definition of a record might be:

> Recorded information produced or received in the initiation, conduct or deletion of an institutional or individual activity, and which comprises sufficient content, context and structure to provide evidence of an activity, regardless of the form or medium.[1]

In the United Kingdom central government all departments and agencies are moving quickly towards the creation, storage, maintenance and retrieval of their records and information solely in electronic form. Paper files and folders are becoming increasingly rare in these organisations. In other areas of the UK public sector, however, while many records are created electronically they are maintained in paper form – often filed systematically but just as often managed in personal systems. Records may also be created on media other than paper or electronic – microfilm, microfiche or computer output microform (COM); or as photographs (prints, negatives, transparencies and x-ray films), sound recordings on disk or tape or moving images on film or video. In some cases records might be in the form of three-dimensional models, scientific specimens or other objects. A set of records, in context, may be in more than one of these formats or there may be close organisational relationships between records in different formats.

---

[1] International Council on Archives, 1997.

THE MANAGEMENT OF RECORDS

Records management provides a framework that aims to ensure that:

- *The record is present* – your organisation should ensure that it has the information that is needed so that it can reconstruct activities or transactions that have taken place. This ensures that the organisation is accountable to its stakeholders (whether they are citizens, parliament or shareholders).
- *The record can be accessed* – the people in your organisation must be able to locate information when required. This is vital in areas where there is freedom of information legislation but just as important to support the efficient operation of the organisation's business.
- *The record can be interpreted* – if required, your organisation must be able to establish a record's context, who created it, as part of which business process and how it relates to other records. This is a vital part of the organisation's accountability and transparency.
- *The record can be trusted* – when you and your colleagues are consulting a record, you need to be assured that it reliably represents the information that was actually used in or created by the business process, and its integrity and authenticity can be demonstrated. Records provide the 'official' evidence of the activity or transaction they document and must therefore be reliable and trustworthy. The reliability of a record is linked to its creation. Who generated or issued the record and under what authority? Can this authority be proved? Not all records have official stamps or seals. The continuous safekeeping of records will also protect their reliability. For example, if the official version of the minutes of a meeting is filed by the records manager and thus protected from change, the unauthorised version will not form part of the official record. This issue of reliability is especially important in the context of electronic records and information.
- *The record can be maintained through time* – your organisation will need to ensure that the qualities of accessibility, interpretation and trustworthiness can be maintained for as long as the record is needed. During its creation a record will develop and change. For example, minutes of a meeting will be produced in draft form and reviewed by the members of the committee before being approved. Once this process of creation is finished the record must be fixed and must not be susceptible to change. If a record is changed or manipulated in some way, it no longer provides evidence of the transaction it originally documented. For example, if someone alters the minutes of a meeting after they have been approved, the minutes can no longer be considered an accurate record of the meeting. This is another issue that becomes more important in an electronic context.

3

● *The record will be disposed of* as part of a planned system, through the implementation of disposal schedules to ensure the retention of the minimum volume of records consistent with effective and efficient operations. Is your organisation keeping more records than it needs? This is the case in very many organisations. The information that does not need to be kept – let's call it rubbish – gets in the way of the important information.

The following principles underpin the management of records.

RECORDS ARE A CORPORATE RESOURCE

Records form part of the corporate memory of an organisation and are a valuable corporate resource. From the point at which a document is created as a record and used in the course of official business, it becomes corporately owned. The records you and your colleagues create and use don't belong to you – they belong to the organisation. They are not kept in your or their filing cabinets or on your computers – they are kept in the organisation's filing cabinet or on the organisation's computer. These cabinets and computers are not even in your or your colleagues' offices – they are in the organisation's office.

ELECTRONIC RECORDS

Electronic records that are generated by or received in an organisation in the course of its business are in this context no different from any other records – they are official, corporate records. Although most current practice is still to print electronic information to paper, your organisations should be making plans to maintain their electronic information as electronic records. In the United Kingdom, policies on modernising government mean that public records must be stored and retrieved in electronic form and their structure must enable that to happen. In any event records should be organised in a way that is able to meet anticipated future business and archival needs, and be reliably and consistently grouped regardless of media.

RECORD KEEPING SHOULD BE INTEGRATED WITH BUSINESS PROCESSES

Records management and archive administration must be built into systems for creating records, to ensure that they are capable of capturing records with all the necessary contextual information. This is vital because you will need to refer to them in the medium, and sometimes longer, term – and this will be regardless of whether they are in paper, electronic or any other form.

RECORDS SHOULD BE RELIABLE, AUTHENTIC AND COMPLETE

Records should be able to function as evidence of business activities and processes through sound record keeping practices. In order to be reliable and authentic they must adequately capture and describe the actions they represent and once created must not be altered without creating a new record. To be considered complete the record should preserve not only content but also the context in which it was created and used, and links to other records.

RECORDS SHOULD BE ACCESSIBLE

Record keeping systems should aim to make records available quickly and easily to all staff and to others who are entitled to access or information from them. Information is the life blood of any organisation; yours or any other cannot hope to function effectively without it.

RESPONSIBILITY FOR CAPTURING, MAINTAINING AND ENSURING ACCESS TO RECORDS RESTS WITH THE ORGANISATION AS A WHOLE

Responsibility for the capture and maintenance of records rests with everyone in the organisation, and all staff should ensure that they are familiar with and are adhering to the records management policy and any procedures and guidelines that are issued through it. Good record keeping is not just the province of the records manager – it's everyone's responsibility.

THE ORGANISATIONAL CONTEXT

There are two essential elements to the function of records management:

- it covers records in all formats (paper, electronic, oral, film, microform, etc);
- it covers records from the moment that they are created until their disposal (either by destruction or preservation in an archive).

Records management is a corporate function in a similar way to human resources, finance and estates management. It should be recognised as a specific corporate programme within an organisation and it should receive the necessary levels of organisational support to ensure effectiveness. The function needs to bring together responsibilities for records in all formats from their creation to their ultimate disposal. All organisations produce records but many do not have a designated records manager with prime responsibility for ensuring an effective and efficient approach to managing records and information across the organisation.

The person or persons responsible for the records management function in your organisation should also have responsibility for, or close organisational connection with, the person or persons responsible for other information management issues, such as freedom of information, and privacy/data protection. This organisational connection should also be extended towards information and communication technology (ICT) units. For example, in the design of information management systems – from simple databases to electronic records management file plans – both the records management and ICT professionals have important roles to play. Such cooperation will ensure a coordinated and consistent progress towards the implementation of effective records and information management systems that accord with legislation and business practices, and will ensure that the best use is made of the latest technology. The person with responsibility for records management should be someone of appropriate seniority, someone who knows the organisation well and can promote and implement the functional requirements. Everyone in your organisation should know who the records manager is. The role needs to be formally acknowledged and made known throughout the organisation – from top to bottom.

The precise location of the records management function in an organisation's hierarchy is largely a matter for local determination. The important thing is that it is recognised as a corporate function.

In this context management studies have provided numerous models for organisations. Among the most common are:

- functional
- divisional
- centralised services.

FUNCTIONAL

The functional structure is arranged according to the key functions of the organisation. Each function is represented by a department that has its own manager who reports to the head of the organisation.

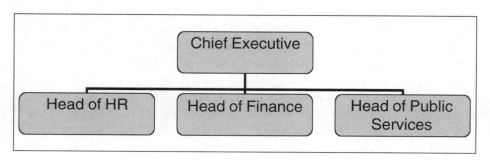

DIVISIONAL

In a divisional structure the business units are arranged, for example, according to geographical areas. The range of functions is then provided within each area.

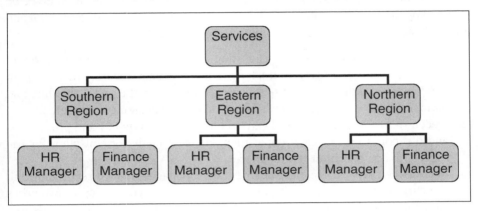

CENTRALISED SERVICES

The centralised services structure revolves round a unit that brings together all the specialised services that other business units will need.

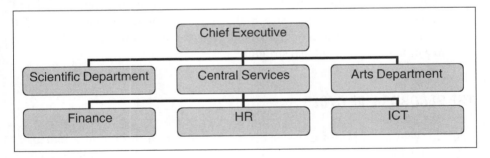

Where would the records management function fit into such organisations?

You could argue:

Functional	a separate department on a par with HR, Finance, etc.
Divisional	regional records managers reporting to a member of the management board
Centralised services	a unit under central services on a par with Finance, HR, etc.

There is no real optimum placement for all types of organisations but it is essential that the function is recognised as being a key process in the operation of the organisation.

The structure of the records management function itself will, of course, be affected by the overall organisational structure, by the size of the organisation and by available resources. The most common structures are:

- Centralised system – where allocation of files/folders, administration of systems, storage, retrieval, tracking and all other records management services are controlled from one point or unit (over the years this has had various names – registry, records office, records management unit, etc.).
- Decentralised system – a small central unit developing policy and procedures and a records unit in each department/division of the organisation for the records and information created there.
- Records centre – where each business unit manages its own records during the current and immediate (semi-current) phases – typically up to two years after the record has finished its active life – and then sends the records to a central store which can be in-house or external.
- Consultancy – where an internal consultant works on projects, developing policy and facilitating and monitoring records management across the organisation.

Each of these models has strengths and weaknesses that are usually only evident when taking into account the size and complexity of the organisation. The important thing is that the model adopted can operate an effective and efficient system within the organisational structure.

THE RECORDS LIFE CYCLE

The life-cycle concept of the record is an analogy from the life of a biological organism, which is born, lives and dies. In the same way, a record is created, is used for so long as it has continuing value and is then disposed of by destruction or by transfer to an archival institution.

The effective management of records throughout their life cycle is a key issue. For example, without a management programme that controls records through the earlier phases of their life cycle, those of archival value cannot readily be identified and safeguarded so that they can take their place in due course as part of the nation's historical and cultural heritage.

In the simplest version of the life-cycle concept (particularly applicable to paper records), three biological ages are seen as the equivalents of the three phases of the life of a record:

THE LIFE CYCLE CONCEPT

- Current – records are regularly used in the conduct of current business and are maintained in their place of origin or in the file store of an associated records office.
- Semi-current – records are still used, but only infrequently, in the conduct of current business and are maintained in a records centre.
- Non-current – records are no longer used for the conduct of current business and are therefore destroyed unless they have a continuing value for other purposes, which, for example, may merit their preservation as archives in an archival institution.

This concept of the life cycle has been seen to be difficult to apply to electronic records. It is true to say that the boundaries between the three phases become very blurred in an electronic context. For example, electronic records that may still have use in the conduct of current business may need to be captured for preservation because the systems on which they were created and maintained are being replaced.

It has also been said that the life cycle concept perpetuates the division of responsibility between records managers and archivists which is untenable in the modern era of record keeping.

In order to overcome these two criticisms a concept of the record continuum has been formulated in recent years.

9

THE RECORD CONTINUUM CONCEPT

The continuum concept defines a consistent and coherent process of records management throughout the life of records, from the development of record keeping systems through the creation and preservation of records to their retention and use as archives. It suggests that four actions continue or recur throughout the life of a record:

- identification
- intellectual control
- provision of access
- physical control.

According to the continuum concept, the distinction between records management and archives management need not be rigidly maintained. The four actions identified can apply at different phases, for example:

Process	Records management actions	Archives management actions
identification	creation of receipt	selection or acquisition
intellectual control	classification within a logical system	arrangement and description
provision of access	maintenance and use	reference and use
physical control	disposal by destruction or transfer as archives	preservation

From this principle a unified model has been developed. The model reflects the pattern of a continuum. Four actions continue throughout the life of a record and cut across the traditional boundary between records management and archival administration. These are:

- the creation or acquisition of the record;
- its placement within a logical, documented system that governs its arrangement and facilitates its retrieval throughout its life;
- its appraisal for continuing value, recorded in a disposal schedule and given effect at the due time by appropriate disposal action;
- its maintenance and use, that is, whether it is maintained in the creating office, a records office, a records centre or an archival repository, and whether the use is by its creator or a successor in function or by a third party, such as a researcher or other member of the public.

RECORDS MANAGEMENT POLICY STATEMENT

A key document in establishing an effective records management system in your organisation is the policy statement. In public authorities in the United Kingdom it has been common practice to draw up such a policy since the introduction of a *Code of Practice on the Management of Records under the Freedom of Information Act 2000*. Many organisations had policies before but often they were informal and, in some cases, not written down. A written statement has the advantage of providing a document that enables everyone in your organisation to be aware of what the corporate policy is in this area and thus eliminates some uncertainty. It also provides an authoritative statement on the management of records and ensures that business information is managed effectively throughout the organisation. The aim of the statement should be to provide a record keeping system that will:

- meet the organisation's business needs;
- address the needs of the organisation's stakeholders;
- conform to relevant legislation, regulations and standards;
- provide a basis for accountability;
- identify responsibilities for records and information, in particular the role of the Records Manager.

The statement should provide the framework for supporting standards and guidance, and cover all aspects of records management, in particular:

- An organisation's commitment to create, keep and manage records which document its principal activities.
- The role of records management and its relationship to the organisation's overall strategy.
- The responsibility of individuals to document their actions and decisions.
- The disposal of records and information.
- An indication of the way in which compliance with the policy and its supporting standards and guidance will be monitored.

Policy statements are best kept short. About two sides of an A4 sheet of paper – certainly no more than three sides – are best. Many people will not have time to read more than this so it is vital to get important points across quickly and clearly.

11

Scope

1   This policy provides for:

- The requirements that must be met for the records of xx organisation to be considered as a proper record of the activity of the organisation.
- The requirements for systems and processes that deal with records.
- The quality and reliability that must be maintained to provide a valuable information and knowledge resource for the organisation.
- Review of the policy and checking the quality of implementation.
- An overall statement of records management policy that is supplemented by detailed procedures.

It covers records in all formats, created in the course of xx's business, including non-conventional records.

Statement

2   Information is a corporate asset and the records of xx are important sources of administrative, fiscal, legal, evidential and historical information. They are vital to the organisation in its current and future operations, for the purposes of accountability, and for an awareness and understanding of its history. They are the corporate memory of the organisation.

3   In consultation with organisations that may be concerned with the management of its records, xx will create, use, manage and destroy or preserve its records in accordance with all statutory requirements.

4   Systematic records management is fundamental to organisational efficiency. It ensures that the right information is:

- captured, stored, retrieved and destroyed or preserved according to need;
- fully exploited to meet current and future needs, and to support change;
- accessible to those who need to make use of it;

and that the appropriate technical, organisational and human resource elements exist to make this possible.

5   All staff of xx who create, use, manage or dispose of records have a duty to protect them and to ensure that any information that they add to the record is

accurate, complete and necessary. All staff involved in managing records will receive the necessary training.

6   The records management policy is a specific part of the organisation's overall corporate programme and relates to other policies, such as:

- following best practice in specific areas
- the organisation's e-government strategy
- Data Protection
- Freedom of Information.

Accountability

7   The *Chief Executive* has a duty to ensure that xx complies with the requirements of legislation affecting management of the records, and with supporting regulations and codes.

8   The *Records Manager* will work closely with Heads of Departments to ensure that there is consistency in the management of records and that advice and guidance on good records management practice is provided.

9   *Managerial and professional staff* are responsible for ensuring that records and information systems in their areas conform to this policy and to the requirements of legislation. *All members of staff* are responsible for documenting their actions and decisions in the records and for maintaining the records in accordance with good records management practice.

Monitoring Compliance

10   xx will follow this policy within all relevant procedures and guidance used for operational activities. Interpretation of the policy will be monitored and there will be regular planned inspections by Quality Services staff and Internal Auditors to assess how the policy is being put into practice. These inspections will seek to:

- identify areas of good practice that can be used throughout the organisation;
- highlight where non-conformance to the procedures is occurring;
- if appropriate, recommend a tightening of controls and make recommendations as to how compliance can be achieved.

Figure 1.1   Model statement

13

2 Compliance and regulation

AIMS

This chapter briefly examines some key aspects relating to the development of modern records and archives legislation. It also describes the current legislative position in the United Kingdom, including related acts, regulations and codes of practice, and briefly examines the role of standards. While it departs slightly from the avowed objective of this book (practicality) the points it raises are relevant to the implementation of records management strategies and systems.

INTRODUCTION

Developing new legislation in our profession has changed fundamentally over the past twenty years or so. Many enactments in the last century have focussed on archives. The management of current and semi-current records was hardly considered until the 1980s, the time at which the use of computers was increasing dramatically and when the creation, use and management of information quickly became a matter of interest to more and more people. It is taken for granted now that new legislation must include records management as well as archive administration.

The basis of all records management authority is comprehensive and up-to-date legislation. Records legislation must ensure complete protection for all public sector records, in whatever format, and provide the governing organisation (be it the National Archives or other body) with comprehensive authority for securing and protecting records.

Unlike many other countries, the United Kingdom does not have a national archives act nor does it have a code of archives or records legislation. There are a number of separate measures which include:

- Central government records
- Local government records
- Records of ecclesiastical authorities
- Records of Scotland
- Records of Northern Ireland.

UK records legislation has two significant characteristics, not always followed by other countries' enactments – it is permissive rather than mandatory and it has no sanctions. In addition none of the legislation contains a general definition of the terms 'records' or 'archives'. These are usually defined in terms of their origin, such as public records and local authority records.

KEY DEFINITIONS

Any records legislation must define precisely all relevant terminology, including 'records', 'public records', 'archives' and 'National Archives'. The definitions must cover records in all media and formats, and records from all sources covered by the legislation (central government, local government, agencies, etc). The following table gives a list of those definitions likely to feature in records legislation:

Table 2.1 Definitions of terms

Term	Definition
Advisory Board	National Records and Archives Advisory Board – a board, comprising prominent people in the records and archives profession, to advise the Minister responsible for the legislation on a specified area of the legislative provisions
Archival repository	A building or part of a building in which archives are preserved and made available for consultation
Archives	Records of enduring value selected for permanent preservation
Current records	Records regularly used for the conduct of the current business of an institution or individual
Department	The National Records and Archives Department – depending on the structure decided upon. The body responsible may be a Department within a Ministry, a Ministry itself, or a separate agency (such as The National Archives)
Director	The Director of the National Records and Archives Department – depending on the term used for the person with executive responsibility for the body responsible for records and archives (other titles used include 'Keeper of Public Records', 'Chief Government Archivist', 'National Archivist'

Disposal schedule	*see* Retention and disposal schedule
Government office	Any institution, body or individual that creates, receives or maintains public records
Heads of government offices	Ministers or other persons responsible for directing government offices
Minister	The Minister for the time being responsible for public records
National Archives	The archival repository in which archives of the central institutions of the [country] are preserved and made available for consultation
Place of Deposit	An archival repository appointed to hold records selected for permanent preservation. Such a place is in addition to the national repository and is usually appointed to make archives more accessible to researchers (either specialist or local)
Private records	Records other than public records – usually specified in a schedule to the legislation
Public records	Records created or held in central government departments of state – as (usually) specified in a schedule to the legislation
Records	Recorded information regardless of form or medium created, received and maintained by any institution or individual in the pursuance of its legal obligations or in the transaction of its business and providing evidence of the performance of those obligations or that business
Records centre	A building designated for the low-cost storage, maintenance and communication of semi-current records pending their eventual disposal
Retention and disposal schedule	A document describing the recurring records of an institution or an administrative unit thereof, specifying which records should be preserved permanently as having enduring value as archives and authorising on a continuing basis and after the lapse of specified retention periods or the occurrence of specified actions or events, the disposal by destruction or other means of the remaining records
Semi-current records	Records required only infrequently for the conduct of current business; for the purposes of the legislation files and other assemblies of records on which no action has been recorded for five years are usually regarded as semi-current records

RESPONSIBILITY FOR RECORDS

In some countries you may see the national archival institution primarily as a cultural institution and responsible to the Minister of Culture or equivalent; in others it may be part of central services such as a Ministry of Public Service; and in others it may be part of the judicial hierarchy, responsible to a Minister of Justice or equivalent. In very few cases is the National Archives a separate body with its own government minister. However, the centrality and significance of the care of public records to sound administration throughout government, and the security implications of that work, make it imperative that ultimate responsibility should rest with the highest authority. This is increasingly the case as the public service relies more and more on the creation, maintenance and retrieval of information electronically. Records professionals need to be at the forefront of information creation and thus the development of information management strategies.

Ideally, the records and archives institution should be made responsible specifically to whoever plays the central governing role within the country, such as the president or prime minister. If this is not possible, the most appropriate minister should be responsible, such as the minister responsible for the civil service in that jurisdiction. Wherever the responsibility may lie, the records and archives function needs high level support as it enters the twenty first century. Our work is becoming increasingly important as information is demanded more quickly and more efficiently.

CARE OF LOCAL GOVERNMENT RECORDS

Ideally, records and archives legislation should also include the records of regions and districts (or their equivalents) by extending the responsibilities for public records to heads of local public offices and by establishing a structure of branch offices for the records and archives institution, which ought to include provision for regional records centres and regional archival repositories. It is hard to generalise on what is the most suitable structure, since this would depend very much on the structure of local government itself. For example, where there are regional assemblies, it would seem to make sense to have regional records centres so that records and information are more easily accessible to regional governments than if they were kept centrally. If the second tier of government were at a more local, rather than regional, level, it would similarly make sense if local record centres and archive offices were established to house material created locally.

In counties that operate a federal system of government, there may be parallel provincial or state systems (as in the United States of America), independent of the national systems but relying on the national archives for professional leadership and guidance. If there is separate state or regional legislation, these inter-relationships should be included in any provisions so that each party is clear about the scope and range of their responsibilities.

LEGAL ADMISSIBILITY

The admissibility of records as evidence in a court of law needs to be covered by the records legislation, although the subject is often included in legislation relating to rules of evidence. In particular, provision needs to be made for the inviolability of government records and for the legal admissibility of records in non-traditional formats, including microform and electronic formats.

In the United Kingdom the British Standards Institute have issued a Code of Practice for Legal Admissibility and Evidential Weight of Information Stored Electronically (SBI, PD 0008).

COPYRIGHT

Records and archives legislation should also address the issue of copyright. More often than not there is separate copyright legislation but the records legislation should take into account the impact in respect of copyright in records held in the archival institution. Typically this would refer to the copyright legislation and authorise the publication of guidance to users of the records. The records provisions should permit the director to make records available for inspection and to provide copies of them without breach of any private copyrights that may subsist in them and also confirm that the director's consent must be obtained before anyone publishes facsimiles, transcripts or translations of public records in which copyright belongs to the state.

THE LEGISLATIVE POSITION IN THE UNITED KINGDOM

PUBLIC RECORDS ACT 1958

The Public Records Act 1958 makes provisions for managing records that have been selected for permanent preservation and deposited at the Public Record Office (in 2003 the Public Record Office merged with the Historical Manuscripts Commission and changed its title to The National Archives). The Act applies only to the records of central government, the courts, the armed services and the National Health Service.

Schedule 1 of the Act gives the Lord Chancellor (the person responsible for supervising the care and preservation of public records) the power to resolve questions as to whether specific records are public records under the Act. The term "public records" has the specialised meaning of a record subject to the Act. The Schedule also defines this term:

... administrative and departmental records belonging to Her Majesty, whether in the United Kingdom or elsewhere, in right of Her Majesty's Government in the United Kingdom and, in particular, -

a)   Records of, or held in, any department of Her Majesty's Government in the United Kingdom, or
b)   Records of any office, commission or other body or establishment whatsoever under Her Majesty's Government in the United Kingdom

shall be public records.

The definition does not apply to records mainly concerned with Scottish affairs, to records relating to the registration of births, marriages and deaths, to certain records of the Duchy of Lancaster and the Public Trustee, and to certain Welsh records (as defined in the Government of Wales Act 1998).

Bodies can be brought within the scope of the Act by an Order in Council under Schedule 1.

The Lord Chancellor is responsible under section 1 of the Act for carrying out its provisions, for supervising the measures to be taken under it for the safekeeping of public records and for the direction of the Public Record Office. Under section 2 he appoints a Keeper of Public Records to administer the Office under his direction.

While the general principle of the Act is that there shall be a central Public Record Office and that public records worthy of permanent preservation shall be housed and made available for inspection there, it also makes provisions for the deposit of any class of public records, at the Lord Chancellor's discretion, in places other than the Public Record Office (termed 'Places of Deposit' – see page xx).

The Act says very little about what is required in terms of creating and managing public records before they are selected for permanent preservation. This is very much a reflection of the time when the Act was passed. In the 1950s there were fewer records to be dealt with than now and fewer pressures in terms of requirements for transparency and accountability. Records management is now a much more developed profession since it needs to cope with increasing volumes of records, increasing complexity (especially in the form of electronic records) and greater demands for access to information and accountability of government.

PUBLIC RECORDS ACT 1967

Under the 1958 Act the deposit of selected public records was expected to take place by the time they were thirty years old but access was not permitted until they were fifty years old. The Public Records Act 1967 amended the section relating to access, reducing this period from fifty years to thirty years. The obligation to transfer records by the thirty year point remained unchanged.

LOCAL GOVERNMENT (RECORDS) ACT 1962

The Local Government (Records) Act 1962 enables all local authorities to promote adequate use of their own records and empowered 'principal councils' to acquire other records by purchase, gift or deposit. Other councils could exercise these powers only under a specific ministerial order.

LOCAL GOVERNMENT ACT 1972

The Local Government Act 1972 section 224 provides for principal councils to make proper arrangements for their records. These proper arrangements have been described in a circular issued by the (then) Department of the Environment. They include:

- preservation of the records
- provision of access
- appropriate storage conditions
- liaison with schools and other educational bodies so that the educational potential of the archives can be realised
- sufficient staffing.

The Local Government Act 1972 section 228 provides local electors with the right to see the minutes of a local authority, an abstract of the accounts, any order for the payment of money, and any record required to be deposited with a local authority.

LOCAL GOVERNMENT (ACCESS TO INFORMATION) ACT 1985

The Local Government (Access to Information) Act 1985 provides for minutes, agenda, reports and background papers of meetings of principal councils, which are open to the public to be available for public inspection

LOCAL GOVERNMENT ACT 2000

The Local Government Act 2000 places a requirement on local authorities to:

- Issue monthly forward plans showing forthcoming decisions and listing related documents;
- Give a minimum of three days prior access to reports, agenda and background papers for decisions;
- Ensure that meetings at which 'key decisions' are to be discussed or taken are open to the public;
- Produce a record of such decisions and the reasoning behind them.

PUBLIC RECORDS (SCOTLAND) ACT 1937

The Public Records (Scotland) Act 1937 is mainly concerned with providing for the transfer of records of central and local Scottish courts to the Keeper of the Records of Scotland. In addition it:

- Outlines the Keeper's powers and duties under the Act;
- Creates the Scottish Records Advisory Council;
- Provides for government departments, agencies, non-departmental public bodies, statutory bodies, corporate and local authorities to transfer their records to the Keeper;
- Prescribes procedures for records disposal;
- Provides for the temporary return of records to their creators, when required;
- Provides for the Keeper to acquire records from private owners (through an amendment introduced in the National Heritage (Scotland) Act 1985).

PUBLIC REGISTERS AND RECORDS (SCOTLAND) ACT 1948

The Public Registers and Records (Scotland) Act 1948 separated the functions of responsibility for historical records from that for the creation and maintenance of the General Register of Sasines (as set out in the Public Records (Scotland) Act 1937).

LOCAL GOVERNMENT (SCOTLAND) ACT 1973

The Local Government (Scotland) Act 1973 is primarily concerned with organisation of local government in Scotland (changes in boundaries, authorities, etc) but section 200 relates specifically to records. It authorises 'proper arrangements' for records and the disposal of those not considered by local authorities to be worthy of preservation. It provides for the transfer of records to the Keeper of the Records of Scotland and defines records as including "charters, deeds, minutes, account books and other documents, and any other records of whatever form which convey information."

NATIONAL HERITAGE (SCOTLAND) ACT 1985

Section 19(2) of the National Heritage (Scotland) Act 1985 gives the Keeper of the Records of Scotland power to accept responsibility for the safekeeping of records other than public records and to acquire records and accept gifts and loans. It also makes minor amendments to the Public Records (Scotland) Act 1937 in respect of the Advisory Council and provides for the disposal by destruction of any records dated prior to the year 1707.

PUBLIC RECORDS ACT (NORTHERN IRELAND) 1923

The Public Records Act (Northern Ireland) 1923 makes several provisions, including:

- The establishment of a national archive of Northern Ireland (the Public Record Office of Northern Ireland – PRONI);
- Powers for PRONI to accept a wide range of records (Northern Ireland courts, departments and public bodies, those created by departments subject to the Westminster Parliament but relevant to Northern Ireland and those held by private individuals, businesses, industry, the professions and local government;
- The making of rules for the disposal of valueless documents.

It does not, however, provide for a right of public access to government records in Northern Ireland; it was established in 1973 (by a House of Commons written answer) that criteria operating in England and Wales are followed. Access issues are now dealt with under the Freedom of Information Act 2000.

The Local Government (Records) Act 1962 does not apply to Northern Ireland. PRONI serves as a record office for the counties as well as a national repository.

The Act named the Minister of Finance of Northern Ireland as the minister responsible for the charge and superintendence of Northern Ireland records. In practice, under direct rule from Westminster, the Secretary of State for Northern Ireland was responsible for record matters. Nowadays PRONI is an executive agency of the Department of Culture, Arts and Leisure.

FREEDOM OF INFORMATION ACT 2000

The Freedom of Information Act 2000 is intended to promote a culture of openness and accountability amongst public authorities by providing people with rights of access to the information held by them. It is expected that these rights will facilitate better public understanding of how public authorities carry out their duties, why they make the decisions they do and how they spend public money.

The following paragraphs describe the background to the Act, its implementation, and the significant effect it has on the management of records in public authorities.

The legislation is the culmination of almost fifty years of debate on the rights of individuals to be able to access information about the way in which they are governed and the way in which decisions affecting their lives are made. The debate has been influenced by many factors – legislation in other countries, the Campaign for Freedom of Information, the Government's commitment to improved public services, and the pressure for greater openness and transparency in government. This influence also works the other way – much of the work in developing the legislation has affected those processes that are needed to make it work.

The Act embraces the whole of the public sector and some parts of the private sector which discharge public functions. It imposes significant duties and responsibilities on these organizations. They need to:

- Know what information they hold;
- Manage their information holdings effectively;
- Have in place the infrastructure for dealing with FOI requests;
- Meet challenging deadlines in responding to individual requests for information;
- Proactively disseminate information through a publication scheme;
- Set up arrangements to handle complaints and appeals;
- Ensure consistency in discharging their duties under the Act.

and undertake many other tasks resulting from these main duties.

The Freedom of Information Act enables people to gain access to information held by public authorities in two ways: from 1 January 2005, they have the right to make a request for any information held by a public authority (although this right is subject to a number of exemptions that permit the withholding of information) and the authority will have to comply with the Act in responding. Prior to that, in the run up to January 2005, every public authority had to make some information available as a matter of course through a publication scheme, with information included in the publication scheme being routinely made available to anyone who consulted it. A publication scheme is both a public commitment to make certain information available and a guide to how that information can be obtained.

The Freedom of Information legislation will only be as good as the quality of the records which are subject to its provisions. Statutory rights of access such as this are of little use if reliable records and information are not created in the first place, if they cannot be found when needed, or if the arrangements for their eventual archiving or destruction are inadequate. In addition the fast-growing use of information technology will increase the pressure on the record keeping system. Good records management practice is therefore essential in implementing the Act, as well as in promoting the efficient business of the Council.

Freedom of Information is affected by several other enactments, most notably the Data Protection Act 1998 and the Human Rights Act 1998 as well as by secondary legislation such as the Environmental Information Regulations. The two main areas in which the Freedom of Information Act 2000 affects data protection are:

- the enforcement of both data protection and freedom of information by one person (the Information Commissioner);
- the definition of personal data.

24

LORD CHANCELLOR'S CODE OF PRACTICE ON THE MANAGEMENT OF RECORDS

The Code of Practice under section 46 of the Freedom of Information Act 2000 lays down best practice for the management of information, in all formats, by public authorities from the moment it is created to the time of its disposal (whether this is by destruction or preservation in an archive). Although the Code has been published in the context of freedom of information, its contents describe efficient business practice for the management of records by public authorities in whatever area they may be operating.

The Code of Practice is an important and highly significant document in the development of the records management profession. It provides an effective framework within which policies and procedures can be drawn up. The Code is reproduced in full at Appendix 1.

MODEL ACTION PLANS FOR REACHING COMPLIANCE WITH THE CODE OF PRACTICE

The National Archives has published model action plans for reaching compliance with the Code of Practice. There is a model for each type of public authority, namely:

- Central Government
- Local Government
- Higher Education and Further Education Organisations
- Police Authorities
- National Health Service
- Schools.

The models are accessible via The National Archives website and can be freely adapted to suit individual needs. The model for local government is reproduced at Appendix 2.

In addition to the model action plans, the UK government is encouraging generally in the public sector a process of self-assessment against the Code of Practice. With this in mind The National Archives has provided on its website an evaluation workbook and methodology (www.nationalarchives.gov.uk/recordsmanagement/code/assessing.htm) to assist public authorities in assessing conformance of their records management systems to the Code of Practice. Completing the questionnaire contained in the workbook will establish the degree to which an organisation complies with the Code. It also provides a mechanism to evaluate the level of risk to the organisation by records management that does not conform to the Code.

25

DATA PROTECTION ACT 1998

With the passing of the Act the Data Protection Commissioner became the Information Commissioner. He is now responsible for supervising the implementation of both the data protection and the freedom of information legislation. At first sight this appears to be a conflict of interest, and there is no doubt that there is a certain tension between the two Acts. However, the Freedom of Information Act counters this quite effectively by making most applications for personal data exempt under section 40.

Definition of personal data

The Data Protection Act 1998 defines data as:

information which -
(a) is being processed by means of equipment operating automatically in response to instructions given for that purpose,
(b) is recorded with the intention that it should be processed by means of such equipment,
(c) is recorded as part of a relevant filing system or with the intention that it should form part of a relevant filing system, or
(d) does not fall within paragraph (a), (b) or (c) but forms part of an accessible record as defined by section 68;[1]

and personal data as:

data which relate to a living individual who can be identified –
(a) from those data, or
(b) from those data and other information which is in the possession of, or is likely to come into the possession of, the data controller, and includes any expressions of opinion about the individual and any indication of the intentions of the data controller or any other person in respect of the individual.

A relevant filing system is regarded under the Data Protection Act as any set of information relating to individuals that is structured by reference to individuals or by reference to criteria relating to individuals, in such a way that information relating to a particular individual is readily accessible. It includes information processed automatically (that is, by computer) and manually (that is, paper and other systems).

The Freedom of Information Act 2000 extends the definition of personal data to include all information – not just that in a relevant filing system – in relation to

---

[1] Section 68 defines an accessible record as a health record, an educational record or an accessible public record. These are defined in great detail in the Data Protection Act 1998.

organisations that are public authorities under the Act. This may have significant implications for managers in particular. Where they have kept loose information on their staff to help them in, for example, annual assessments, such information may now be requested by individuals. However, not all the data subject's rights are applicable to this extended category of data. They can see the data and request any inaccuracies to be amended, but they cannot prevent use of the data for the purposes of direct marketing and retention of the data for longer than is necessary for a specific purpose. In addition there are some procedural requirements for accessing unstructured data.

In essence the right of access to information about third parties under the Freedom of Information Act is subject to three main conditions:

- Disclosure should not contravene the eight Data Protection Principles, that is,
    - Fair and lawful processing
    - Processing for a specified and lawful purpose
    - Data not to be excessive
    - Accuracy of the data
    - Data not to be kept longer than necessary
    - Data subject rights
    - Security
    - Transfer outside the EU.
- Information would be disclosed to the data subject (of the information) if they applied under the Data Protection Act 1998 provisions.
- The data subject(s) have not exercised their rights to prevent processing likely to cause damage or distress.

Whereas private personal data (home address, marital status, personal life, etc.) would not be disclosed under the new arrangements, it is likely that some information about public servants in connection with their work will be accessible, for example work telephone number and address, role and responsibilities and grade.

HUMAN RIGHTS ACT 1998

All public authorities, including those that for one reason or another are not subject to the Freedom of Information Act 2000 and those bodies that have a mixture of private and public functions, are public authorities under the Human Rights Act 1998. This Act makes it unlawful for any public authority to act in a way that is incompatible with the European Convention on Human Rights.

There are five articles of the Convention that have a bearing on freedom of information:

- Article 2: Right to life – the provision of information relating to health and safety may affect this protection of the right to life.
- Article 5: Right to liberty and security – the right to access to information may be necessary in providing an individual with the right of access to a court to test the lawfulness of detention under this article.
- Article 6: Right to a fair trial – defendants in criminal cases may be able to argue that it is in the public interest for information on the investigation to be disclosed.
- Article 8: Respect for private and family life – as well as private and family life, this includes the individual's home and correspondence. Thus there may be a request for access to information that contravenes this article.
- Article 10: Freedom of expression – the right also includes freedom to receive and impart information.

Like the Data Protection Act 1998, there seems to be a tension between freedom of information and human rights, and the relationship is no less complicated. Where the European Convention on Human Rights allows the release of information, it will be unlawful for a public authority to withhold that information. The Information Commissioner will be able to interpret the Act in such a way that the public interest test can be applied in such circumstances.

LIMITATION ACT 1980

This legislation lays down periods after which legal action cannot be taken in respect of different kinds of transactions, for example in financial transactions this is 6 years, and in land transactions, 12 years.

For records managers this means that some records created by these functional areas might need to be kept for the stated periods to meet any claims for damages, etc. Essentially this is a risk assessment process – what are the risks of receiving claims where records have been destroyed? – and a cost analysis process (do the costs of preserving records outweigh the cost of any claim that might have to be met?).

OTHER PROVISIONS

Environmental Information Regulations

Prior to the Environmental Information Regulations 1992, 1998 and 2004, the Environmental Protection Act 1990 granted public access to various pollution registers.

A right of access to information relating to the environment held by public authorities is now provided by the Environmental Information Regulations (EIRs) 2004. These regulations require public authorities to make available information about the condition of the environment, anything that has a negative effect upon it, and what measures are being taken to counter the negative effects. In replacing the earlier regulations they provide:

- Clarification of the term 'public authority';
- Amendment of requirements on the handling of information on emissions;
- Tightening of requirements on charging for environmental information to allow public authorities to charge for the cost of supplying information only;
- Introduction of personal data provisions to align the environmental requirements with data protection.

From a practical point of view these regulations:

- Apply to a wider range of public authorities than the Freedom of Information Act;
- Apply to all requests for environmental information (not just written requests);
- Have fewer potential grounds for refusal;
- Override domestic information regimes.

It was agreed in 1999 that the Environmental Information Regulations should be exempt from FOI to avoid the risk of not meeting international obligations and to allow for updating the regulations. It was also agreed that environmental information should be treated no differently from any other information and that the provisions of the FOI Act relating to the Information Commissioner and the Information Tribunal would also apply to the Environmental Information Regulations.

Under the Environmental Information Regulations the definition of environmental information is very wide. It includes:

- Information about air, water, soil, land, flora and fauna, energy, noise, waste and emissions;
- Any decisions, measures and activities affecting or likely to affect any of the above;
- Financial and cost benefit analysis used in relation to the above;
- Information about human health and the food chain, built structures and cultural sites.

The regulations have their own set of exemptions (termed 'exceptions' in the regulations themselves). A request for information can be refused if:

- The information is not held
- The request is manifestly unreasonable
- The request is too general

- The request is for unfinished documents or data
- The request is for internal communications.

Public authorities can refuse to release information in order to protect:

- Confidentiality of proceedings
- International relations
- Public security
- Defence
- The course of justice and the right to a fair trial
- Commercial confidentiality
- Intellectual property rights
- Personal/voluntary data
- Environmental protection.

If information relates to emissions, the authority cannot refuse to disclose it on the grounds of confidentiality of proceedings, commercial confidentiality, personal/voluntary data or environmental protection.

All information under the EIRs is subject to a public interest test.

NEW UK LEGISLATION?

Over the past decade or so there have been quite a number of suggestions for new records and archives legislation in the United Kingdom. Why is it felt that new legislation is required? Several reasons have been put forward:

- Scope – the coverage of current legislation is limited. This is perhaps a reflection of the time at which it was promulgated.
- Permissive nature of current legislation – the records and archives law as it stands has no teeth. It is difficult, however, to be proscriptive over issues such as selection and disposal, and records management generally.
- The electronic age – while the Public Records Act 1958 does not appear to exclude electronic records (it defines public records in terms of the bodies creating them not their physical form), legal advice is that this is unlikely to be adequate. For example, electronic records raise numerous issues about authenticity, security and preservation.
- Accountability – in the modern era new demands of accountability, transparency and corporate governance need to be reflected in records and archives legislation.

STANDARDS

Legislation in the field of records and archives is often 'enabling' – in other words it requires interpretation. This interpretation is provided by the records profession, usually in the form of standards and best practice guidelines. In the United Kingdom the pivotal document in this respect is the Code of Practice on the Management of Records under section 46 of the Freedom of Information Act 2000. The advice and guidance in this book draws very much on the framework set out in that Code of Practice. The Code is reproduced in full in Appendix 1.

In the UK health sector the Department of Health has recently published Records Management: NHS Code of Practice. This succeeds and replaces previous guidance contained in the Department of Health circular HSC 053/1999 For the Record. The Code provides a key component of information governance arrangements for the National Health Service in the United Kingdom.

The great thing about standards and codes of practice in our profession is that they are not imposed from above (often from somebody or some organisation that has little or no connection to records management) but are formulated by our community in response to particular needs.

The most important standard in recent years is BS/ISO 15489 Records Management. It was based on the Australian records management standard AS4390 and promotes the standardisation of policies and procedures to ensure that appropriate attention and protection is given to records and that they can be retrieved more efficiently and effectively. The standard is accompanied by a technical report that explains how the desired standards might be implemented. In addition the British Standards Institute has produced three publications relating to the standard:

- Effective Records Management: Management Guide to the Value of BS/ISO 15489 (ref: BIP 0025-1).
- Effective Records Management: Practical Implementation of BS/ISO 15489 (ref: BIP 0025-2).
- Effective Records Management: Performance Management for BS/ISO 15489 (ref: BIP 0025-3).

The British Standards Institute has also published guidance on implementing and operating information management systems, particularly where issues of legal admissibility are important. There are three very worthy of mention:

1. BIP 0008 Legal Admissibility and Evidential Weight of Information Stored Electronically – provides a common framework that helps to maximize the value and integrity of information in a court of law.
2. PD 0010 Principles of Good Practice for Information Management – identifies

features common to all information handling processes, independent of specific technological devices, setting out five principles that would be applicable however the technology changes. The principles are to:

- Recognise and understand all types of information
- Understand the legal issues and exercise 'duty of care' responsibilities
- Identify and specify business processes and procedures
- Identify enabling technologies to support business processes and procedures
- Monitor and audit business processes and procedures.

3. BS 7799-1 Code of practice for information security management – has been explicitly produced for an environment that is increasingly confronted by a range of threats (fraud, espionage, sabotage, vandalism – the list is almost endless). Much of the detail of the standard is for ICT professionals but even this has to be backed up by appropriate procedures in records and information management.

3 Record creation and classification

AIMS

This chapter examines the creation phase of records and information. It provides guidance on business analysis – a prerequisite of planning for systems of record keeping – on information audits/surveys and on the design and implementation of file plans (often called business classification schemes) for both paper and electronic records. A case study at the end of the chapter covers recent work undertaken by The National Archives in a small development trust.

BUSINESS ANALYSIS

The overall purpose of creating, using and managing records is to support the business of the organisation. These business needs, the benefits that the organisation expects to gain, for example, from a move to electronic working and other relevant external requirements on the organisation are the general determinants of the way in which records should be organised, and the means by which they may be accessed. While business analysis originated with and has been more widely used in the private sector than in the public sector, the approach is equally applicable in both. The word 'business' in this context is used in its more general sense of any purposeful work or activity rather than in its more particular sense as commercial trade.

THE PROCESS OF BUSINESS ANALYSIS

The process of business analysis involves identifying and then examining the component parts of an organisation, in order to gain information about how the organisation functions and the relationships between various tasks, jobs, people, structures and other elements. This includes identifying broad organisational goals and supporting business areas and processes, and business process definition and decomposition. You will often find that these analytical projects can lead to enhanced performance in your organisation by improving the way work is carried out. For example, available resources can be linked more directly to the aims and goals of the organisation; and similarly – which, of course, is the point of examining this subject here – records and information systems can function more effectively if they are more closely linked with the institution's day-to-day work.

Business analysis allows managers to see their organisations as an integrated whole, preventing them from getting lost in the complexity of the organisational structure or the details of their day-to-day job. When managers apply such thinking to an understanding of their organisation, they see that the best performance will be achieved when all the component parts of the organisation, or business system, are working together harmoniously to achieve the organisation's mission and objectives. Optimum performance can only be achieved when organisational change or redesign takes into account the entire system – the corporate whole. For example, there have been many public sector reform projects aimed at improving financial and human resource management systems that have failed because they have overlooked how these functions interrelate with and need to be supported by record-keeping systems. Similarly, many projects aimed at redesigning record-keeping systems fail because they are not integrated with and do not support other organisational systems. This theme of corporate working will crop up again and again in the following pages; if you do not recognise its importance, life will be more difficult for you.

Where the redesign of records and archives management functions and requirements take place as part of wider public sector reform exercises, for example in developing countries, there may be limitations on the scope of the changes that can be made to organisational functions and processes. This can often be the case when not all government agencies are committed to undertaking such organisation-wide restructuring.

There are several good examples of the business analysis process. Two well worth looking at are detailed below.

DIRKS (Design and Implementation of Record Keeping Systems)

The DIRKS methodology was developed some years ago by the National Archives of Australia. It is an eight step process for the improvement of recordkeeping and information management practices. Practical guidance on using the methodology is in the DIRKS Manual which includes a step (B) on the analysis of a business activity. See the website of the National Archives of Australia: www.naa.gov.au/recordkeeping/dirks/summary.html.

JISC (Joint Information Systems Committee)

JISC commissioned a study of the records life cycle in 1999. An integral part of this study was the business function activity model (FAM). It was drawn up originally as part of an overall functional approach to records management for higher education authorities. It presents a very practical approach to business analysis, and was recently revised. See the JISC website: www.jisc.ac.uk.

ROLE OF RECORDS MANAGERS IN BUSINESS ANALYSIS

Records managers are usually confronted with two broad options:

- Forego making any changes to the flow of information and associated record-keeping systems, since they can change only one part of the system.
- Forge ahead with changes, knowing that the entire system has not been changed but that at least some processes will be strengthened by the improved management of records. However, changing records systems on their own, when the underlying processes are not operating efficiently is not recommended.

In order to make effective changes, the records manager should be part of any larger organisational redesign processes. This participation rests on a commitment from senior management to the comprehensive re-engineering of processes, including the fundamental information management process, but often this commitment does not exist. Indeed, programme managers may resist the recommendations of records management professionals because they perceive records managers as not understanding their business or, worse, interfering with their work. This is where records professionals need to sell their ideas to senior management and strive to be treated as equals.

Even if there is no organisation-wide reorganisation of business functions underway, or if the record-keeping component of public sector reforms is limited, records managers can still use business analysis as a tool to restructure record keeping operations and develop file classification schemes and disposal schedules, as well as carry out a number of other projects designed to improve records management.

Business analysis is relatively new to records and archives management professionals. Traditionally, particularly when appraising records and developing disposal schedules, records managers and archivists have concentrated on relating records to their administrative origins, in keeping with the archival principle of provenance. You may think that this is because records management has not usually been thought of as a requirement for business and therefore the profession has not had the recognition it deserves. This is true, but it was also embedded in the paper environment where relationships between government business and the records were often only analysed when records became archives and were pored over by historians rather than business managers. We generally have not linked records to organisational mission, functions, processes and transactions. Business analysis is a tool that records managers can use to map the relationship between an organisation's mission, administrative structure, functions, processes and transactions and the records it generates over time. With this understanding and knowledge, they are better positioned to improve the state of records in their care, improving access and also making their own work easier. Ultimately, good record keeping will contribute to strengthening the organisation and achieving the goals of efficiency, accountability and good governance.

PRACTICAL APPROACHES TO BUSINESS ANALYSIS

The ideal approach occurs when people responsible for the business process, usually senior or line managers, have initiated and are committed to revising (usually called 're-engineering') their procedures, and records managers are brought in to work with managers, technical experts and other stakeholders as part of a corporate team. The team works together to design policies and procedures that function optimally in all areas, including records management. When this approach is taken, experience shows that business managers develop a much greater appreciation of the importance of records to their function(s) and more readily accept the requirements for effective management of recorded information.

Unfortunately, records managers are often forced to deal with less than ideal situations. With files piling up in offices, hallways and any other available space and the complete collapse of record systems, they may be forced to take a more pragmatic approach. Short-term quick fixes, such as the immediate removal of files, may be necessary but fail to strike at the heart of the problem. There is a need to convince senior managers that quick fixes do not solve the problem in the long term and that there is a need for changes in business procedures if real progress is to be made. Let us not be backward in coming forward. When an organisation is reviewing its business practices, we must get in there to make it clear that any re-engineering of business processes will affect record keeping procedures.

Don't forget, of course, that records managers also have scope for redesigning procedures and driving organisational change for the procedures that they themselves own, such as those carried out in records offices, records centres and archival institutions. However, even here records management staff may experience some difficulty because organisations carry out their record-keeping functions through a variety of organisational structures. Records creation and management may be divided up between any number of offices, divisions, branches and agencies. The people involved in each may have differing organisational and professional allegiances. For example, the records manager and the archivist may each work within and be responsible to separate offices or separate parts of the same organisation. Consequently, the organisational structures can create significant barriers to re-engineering even those procedures over which records managers and archivists might seem to have a large degree of control. Thus business analysis can provide an easing of organisational change in that change is not seen as 'change for change's sake' but has some business rationale behind it.

To succeed at redesigning record-keeping systems, records managers must become adept at working with people in all parts of the organisation. Just as senior management must remember to include records professionals in organisation-wide business analysis activities, records managers and archivists must also include other stakeholders – including programme managers, information technology specialists, information managers, legal experts, internal auditors and other stakeholders – in the analysis of records systems.

PROJECT MANAGEMENT

Business analysis is an analytical approach to organisational change. When used as a tool, it usually takes place as part of a specific project. The project may be designed to serve a range of different purposes, such as redesigning business processes, designing automated systems, restructuring record keeping operations, developing file classification systems, or developing records retention schedules.

A critical skill in any project is the management of change. This includes identifying and taking into consideration the point of view of all project stakeholders; identifying and minimising points of resistance; evaluating and countering risks; assessing and encouraging people's willingness to change; and evaluating the process of change.

Key stages in the management of business analysis projects are:

- planning the project
- analysing the organisation
- designing solutions
- implementing the design
- evaluating the results.

There are several methodologies available for the management of projects of all kinds. One commonly used in the public sector in the United Kingdom is PRINCE 2.

PRINCE (**PR**ojects **IN** Controlled **E**nvironments) was established in 1989. It is a *de facto* standard used extensively by the UK Government and is widely recognised and used in the private sector. The key features of the methodology are:

- Its focus on business justification;
- A defined organisation structure for the project management team;
- Its product-based planning approach;
- Its emphasis on dividing the project into manageable and controllable stages;
- Its flexibility to be applied at a level appropriate to the project.

For more information on the methodology see http://www.ogc.gov.uk/methods_prince_2.asp.

KEY FEATURES OF A BUSINESS ANALYSIS PROJECT

Identifying the Issue

It may not be as easy as you think to identify a records management issue or problem. Different people in the organisation may have very different perceptions about its nature. For example, a common complaint is that people in the organisation cannot find information as and when they need it. If this is a general concern, how might different people in the organisation perceive that issue?

- A senior manager may perceive this to be a records management issue – 'no one knows what information is being created and where to find it when it is needed'.
- A middle manager might see the issue as resting in the office – 'uncontrolled and duplicate files are building up in filing areas'.
- The organisation's records manager might identify the issue as a resting with the records – 'staff in the organisation have stopped using the record keeping system because of the poor service it provides'.

All of these differing perspectives must be taken into account in order to define the issue accurately and effectively. Not doing this could result in analysing the wrong level of the business system. It's the old corporate approach again. Don't be too narrow in the analysis of the problem. For example, if only the perspective of the records manager were taken into account, the focus of the analysis would be on the record keeping system alone. However, the perspectives of the middle manager and senior manager suggest that a broader definition of the issue is preferable (and would meet basic business analysis requirements as set out above). If the wrong level of the system becomes the focus of analysis, the redesigned component of the system may function perfectly well within its strictly defined limits but reduce the overall effectiveness of the organisational system, thereby creating additional problems. Further, if the definition of the issue focuses only on one functional area, such as the record keeping system, important relationships between that functional area and other parts of the organisation may be overlooked.

One way to ensure the issue is not defined too narrowly is to take a comprehensive view of the organisation. This can be done by examining the organisation's environment, resources, goals, activities, achievements and probable future trends. Look at corporate and business plans, if they exist. Talk with selected managers and other key people both inside and outside the organisation. In doing so, it is important to start with a general overview and move to the more specific. Avoid becoming immersed in too much detail. At this stage, it is more important just to try to define the issue to be investigated, not to undertake the detailed analysis of the issue; this in-depth study can take place later.

Also note that, at this stage, no attempt should be made to analyse the causes of the problem or to suggest solutions for it. Making assumptions at this stage can be detrimental. Incorrect assumptions may lead people to rule out important possibilities.

Aims and objectives of the project

Once the issue is identified, it is possible to define the project's aims and objectives. It is essential to consult with stakeholders in order to formulate a coherent set of aims and objectives.

Project scope

Defining the scope of the project is important. Business analysis projects can quickly become unmanageable if their scope is defined too broadly, and they can be ineffective if their scope is too narrow. Defining the project scope entails assessing the feasibility and likelihood of successfully realising the broad project objectives. To arrive at the project's appropriate scope, it is necessary to refine the broad project objectives to ensure a greater likelihood of success. A number of factors may bear on the feasibility of a project, including:

- the authority of the person undertaking the project (for example, whether the person is the owner of the business functions or processes under analysis);
- organisational capabilities (such as levels of expertise, numbers of available workers and affect on other operations or projects);
- resource commitments (such as labour costs, costs of material, funding);
- anticipated benefits of the project (for example, whether large or small, time elapsed before benefits are fully realised and duration of the benefits).

In order to maximise the likelihood of success, it may be necessary to narrow the focus of the project to a particular component or area of the organisation, such as information systems, and to establish a time-frame.

Project activities

Having determined the project's vision, scope and objectives, the next step is to identify the activities and tasks required to complete the project. There may be hundreds in a large business analysis project. For example, the organisation's vision for records and archives project might be:

> establish an effective record-keeping system that provides the right information in the right form to the right person at the right time.

The objective would be

> review the operations of the record keeping system with a view to establishing an effective system that provides the right information in the right form to the right person at the right time, and to report within three months.

The tasks involved within the review might include:

- interviewing records staff (part of the data gathering phase);
- assessing the quality and effectiveness of forms and procedures (part of the analysis phase);
- determining the way the records office is used by members of the organisation (part of the analysis phase);
- etc.

Although it is not possible or logical at the beginning of the project to know what actual tasks will be undertaken when a solution is implemented, it can be helpful to consider what tasks might have to be undertaken. Therefore, at this stage it is useful also to consider briefly the possible tasks that might be involved in establishing an effective record-keeping system, such as:

- revising forms and procedures as required;
- reorienting members of the organisation to the purpose and functions of the records office;
- retraining records personnel in the new procedures.

However, the precise activities and tasks will not be determined until the actual problem has been defined and strategies developed for solving it.

Project personnel

Once the what and how of the project have been determined, it must be decided who will carry out the project work. Although it is possible for a single person to undertake a business analysis project, it is much easier when it is performed by a team of individuals consisting of the system's stakeholders. Moreover, when the purpose of the project is to redesign business processes, wide-scale input and involvement is critical in order to reduce resistance to organisational change. Thus, establishing a temporary organisational structure is an important part of project planning. A typical structure (in line with the PRINCE 2 methodology mentioned above) will consist of:

- project manager
- business, technical and user representatives
- team administration
- steering committee.

While this represents a model organisational structure for a project, such a formal and complex structure may be neither necessary nor possible. For example, if the scope of the project is limited to a review of a single process, the project manager and the business representative may be one and the same person. The project organisational structure should be adapted to suit the scope and objectives, the available resources (human and financial) and the organisational context of the project.

IMPLEMENTING PROJECT RESULTS

Changes to the organisation's processes as a result of a business analysis project might range from a complete redesign of systems to small improvements in select functions. The choice made will depend on a number of factors, including:

- the seriousness of the problem;
- the scope of the records manager's authority;
- the likelihood of successfully re-engineering the process;
- the degree to which staff members might accept dramatic changes in their work.

There are no cut and dried methodologies, techniques or tools for redesigning or improving business processes. However, the following are points to keep in mind when thinking about how to resolve internal process problems.

- Be creative; try to think in new ways.
- Challenge assumptions (for example, ask: 'What is the worst thing that would happen if we just did not perform this activity or task any more?')
- Look for duplications in activities or tasks that can be eliminated or combined.
- Look for activities or tasks that can be moved to another stage in the process, simplified or carried out simultaneously.

- Look for ways that information technology can be used to eliminate the need for certain activities and tasks or increase process performance.
- Ask: 'How would we do this work if we had less staff to do it?'
- Organise new processes around outputs not activities.
- Seek the ideas of outsiders (those unfamiliar with the specific process under review), as they usually find it easier to look at a process objectively and challenge assumptions.
- Look for who is performing each activity (for example, ask: 'Do several people in different organisational units assist with the process?'). This may indicate areas where too many hand overs in the process are slowing it down.

The first step in implementing proposed solutions is to assess in detail the anticipated benefits of implementing each recommendation. Assessment of the benefits must be SMART:

Specific
Measurable
Achievable
Realistic
Timely

For example, if you recommend the establishment and implementation of a records retention schedule, the benefits might be expressed in terms of the number of linear metres of records or the number of filing cabinets that destruction of valueless records will release. However, certain benefits associated with the redesign of a business system may be difficult to quantify. For example, it may be impossible to measure improved reliability or greater customer satisfaction. Nevertheless, where possible, benefits should be defined in measurable terms.

It is also necessary to assess the requirements and time frame for implementation of the recommendations. Funding, for example for the acquisition of new equipment, is an obvious type of requirement to be considered, but it is important to factor in the time involved in rewriting policies and procedures to incorporate proposed changes. Staff training must also be considered when determining a time frame.

EVALUATION

Evaluating the success of any project is critical to ensuring its success and sustainability. One method of evaluation is to conduct an audit. If the objectives of implementation were specific, measurable, achievable, realistic and timely, the audit should reveal that they have been successfully achieved.

You might find that the audit will also identify recommendations that have not been fully implemented and highlight those recommendations that are not producing the desired effects. If approved recommendations have not been fully implemented, it will be necessary to determine the reason and take steps to ensure their full implementation. If, however, implemented recommendations are not producing the desired effects, there will be a need to review the original problem again in order to ensure that root causes have been properly identified and that solutions address the causes.

INFORMATION AUDIT

One of the key undertakings in the examination of records management systems, prior to proposed changes in policies and procedures, is the information audit. You may know it also by the name of records audit or information survey. It is one of the most important processes that a records manager will undertake.

An information audit must provide an objective assessment of an organisation's record and information keeping practices and procedures. It is the first and most important step in gaining control of records and information. It is also a useful tool in assessing the level of knowledge of records management in an organisation. Information audits are primarily concerned with the examination of active records but occasionally it may be necessary to survey semi-active or inactive material when, for example, retention and disposal periods are being re-examined. It can be, and inevitably is, a time-consuming and very resource-intensive undertaking – but it is time and resources well spent. 'Invest to save' is a phrase often used, sometimes rather glibly, but it is one that is very relevant to this aspect of records management. The time and resources invested at this stage will make subsequent work in the records and information management life cycle much easier to execute.

Some of the outcomes of recent audits have been evidence and indication of:

- Unnecessary duplication of records;
- Likely cost savings;
- Too many records being kept for too long;
- Lack of corporate record keeping (silos of records);
- Uncertainty over what should be confidential and what can be open.

Highlighting such issues is a prerequisite to the achievement of effective records management procedures. Records are the reflection of an organisation's activities. The audit provides access to these activities and the records that arise from them. It profiles each record series and system, and helps to identify any problems, establish a records management programme, and quickly design a filing system or produce a disposal schedule. It also helps to determine what is required to install and maintain the records management programme (space, equipment, personnel, etc.) as well as how to evaluate the efficacy and economy of records management systems.

In order to meet records management objectives and users' needs, having regard to the likely availability of resources, the information audit needs to include the following:

- a full understanding of the organisation – the nature of its activities, its mission, objectives, components and operations;
- level of staff awareness of records management;
- what records are held and the activities to which they relate;
- an inventory of record containers (cabinets, shelves, etc.);
- records documentation (file lists, indexes, etc.);
- amount of records;
- copies of records;
- date range of records;
- frequency of consultation of the records;
- tracking systems for the records;
- current records management system and competence levels of records management staff.

METHODOLOGY: PLANNING

Many of the difficulties associated with introducing new records management procedures can be overcome by careful planning of the information audit. This planning should include:

- commitment from top management
- organisation of the audit
- aims and objectives
- communication
- data collection
- compilation of forms

Commitment from top management

The first step is to obtain senior management support. This should take the form of a directive from the Chief Executive/head of the organisation, informing staff that the audit is taking place and that they are expected to cooperate. The passage of the audit will be eased significantly with such a directive.

Organisation of the audit

The person or persons who will carry out the audit will depend very much on the nature and size of the organisation. For example, in a small organisation it would be possible for it to be undertaken solely by the records manager. In most cases, however, it will be more effective if a small team, representative of the organisation as a whole, were to drive the audit forward. The records manager must maintain control of the survey and provide any advice and guidance required. Ask yourself also how far the internal auditors of the organisation will want to be involved (if there is such a unit in the organisation). There will often be an internal audit programme, sometimes on a rolling basis, and many organisational difficulties may be overcome by tapping into this.

Aims and objectives

Aims and objectives must be established before the audit is undertaken. These parallel the aims of records management in general and are actually part of the strategy in achieving these aims. They may be short-term or long-term. Short-term aims are usually the basics of records management improvement programmes:

- Introduction of economical records storage and retrieval: currently most storage methods for paper records are highly uneconomical. For example, many records – particularly current files – are kept in four drawer filing cabinets. A simple 'storage factor' calculation will illustrate this: a four-drawer filing cabinet takes up about 1 square metre of space; it holds about 2 linear metres of records; thus the storage factor will be **2** [metres per sq metre]. A storage cupboard (with roller front) also takes up about 1 square metre of space but it will typically hold six linear metres of records; thus the storage factor would be **6**. The higher the storage factor the more economical is the storage of records. While the initial cost of replacing uneconomical furniture may be high, the medium to long-term costs will represent a saving.
- Questions may concentrate on how current records are created and managed rather than on their eventual disposal. If the overriding problem is considered to be the management of active records, the audit's objectives will likely be the establishment of a standard or corporate system of record keeping.
- Development of disposal schedules: while the current records may be managed effectively, it may be evident that too many records are being kept for too long (a common complaint). People are often reluctant to dispose of or destroy records; the risk factor – usually in the form of 'I'd better keep it just in case…' – comes into play, but usually without regard to efficient record keeping.

In general the objectives of the audit will be one or more of the following, depending on circumstances and what is being aimed for:

- Reappraisal of the records management structure of the organisation;
- Link between business functions and records creation;
- Equipment and accommodation used for record keeping;
- Use of records;
- Who controls the creation and management of local records and information;
- How long records are required for business purposes;
- Long-term (historical) value of records;
- Legacy systems and hybrid records;
- Identification of vital records;
- What information is held (for example, to meet freedom of information requirements).

The overall objective of the survey should therefore be to gather only the information that addresses the aims and objectives cited above. For example: identification of all the organisation's records by series or collection and an understanding of their functional context and business needs will provide the basis for the disposal schedule. Similarly, categorisation of the types of equipment will assist in systems improvement and in calculating savings.

Communication

There should be a communication strategy. People need to know not only that an audit is taking place but also why it is necessary. It needs to be put into context. Prior to carrying out the audit a notice should be sent to all managers and staff concerned, identifying the nature of the audit, its objectives, how it will affect their work, and when it will begin. It is often useful to hold orientation sessions with key staff, and to keep managers informed by the issue of progress reports. The communication plan needs to include a timetable of visits. Don't just turn up one morning, but at the same time don't give the client so much notice that they forget about it. Two weeks maximum is usual.

Consider what are the best ways to communicate this information. Is it departmental meetings, newsletters, intranet, or, fnformal discussions?

Data collection

Before conducting the audit several items should be collected and studied:

- costs of office space, equipment, supplies and staff. Organisational unit costs are often calculated regularly for accommodation (including maintenance and running costs) and for staff (including support services);

- maps and plans of buildings, showing furniture and equipment;
- copies of contracts with commercial storage companies, microfilming bureaux, computer services, etc.;
- inventory of equipment, including computers and photocopiers;
- organisation charts that will give an understanding of the flow of information;
- procedural manuals and forms;
- copies of file lists or databases;
- copies of previous studies.

Compilation of forms

If the audit requires that participants complete a form (as may often be the case), this form must only ask for information that is relevant to the aims and objectives of the audit. In this respect, therefore, there is no one standard form that is recommended.

Examples of forms that have been used in the recent past in the UK are shown at the end of this chapter.

Information collection

The collection phase of the audit needs careful consideration. You should only be collecting information that accords with the aims and objectives of the audit. There is no point in seeking out information that you are not going to use; it is a waste of time and resources.

All records within the scope of the audit must be included, not forgetting onfidential material (for example, personal files), private collections of official material, and, all formats (including electronic, sound recordings, videos, etc.).

Collecting information during the audit is a time-consuming and labour intensive exercise. There is no easy or quick way. There are three main methods:

Physical observation

A physical survey requires records staff to visit business areas and look into each item of records storage equipment, ask questions and complete a standard survey form. It is usually sufficient to sample a series or collection of records rather than examine individual records.

The physical survey needs to be planned carefully and executed with a minimum of disruption. An initial investigation to establish the whereabouts, ownership, volume and condition of the records may be required to make the plan more effective. When the plan and timetable have been drawn up the detailed survey can take place.

Four main actions form the key to finding out information from the survey:

- *Find* every storage place (including tops of cabinets, disks, commercial storage, under desks).
- *Look* at all the records and information in the location.
- *Ask* questions until understanding is complete.
- *Record* the information acquired for future analysis.

Don't believe everything you are told! Seek evidence for the information given to you.

Questionnaire

The reliability of data that might be required to develop or support a hypothesis or serve as a prerequisite for introducing new procedures, is closely related to the size of the survey through which the data is obtained. Physical surveys can be programmed to cover all parts of an organisation. The use of questionnaires, however, relies on individuals to complete them accurately and in a timely manner. Much time can be wasted chasing up missing questionnaires and following up unclear information on completed, or partly completed, question-naires. Because of the heterogeneous nature of information resources, careful consideration should be given before deciding whether the use of a questionnaire will provide results comprehensive enough to enable crucial decisions to be made. Although a well-constructed questionnaire that produces a high percentage response can be a sound, cost-effective approach to gathering information, greater coverage may be achieved through physical observation.

In addition, questions must be framed so that they elicit relevant and accurate information. Open questions will encourage opinions and give freedom to respondents but the analysis of free-ranging responses can be difficult. Closed questions lessen the chance of obtaining information that might be useful but that may not have been thought of. A balance of closed and open questions is ideal.

Open questions should direct the respondent to as specific area as possible. For example, the following questions, while meaning much the same thing, will produce different responses:

A. Having recently attended a records management course, what are your thoughts?

B. You recently attended a records management course. What new skills do you think you acquired?

Closed questions can be asked in a variety of ways, seeking a yes or no answer, providing statement or answer boxes for ticks, ranking scales, for levels of agreement to statements or order of priority of certain issues.

Whatever method or type of questioning is used, only one answer should be sought to one question. For example, the following is actually asking two questions:

> There have been too many leaks of confidential papers and managers should be doing more to prevent leaks occurring.

> Agree_____l_____l_____l_____l_____l_____Disagree

Consideration should be given to the issue of anonymity. If names are not included on completed questionnaires it may cause difficulties in checking the extent of replies received. However, replies might be more honest and open if the respondent is not required to include their name on the form.

Interviewing

Formal or informal interviews can be held with key members of staff to elicit the information required by the audit. These might be carried out in one-to-one situations or with small groups of staff from discrete areas of the organisation's business.

It is vital to target the person or persons who have most knowledge about the records in the framework in which the audit is set. For example, it is not always the head of a unit or department; it may be a clerk who has been in charge of record keeping for several years.

Probably the best approach to interviewing is a combination of the following methods:

- send the questionnaire to key personnel in each business area;
- ask them to complete the questionnaire as far as possible and retain it;
- make an appointment (for up to one hour) at which the issues raised by the questionnaire can be discussed and clarified;
- use the appointment as an opportunity to look at some records and storage equipment.

AUDITOR

Who undertakes the audit will depend on the size of the exercise. Ideally it should be the records manager but it may be too much for one person. If there are staff in the records management unit, it may be a good training/development opportunity for them to participate in the audit under the guidance of the records manager.

EVALUATION OF RESULTS

The task of analysis and evaluation of the data from the audit should be carried out promptly as delay can make the findings obsolete. Evaluation should be made with a use for the information in mind. Records management is meant to improve records and information systems for the people who use them. An audit that results in only a statistical report is of no use. Information gathered from the audit will enable consideration to be given to several issues, for example:

● records that are valueless and could be destroyed immediately – identified from the audit form by low or nil usage rate, or duplication;
● inactive records that could be removed to storage – closed files no longer required for reference that can be removed to cheaper accommodation;
● filing equipment that could be emptied, removed or re-used – the audit may identify partially-filled equipment in which records could be consolidated;
● computers being used inefficiently – the evaluation should take the opportunity to assess whether computerised filing systems, indexes or databases are being put to good use and are improving the efficiency of the information systems;
● records or information that could be consolidated, including the elimination or reduction of duplication – evidence of duplication should be highlighted so that resources are used most efficiently;
● protection of the records against loss, damage, etc – the type of equipment used should take into account the value of the records, including those which may be of archival value;
● effectiveness of systems (filing, indexing, etc.) – staff and user comments may point the way to the need for improvement.

Only when issues such as these have been considered can plans for improvement, appraisal or new programmes begin.

REPORTING

Quantitative data from the audit can be presented in tabular form (for example number of different types of storage equipment), with charts (for example percentage of records covered by disposal schedules) or by graphs (for example comparison of number of staff and amount of records serviced).

Qualitative data, such as physical condition or staff comments, will need to be presented in narrative form.

The audit report should frame recommendations that are clear and that are constructive proposals for improvement or development. They should be short and supported by facts in the report. They may be one of several types:

- Educational – where the recommendation is long-term or developmental, a timetable should be considered.
- Influential – where contact or negotiation and persuasion are needed, consideration should be given to who the important figures might be, whether they have been involved, and who might be able to contribute to implementation of the recommendation.
- Threatening – where some areas might be threatened by a recommendation, the balancing advantages must be taken into account.
- Enforcing – tightening up of procedures may lead to significant changes in culture or attitude.
- Redeploying – where existing procedures or systems may have to change, there may also be implications in budgets, timetable, training, etc.
- Cost saving – where costs can be measured with reasonable certainty, the report should set out the cost benefits clearly.

The audit report should be as short as possible. There should be a summary, which should concentrate on major findings and recommendations, a brief narrative to illustrate evidence gathered during the survey, and factual data.

Recommended structure of the report:

- Executive summary (this is often the only part of a report that many people will read, so it needs to highlight major issues and recommendations in a clear and concise way);
- Introduction and background (why the audit was commissioned, respective roles of the client and auditor in the process);
- Methodology;
- Findings (general and specific to business areas; data should be in annexes, for example people seen, file list, breakdown of storage equipment, etc.);
- Recommendations;
- Summary of recommendations (number and short/concise, referring to paragraphs in the main body of the report).

NEXT STEPS

It is important to take action on the report – not let it sit on a shelf/desk indefinitely. Often a good way to take it forward is to include specific recommendations or proposals in the next corporate/business plan of the organisation.

Consider giving presentations on the outcomes of the audit – to management boards, departmental meetings and similar gatherings. Use established channels of communication to promote the report's recommendations – the intranet, newsletters, etc.

Records managers and others involved in information audits need to be patient and flexible. It can be frustrating when much work has gone into the audit and there is a slow response to the recommendations. This is often the result of budget restraints but can also be because the rationale behind the audit has been lost. Even though some of the data gathered during the audit may not be used immediately to improve record keeping practices, it will be a valuable source of information for future developments.

FILE PLANS

The departmental business classification scheme (file plan) should be recognised as the principal intellectual instrument in records management activities and should be devised and implemented to support the management of the creation and disposal of records and, where possible, the management of security of and access to the records.[1]

INTRODUCTION

New considerations on file plans (business classification schemes) have arisen over the last few years largely as a result of the increasing use of electronic records management systems. This is not to say that the new approaches are not equally applicable to paper systems. Indeed, it has often been said, with some justification, that paper record keeping systems and electronic records management systems should mirror each other. It is clearly not conducive to good business practice to have two different systems operating together. In the increasingly complex operation of public and private sector organisations paper and electronic records are often arranged in mutually exclusive systems. The purpose of the file plan is to achieve intellectual control over both by ensuring that the records are maintained consistently.

A corporate filing system should form the basis of an organisation's information resource. A standardised file classification system has the following advantages:

- it ensures that a clear record exists of how various series of records were created, by whom they were created, when they were created and for what purpose – this is important in meeting the demands of business efficiency and transparency, and also in providing contextual information for future researchers;
- systematic and economical storage of records;

---

[1] Business Classification Scheme Design (The National Archives, 2003).

- timely retrieval of records;
- ready identification of records for review and disposal;
- prevents the duplication of information.

A file plan (business classification scheme) is required by BS ISO 15489 (the international standard on Records Management) and, together with the folders and records it contains, comprises what in the paper environment was often called a file classification scheme or registered file structure. A file plan is thus a full representation of the business of an organisation. As such, it is a useful method of organising information for purposes such as retrieval, storage and more involved processes of records management, such as disposal scheduling.

Some systems (including many proprietary document management systems, shared drive directories in either an 'explorer' or other folder view) can be used to manage documents effectively but without the disciplines of a proper file plan based on business classification. This is insufficiently robust for the management of formal records of business activity.

A file plan should not be tied to organisational structure – that is all too often prone to change or modification. For long-term viability, it should be organised according to more stable or independent criteria.

Inadequate or failing file plans for paper systems should not be transferred or replicated for the implementation of electronic records management. Moving to the electronic environment provides an opportunity to make improvements and develop a tool to meet business needs.

The main purposes of a file plan may be summarised as being:

- providing links between records that originate from the same activity or from related activities;
- determining where a record should be placed in a larger aggregation of records;
- assisting users in retrieving records;
- assisting users in interpreting records;
- assigning and controlling retention periods;
- assigning and controlling access rights and security markings.

DEVELOPING A SCHEME

User consultation is important for successful implementation of the file plan. Support will be needed to help users adapt to viewing, browsing and retrieving information in a variety of new ways. The user interface needs to present a comprehensible and friendly aspect to the end user. Substantial consultation should be conducted with user groups on draft file plans to ensure that there is sufficient acceptance and buy-in by end users. Training on the file plan during implementation will also be required to ensure they know how to use it and understand its uses.

It is also important that users can adapt to being able to view and browse and retrieve information in a variety of new ways in an electronic environment. Realising these benefits is an important part of the business case for electronic records management as well as wider information and knowledge/content management ambitions.

In the paper environment, as the main view of the corporate holding was only normally available to registry staff, users tended to interact with those staff as intermediaries and with a limited subset of the organisation's records (usually closely related to the business unit in which they were employed). Records were generally under the physical control of the business unit that created them until such time as access requirements had declined to such a low rate as to allow their transfer to off-site storage facilities. Once there, if they were viewed at all prior to disposal, it was most likely that any retrieval would be by the same organisational units. Secondary purposes of records emerged haphazardly in some instances but were hardly facilitated by accepted information management practices.

In the electronic environment, the full file plan will be made available to all users. Staff can independently identify almost any existing records that may inform their work. Those records may have been created by a different business unit and not accessed for some time, but will be available to meet a current information need. Not having to 'reinvent the wheel' can lead to significant savings.

FILE PLAN STRUCTURE

Commonly, the intellectual structures for a file plan fall into four types, as detaailed below.

Functional

The functions that an organisation carries out change less frequently than its organisational structure. As changes move functions between organisations, it is easier to restructure corporate filing systems. A strict functional approach will not support case files well. Records managers like functional structures (management is easier); users dislike and do not understand them (hard to use).

Subject/thematic

This structure enables a more common approach across information systems: EDRM, websites, Intranets, etc., it is more easily recognised and understood by users, but interpretation and understanding may vary considerably between user groups.

Organisational

The organisational structure is familiar to end users, perhaps from the paper environment, but is high maintenance and subject to frequent change. Continuity over time is difficult.

Hybrid

A hybrid approach enables compromise between a strict purist approach and operational flexibility. For example: it is functional at a broad level (with disposal rules mostly operating at that level), with subject-based sub-classes.

Table 3.1 Advantages and disadvantages of the four structures

Structure	Advantages	Disadvantages
Functional	Highly rigorous; provides future proofing against changes in organisational structure; the business analysis required to set it up can prompt effective business change; best suited to situations where the functions are discrete, regular and simple	Requires extensive change management programme; may be alien to end-users and services customers; some issues arising with case files
Subject/thematic	Easy to map to other subject classifications	Some users do not find subject indexing and retrieval easy; may be difficult to maintain without full thesaurus support
Organisational	Easy to map on to organisational structure	Frequent changes usually necessary to keep abreast of organisational changes
Hybrid (e.g. functional at high level, subject based lower down with optional flatter case files area)	Can, if implemented successfully, gain most of the advantages of the functional and subject approaches whilst minimising the disadvantages	Perceptual difficulties in set up; often confused for the purist functional approach

RECOMMENDED: THE FUNCTIONAL APPROACH

An organisation's administrative arrangements often change, for example when priorities change or opportunities for efficiency gains are identified. In these instances, functional responsibilities may be moved between departments. Alternatively existing departments may be merged or split. When functions move, current and recent records usually follow.

Although their allocation is prone to variation, functions themselves tend to be quite stable and change little over time. Thus a functional approach to file planning can make the relevant records easier to identify and relocate during times of administrative change.

Functional analysis involves identifying the business functions of an organisation and breaking them down into activities, transactions and perhaps sub-tasks as opposed to existing records or the organisational structure. Various methods may be used, singly or in combination, including hierarchical analysis (top-down) and process analysis (bottom-up). The product is a functional file plan.

Records are created, received or maintained as evidence of business transactions. Therefore, where appropriate to business needs and organisational culture, a file plan can be designed to directly reflect the hierarchical relationship of functions, activities, transactions and records.

One potential huge benefit of the functional approach is the appraisal of the business function (as opposed to the records themselves produced – a costly process involving examining individual files and records within them) and the application of disposal criteria at a higher level as a result of this activity (this disposal undertaking is vital to effective management of records and information – see the chapter on Records Appraisal); both these activities are integral to overall operations. Secondly, any changes in organisational structure need not affect the operation of disposal, so long as records are allocated to a particular function.

DESIGN

The design of the functional file plan should be based on the simple framework of:

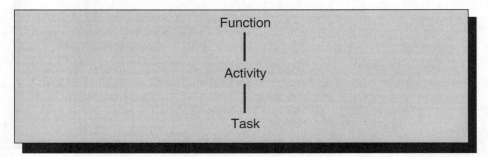

Function	Activity

Function   The largest unit of business process/procedure in the organisation; major responsibilities, managed by the organisation to fulfil its goals; high level aggregate of activities.

Activity   The major pieces of work performed by the organisation to accomplish each of its functions; several activities are often associated with each function.

Task   The smallest unit of business activity; tasks, not subjects or record types.

These definitions depend largely on the way the organisation is structured and, to a certain extent, its traditions and culture. It is not easy to get everyone to agree on these levels and indeed, in some cases, on the definitions themselves. Another way of looking at it might be to regard functions as those high level corporate undertakings that often feature in corporate plans and objectives. Apart from generic functions – such as HR, finance, buildings/estates/accommodation, health and safety, press and public relations/marketing, records management, and freedom of information – they are those for which the organisation was established.

For example, the Department of Health Primary Care Trusts should function to engage with local populations to improve health and well being by improving health status, contributing to well being and protecting health. They should also be commissioning a comprehensive and equitable range of high quality, responsive and efficient services such as: assessing needs, reviewing provision and deciding, priorities, designing services, shaping the structure of supply, managing demand and performance-managing providers. Another function is to directly provide high quality responsive and efficient services such as physiotherapy and a pharmacy service, etc.

Aylesbury Vale District Council provides community services such as housing needs and advice, environmental health, licensing, environment support, recycling, a dog warden and pest control. It also deals with environment and planning issues such as planning, development control, architecture, quality surveying, landscape and historic buildings, etc.

Essex Police functions with many services such as dealing with firearms applications, taking crime reports, collecting road collision information and acting as secure keyholders. They also deal with crime issues such as child protection, community safety and investigation, etc.

Activities might also be seen as those pieces of work that are typically undertaken by teams, units and sections within the functional department, division or group. For example, the human resources (HR) function will have the following activities:

- Recruitment
- Training
- Welfare
- Discipline.

Tasks are typically undertaken by individuals or smaller teams and units. Using the same HR example, the recruitment activity may comprise the following tasks:

- Advertising
- Interviewing
- Examinations and tests.

In some organisations the recruitment tasks might be arranged by staff grades.

Three important considerations should underpin the design of the file plan:

Simplicity

The file plan must reflect functions, activities and tasks that are easily recognisable by users (this usually means that it must align itself with business processes as set out in corporate documents such as visions, policy statements, business plans, aims and objectives). The bottom line is that (as far as possible) in every case it must be obvious into which file or folder a document should be placed.

Consistency

The file plan must have rules and guidelines that ensure all staff/users follow the same procedures. Inconsistencies typically manifest themselves as duplicate files/folders, documents on the same activity being separated, and mis-naming of documents.

Flexibility

The file plan must be adaptable. It must be designed so that new files and folders can be fitted in as and when required, while still adhering to the *function-activity-task* principle.

The focus throughout compilation of the plan should be on functions and activities. Generic terms such as 'committees', 'procedures' and 'minutes" must be avoided, particularly at the top two levels. The view is that, if someone is looking for committee minutes or papers, the search relates to a committee on a specific function or subject.

The design approach describes three levels. It is possible that one or two more level(s) may be required, although these should be kept to a minimum to avoid complex and confusing structures (where, for example, it becomes uncertain in which folder to place a document). Procedurally the Records Manager must control the top two levels of the plan; staff themselves should be in a position to allocate folders at subsequent levels but the records managers should be able to satisfy themselves that accepted file plan procedures are being properly followed.

The plan should incorporate a system of naming conventions so that records are described in a consistent manner over time. This will promote the efficient retrieval and disposal scheduling of records. The organisation should be able to issue lists of accepted terms for particular descriptions or wording, and may even wish to go as far as compiling a thesaurus. In this context much work has recently been completed in the United Kingdom on the development of an Integrated Public Sector Vocabulary (IPSV) – an encoding scheme for populating subject metadata to index and categorise information across the public sector. This controlled vocabulary contains approximately 3,000 preferred and 4,000 non-preferred terms. Using a device such as this can make it easier for people to find the information resources they want on networks and systems such as the Internet or internal documentation systems. For example, using a keyword such as "jobs" typically fails to retrieve items described as 'vacancies', 'recruitment opportunities', 'situations vacant', etc. The IPSV needs to be used together with tools for applying the consistent names in metadata and search engines that read metadata. Detailed information on this can be obtained from the Cabinet Office website at: www.esd.org.uk/standards/ipsv/.

METADATA

A great deal has been written and said about metadata – its definition, its management and its role in records management. For our purposes there are only a few non-technical aspects that we need to understand.

Metadata is often described as 'data about data'. It may be more helpful to describe it as 'descriptive and technical documentation'. A surf of the Internet will reveal numerous slightly different definitions. What is certain, however, is that the term is used differently in different communities. Some use it to refer to machine understandable information, while others use it only for records that describe electronic resources. In a paper environment metadata has often been collected on an ad hoc basis. For example, a series of files or papers sometimes contains a file containing information about the series or collection (in some circles this is referred to as the 'zero file'). The information usually comprises a list of files in the series, the background to its formation (such as legislation, administrative changes, acquisition of new functions), links to other series and a disposal schedule.

There are three main types of metadata: 1) *Descriptive metadata* describes a resource for purposes such as discovery and identification. It might include elements such as title, abstract, author and keywords. 2) *Structural metadata* indicates how compound objects are put together, for example how pages are ordered to form chapters. 3) *Administrative metadata* provides information to help manage a resource, such as when and how it was created, file type and other technical information, and who can access it.

Metadata is key to ensuring that resources will survive and continue to be accessible into the future. Archiving and preservation require special elements to track the lineage of a digital object – where it came from and how it has changed over time – to detail its physical characteristics and to document its behaviour. Only in this way can we emulate it on future technologies.

What metadata might we require for an archival record that we will present to the public? It might include the following: reference, date(s), description of content, former reference, access, format/size, links, creator and language.

Many different metadata schemes have been developed over the years in a variety of user environments. Some of the most common ones are Dublin Core; Text Encoding Initiative (TEI); Metadata Encoding and Transmission Standard (METS); Metadata Object Description Schema (MODS); Encoded Archival Description (EAD), and E-Government Metadata Standard (e-GMS).

For more information on this subject, have a look at the *GovTalk* website: http://www.govtalk.gov.uk/schemasstandards/metadata.asp.

CASE FILES

Where organisations are heavily involved in casework and the case file is a major part of the filing structure, there are important issues that need to be addressed when setting up a new file plan.

A case will normally possess an identifier ('ID') that is perfectly adequate for most purposes and generated from outside the immediate environment of the file classification scheme. Such things have evolved to suit the business needs of organisations in the paper environment. For example an ID from a case management application, a citizen's personal name, an organisation's name or reference number from an authoritative source, or a case ID (or other) as a structured element in folder titling.

Given that it is likely the case is also formed of a number of slightly different transactions, it is perhaps not necessary for the same number of levels of the file plan to classify these records. They may simply be classified as function – activity/task, that is within a 'shallow' area of the classification scheme.

Fitting the electronic equivalent of the traditional case file within a file plan constructed on functional principles is therefore possible, but it means that the scheme, strictly speaking, is probably a hybrid structure. Some examples of case files in a file plan follow.

Table 3.2   Personal files/folders of members of staff within HR

Function	Activity	Task
HR	Recruitment	Advertising Interviewing Examinations and tests
	Training	Senior management courses Middle management courses Planning and strategy
	Welfare	
	Discipline	
	Personal files – by name	

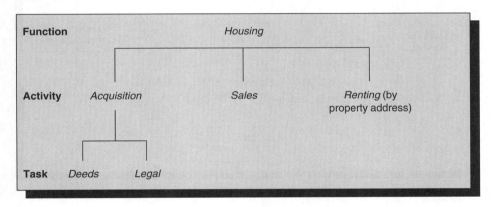

Figure 3.1   Housing rent files/folders

CASE STUDY – THE W DEVELOPMENT TRUST

BACKGROUND

The Trust is a registered charity and was established to provide opportunities and community support in an area of London hugely affected by a major road construction project. Its overall brief is to develop 23 acres of land for community benefit.

61

The Trust wanted to introduce more robust records management policies and procedures so that it could function more effectively and more economically in a professional and efficient way. Particular focus was placed on the establishment of new procedures relating to the creation and disposal of records and information.

W Development Trust is a small organisation, comprising about 30 staff, but covers a wide range of functions and maintains a high profile in the local community. Its structure is as follows:

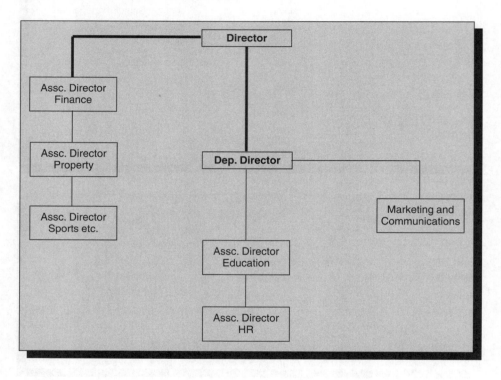

METHODOLOGY

A survey of record holdings in WDT was carried out by employing a standard questionnaire (sample 1 on page xx) and this was supported by informal interviews with key members of staff. The survey was conducted in accordance with standards in common use throughout the UK central government. The aim of the survey was to gauge views on the record-keeping arrangements within WDT and to confirm needs in this area. The opportunity was also taken to study the organisation of folders and sub folders on the Trust's local area networks (F:/ and L:/ drives).

Various sources were consulted during the survey, including:

- Code of Practice on the Management of Records under section 46 of the Freedom of Information Act (2002) – although the Trust is not subject to the provisions of FOI, this code sets out best practice in records management generally and can be used or adapted for most organisations.
- BSI ISO 15489 – Information and documentation records management Part 1.
- Retention Scheduling Guidelines: various types of records.
- The Trust's website.
- Data Protection Act 1998: A Guide for Records Managers and Archivists
- Modernising Government: Framework for Information Age Government: Electronic Records Management.
- Health & Safety at Work Act 1974, Fire Precautions Act 1971, Fire Precautions (Workplace) Regulations 1997.
- Various British Standards such as BS 7799, 5839, 4737, 7042 and 5979.

FINDINGS

Storage facilities for records varied – the main method being lever arch files/ring binders and loose files on open shelves. There were some two and four drawer filing cabinets in the offices. Accommodation to store records is limited with the inevitable result that innovative use of floor space had been made.

It was common practice throughout WDT for individuals to keep files on the area(s) for which they were responsible and these were stored within the appropriate business unit. The accessibility of information was impaired by this method of record keeping; the absence of individuals or small work groups meant that records and information could not be located in a timely fashion. Information was usually stored according to locally devised filing systems with manually controlled indexes that were often not available to other WDT staff, even within the same business unit. These individual filing arrangements ranged from controlled and organised collections to extensive and disorganised personal archives containing material that should have been disposed of years before, which may also have been infringing Data Protection provisions.

There was no central guidance on records management, and systems and procedures had evolved piecemeal as the organisation grew. Each business unit tended to work in isolation and to follow its own practices for creating records, tracking and retrieving information. This promoted a disjointed organisation in terms of the management of information. The need to share information was considered to be increasing in importance as organisations like WDT need to meet business targets and become more accountable and transparent. Whilst it was felt that a few areas of WDT could operate in isolation (for example Human Resources), the overwhelming majority of WDT operations needed to consider this important aspect of working.

A sizeable majority of administrative and corporate information was kept in paper form (that is files, folders etc.,) and often as multiple copies. For example, documents were invariably created electronically but, in all likelihood, authors and recipients printed them out for filing as well as retaining them electronically.

WDT staff used office software and e-mail to create and exchange electronic documents. However, they usually attempted to manage these documents as records in a paper format, with a general 'print to paper' policy for information. In some instances the content of the paper and any electronic versions of files did not match. Some WDT staff were aware of this situation and invariably treated the paper files as the authoritative source. This was considered an area of vulnerability for WDT and it was felt to be fortunate that any legal/professional repercussions resulting from inconsistent file formats had been avoided at the time of the survey. The authenticity of the 'record' might also have been called into question. Overall, this situation was not at all surprising and occurs frequently in organisations that operate 'hybrid' paper and electronic records systems. In part, it is a training matter that should reflect corporate policy in this area, but staff need to appreciate the importance of maintaining a complete corporate record in whatever format is pertinent.

Users saw printing electronic documents and placing them in paper files as an increasingly burdensome process. On the other hand, the practice within WDT of relying on paper files meant that the electronic version of documents was not consistently managed. Without any central guidance or imposition of a coherent records management system/file plan, documents were stored unpredictably in a variety of locations and under varying names.

There was no corporate disposal policy for WDT records and there were many instances of records and information probably being kept unnecessarily. A minority of business units did have some form of disposal guidelines but any scheduled actions often fell prey to other priorities, leading to failure to take required actions. There was no defined corporate policy for the retention, storage or disposal of electronic versions of files or e-mails.

There were occasional clear outs of paper when, for example, it became apparent that information was also kept in electronic form or room was required for office space. In some areas the Trust was keeping information unnecessarily – long after its operational use had disappeared – while at the same time not identifying those records that might have had long-term value (historical or legal).

There was significant duplication between paper and electronic records. In a paper environment some duplication is expected (in order to facilitate accessibility) but with electronic access only one source for each document/record is required. It was felt important that WDT's corporate record should be identifiable; duplication made this difficult.

RECOMMENDATIONS

The effective management of its information is crucial to the Trust's business processes and objectives. It is important that not only technical data but also administrative and management information is handled efficiently and made accessible as and when required. WDT needs to co-ordinate and share information in a much more coherent fashion if it is to function well in the modern business environment.

The Trust must be clear on what is its corporate information. As office procedures become increasingly electronic and business processes rely more and more on electronic information, there is a danger that there will be confusion over what are the up-to-date corporate documents within the Trust's workflow. It was strongly recommend that one electronic drive on the computer system be identified to hold the corporate record. Other drives must only be used for personal records and non-corporate information. Becoming used to this practice will be important when (as seems inevitable) the Trust acquires an electronic records management system.

It was recommended that a records management policy statement be compiled, covering all aspects of records management, such as:

- commitment to create, keep and manage records which document WDT's principal activities;
- the role of records management and its relationship to WDT's overall strategy;
- the responsibility of individuals to document their actions and decisions.

File plan

It was recommended that a corporate filing system should form the basis of the Trust's information resource. Individuals could still have responsibility for their own records but there should be central control of the system (from the Records Manager).

A draft file plan was provided (see below). The design of this was based on the simple framework of

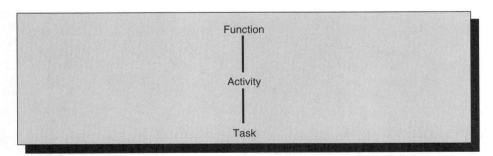

The design was based on the premise that WDT ought soon to be considering and implementing an electronic records management system. With this in mind there should be no need for the duplication of records that is the norm for most paper systems. Access can be provided across sites and, through access control mechanisms, controlled to the relevant staff. Managers, for example, can access the same records as finance and HR staff to exercise their devolved responsibilities although the specialist staff remain at the centre.

Implementing the File Plan

It was suggested that a 'vesting day' be assigned for implementation – a specific day on which the new file plan would come into operation. The actual date of this depended on how the change might be fitted in with current work and deadlines. Consultation with staff/users, of course, was essential.

It was recommended that, rather than use lever-arch files or ring binders, conventional file covers be used throughout. This system of keeping paper records was considered to be more economical and made the documents more accessible.

The Trust had to decide which format would be considered their *corporate* record. Until it was able to obtain and implement an electronic records management system, it was recommended that this is paper. Nevertheless, WDT would clearly want to manage some of its information in existing shared drives (local area network) system. Electronic folders allocated should fit in with the file plan – it may often be the case that there will be paper and electronic files/folders with the same title so that there is one corporate system; this was considered not only acceptable but highly desirable.

At vesting day all existing paper files should be closed (a final sheet of paper on the file or large writing on the cover should indicate this (for example: *File Closed. No Further Papers to be Added. See new file* ...). All existing electronic folders should be made "Read Only" and staff required to place documents in the new folder structure that accords with the file plan.

Table 3.3   File plan structure

Function	Activity	Task
Arts		
Communication	Events	
	Marketing	Advertising
		Reports
	Press and Public Relations	
	Publicity	Newsletter
Community Development	CEA Sub Committee	
	Charities	
	Grants	
	Member organisations	Individually named files
Corporate Governance	Annual General Meetings	
	Audit	
	Compliance	
	Development projects	*individual project files*
		Management
	Director	
	Management committee	
	Performance management	
	Policy management/development	
	Risk management	
	Strategic planning	
Education	Appraisal	
	Administration	Management reports
	Courses	
	Funding	Applications
		individual funders
	Grants	
	Learners	Attendance
		individual files
		Policy
	Policy and development	
	Projects	*individual projects*
	Stakeholders	*individual names*
Facilities Management	Buildings maintenance	Cleaning
		Repairs and refurbishment
	Car parking	
	Contracts management	Individual contracts
	Emergency planning	
	Energy management	
	Equipment	
	Grounds maintenance	

67

	Health and safety	Accidents/incidents
		Administration
		Fire precautions
		Inspections
		Manual
	Licensing	
	Mechanical and electrical services	
	Pest control	
	Planning and development	
	Postal services	
	Reception	
	Security	Advice and guidance
		Equipment
		Inspections
		Liaison with police
	Telecommunications	
Financial Management	Accounting	Audit
		Guidance
		Invoices
		Payments processing
		Receipts processing
		Rents
		Reports
	Asset management	Assets audit
		Asset register
		Current assets
		Current liabilities
		Depreciation
		Disposals
	Budget management	Planning
		Reconciliation
		Reports
	FS Sub Committee	
	Insurance	
	Investments	
	Pay	
	Pensions	
	Planning and strategy	
	Procurement	
	Tax management	
Human Resource Management	Agency staff	
	Attendance management	Leave
		Overtime
		Sickness recording
		Timekeeping
	Conditions of service	
	Discipline	
	Employee relations	

	Manpower planning and organisation	
	Performance management	
	Recruitment	Advertising
		Interviewing
		Job descriptions
		Vacancies
	Staff records	*individual files*
	Training	Courses
		Development programmes
		Induction
	Welfare	
	Work experience	
IT Management	Database management	
	Maintenance	
	Software development	
Knowledge and Information Management	Data protection	
	Freedom of Information	
	Library	
	Records management	
Legal	Legislation	
	Litigation	
Property management	Key holders	
	P & P Sub Committee	
	Tenants/Property	Policy
		named tenants/property files
Sports and Fitness	Community sports	
	P G Fitness Club	Administration
		Community
		Gym
		Reception
		Sales and marketing
		Studio
	SF Sub Committee	
	Sports Centre	Accommodation management
		Customer care
		Duty management
		Income allocation
		Induction pack
		Lost property
		Policy and procedures
		Reception
		Registration
		Staffing
		Waiting lists

SAMPLE FORM/QUESTIONNAIRE 1

Survey Questionnaire

XXX District Council

Questionnaire on the Management of Records and Information

I should be most grateful if you could take some time out to complete the attached questionnaire prior to our meeting on xxxxxxxxxx. It should help to save time at the meeting and give us a good pointer to the type of information held and how it is used and disposed of.

If you would like to include any extra information or need to use an extra sheet, please attach the papers to the form. You need not return the form – it is being used to guide you in the direction of the records issues that will be raised.

Glossary of terms used:

Section	a section/unit within a division working on a specific area of work (eg sustainability team in environmental health; countryside services in leisure). Where the division has a single function the term section should be interpreted as the division
Disposal	the review and subsequent retention or destruction of records
Information	covering records in all formats (paper, electronic, etc)
Registered file	official file forming part of a discrete series, classified and referenced in accordance with accepted practice (eg DAN/1/4/6)
Review	examination of a record to see if it has any further administrative or historical use

Unregistered file informal folders or information held by individuals, neither of which are on a standard system

Vital records those records without which a section could not continue to operate, and which contain information needed to re-establish the section in the event of a disaster

Thank you for your cooperation

1. Date Completed:	2. Branch and Function:

3. Person completing form and contact details:

4. What main categories of information does your section hold? (eg planning applications, registers of electors, policy files)

5. How information is held in your section. Please tick formats below (take all categories as one source of information): – registered files – personal network drive (h) – unregistered – ersonal disk drive 9c) – floppy disk – other – network drive (f)	6. How much of this information is held on more than one of the forms (%)?

7. Does your section have a policy for disposal of your records, including electronic?

If so, please give outline details (continue on a separate sheet)

8. What do you consider to be your vital records?	9. What indexes/finding aids does section hold to help you locate records? (eg manual list, database) Do you use standard terms/naming conventions?

10. How much of the information held by your section is not used for current work (%) (including off-site storage)?

11. Where and how does your section store records (eg 4 drawer cabinets, open shelves, etc)? Please indicate how many items of teach type of equipment.

12. What and how much (%) information is currently made available to:
the general public?

13. Please indicate what and how much other information in your section, if any, could be made available to:
the general public?

shared with other branches in XXDC?

shared with other branches in XXDC?

other authorities/organisations?

other authorities/organisations?

14. What requests do you receive for the information that your section holds (please tick)?

     Public representatives (MPs etc) Internal

     Companies/organisations   Public

15. How much time do you spend looking for information each week (please tick)?

Less than 1 hr   1 – 3 hrs   4 – 6 hrs   7 – 10 hrs   Over 10 hrs

16. How often do you NOT find what you want (please tick)?

Never   Rarely   Sometimes   Often   Constantly

SAMPLE FORM/QUESTIONNAIRE 2

Survey Questionnaire

- *Complete this form electronically*
- *Do not remove the form's protection*
- *Use the tab key to move between questions*

Who is filling in this form?	
1. Name	
2. Job title	
3. Section/subject	
4. Date	

Description of the record series/collection	
5. Record series title	
6. Alternative title or reference code	
7. What information is in the series?	
8. Earliest date (year only)	
9. Latest date (year only)	

10. What format are the records? (Select all that apply. Some collections may contain both paper and electronic information)

Paper:	Electronic:
Loose papers	Word
Loose papers in folder	Excel
Cardboard files	PowerPoint
Ring binders	Access database
Lever arch files	HTML
Bound volumes	PDF
	E-mails
Other (please specify)	Other (please specify)

11. Approximately how many individual files are there?	

12. For paper records, how many linear metres of shelving do the records occupy?	
13. For electronic records, how many megabytes of storage do the records occupy?	
14. How is the collection organised?	
15. Do you have a list or index of the records in the collection?	

Information about the use of the collection

16. What function gives rise to the records	
17. Who creates the records?	
18. Who uses the records?	
19. What are the records used for?	
20. How long are the records needed?	
21. How often are the records consulted?	

Information about the management of the records series

22. Who is responsible for the series?	
23. Does someone know how to use/maintain the records?	
24. Is the collection still accruing?	
25. If yes, what is the rate of the accrual?	
26. How long do you keep the records?	
27. Why?	
28. Does legislation require you to keep the records?	
29. If yes, please give further details	

30. Where are the records stored?	
31. For paper records, do you have systems for tracking who has a particular file?	
32. If yes, please describe the system	
Access and security	
33. Who should have access to the records?	
34. Is the information in the records disclosed to anyone outside the organisation?	
35. If yes, to whom is the information disclosed?	
36. Are these records vital records?	
37. If the records are vital records, what arrangements have you made for their protection?	
38. What measures are taken to keep the records securely?	
39. Do the records contain sensitive or confidential information?	
40. What type of sensitive or confidential information do they contain?	
41. Do the records contain personal information?	

42. If the records contain personal information, what group of people is the information about? (select all that apply)	
Students	Staff
Customers and clients	Suppliers
Applicants	Research subjects
Others (please specify)	

43. If the records contain personal information, what personal details are included? (select all that apply)	
Name	Contact details
Date of birth/age	Nationality
Financial details	Physical or mental health or condition
Racial or ethnic origin	Sexual life
References	Education and training details
Employment details	Gender
Goods or services provided	Offences (including alleged offences)
Criminal proceedings, outcomes or sentences	Others (please specify)

44. If the records contain personal information, who provides that information? (select all that apply)	
Data subject	Staff
UCAS	Other (please specify)

Relationship with other records	
45. Are the records direct copies of records held elsewhere?	
46. If yes, please give further details	
47. Do the records duplicate information held elsewhere in the organisation?	
48. If yes, please give further details	
49. Do these records relate to other records?	
50. If yes, please give further details	

4 Records maintenance

AIMS

This chapter covers general maintenance procedures for records and information, focussing particularly on the semi-active phase of the life-cycle and the management of records centre operations. It examines the storage of records, retrieval and replacement, tracking and business recovery planning. Most of what it has to say is relevant to records in all media, but attention is drawn specifically to issues where special arrangements need to be made for electronic records.

SEMI-CURRENT RECORDS

As we have seen in Chapter 2 (Compliance and regulation), records that are in regular use in an organisation that created them are generally called 'current records'. When they are no longer required for the conduct of current business, but still need to be kept for reference or legal purposes, or may have potential for permanent preservation because of their historical value, they become 'semi-current records'. At this point they should be removed from business areas and current systems, so that they do not take up space unnecessarily. They should be stored in a records centre or intermediate repository pending their disposal under schedules or as a result of appraisal. Such a place provides more economical storage and maintenance, and facilitates systematic disposal. Many private companies provide records centre facilities. The choice between using an external provider or keeping the operation in-house might be based on a number of factors but economy and security are usually paramount.

RECORDS CENTRE OPERATIONS

You should ensure that a records centre provides a general service to all parts of the organisation (that corporate approach again). It should be a high-density, low-cost storage area, equipped with a system for retrieving and consulting the records held. The records centre receives and makes available all records that have any continuing use, regardless of their bulk or form. The centre should be safe, secure, clean, efficient and economical. It should be capable of holding all designated semi-current records in all media and able to provide a dependable retrieval service. It is a fundamental rule that no records should be transferred to a records centre unless appraisal has taken place and there is an action date attached to the records. Records that are deposited in a records centre and that have no date for disposal or review soon become forgotten about and store up extra work for the future.

SECURITY

You should not contemplate transferring records to a records centre if it is not completely secure. A high level of security must be maintained both externally and internally at all times. If there is any suspicion of poor security, how can you or your colleagues have confidence in it? To all intents and purposes its services will be rendered useless. It is important that all users of the records centre know that the facility is safe and secure. A records centre must be:

- externally secure;
- environmentally secure so that records and information can be maintained in a usable state for long periods;
- clean and orderly.

It should not be possible for unauthorised persons to gain access to records in the records centre. All of the storage conditions and access controls in the records centre should conform to the same requirements that were in force when the records were current. In some cases it may be necessary for a special area to be set aside for confidential records, in order to satisfy business security concerns. These areas should be separated from the rest of the storage area by a locked enclosure, and access should be restricted to staff who have been specially authorised for this purpose. However, records management staff should seek to declassify records according to regulations and guidelines whenever possible. Don't allow obsolete restrictions to remain in effect, preventing the full and appropriate use of the information in the records.

Everyone in the records centre should be identifiable. Usually, all people in the facility are required to wear a visible identity card. Staff should wear a card carrying their photograph, and visitors should wear a temporary identification card issued to them at the entrance. Anyone on site without a visible identity card should be challenged. The entrance to the records centre should have a prominent notice that no unauthorised persons are permitted. Intruder alarms should connect automatically with the appropriate police or security authorities.

Keys to the building should be controlled by the centre manager who should keep a record of all keys issued to personnel. If push-button control pads or combination locks are used, the manager should take care to control the security codes used. These ought to be changed on a regular basis (like you are required to change the password on your computer at frequent and regular intervals). All external doors must be kept locked, subject to health and safety regulations. Keys should be numbered and kept in a locked security cabinet. Spare keys for use in an emergency should be kept in a location set out in the business recovery plan.

The records centre should be isolated from any dangers that might threaten the safety of the records, including fire, flood or natural disaster. This system of isolation should be supported by the installation of automatic alarm systems and by constant monitoring of the area. Smoke, fire and flood alarms should connect with the appropriate fire service. Staff should be trained in the use of extinguishers and should know what to do in an emergency. All alarm systems should be tested regularly. How many records stores have you seen with sprinkler systems? Hopefully, not many. It is generally accepted that the water from such systems will, in the event of a fire, do more damage to the records than a fire. Much better to use hoses and fire extinguishers with a smoke detection system.

Boxes of records transferred to the records centre should themselves carry no markings that give a direct indication of their contents. Usually the reference numbers of the records contained therein is sufficient for retrieval purposes. This form of anonimity is one of the best forms of security as far as access to the records is concerned.

CLEANLINESS AND ORDER

The records centre must be clean. This means that the records in it must be protected from damage by dirt, insects or rodents or infestation by moulds. To maintain cleanliness, no one should be allowed to eat or bring food into the records centre. Smoking must be prohibited in the records centre at all times, and there should be prominent notices to this effect. The records centre should be cleaned, dusted and inspected on a regular basis.

The records centre should also be orderly. This means that the records kept in it must be in proper order on the shelves, so that any record can be found at any time with a minimum of delay. Records should be kept in proper containers or wrappings, clearly labelled with their reference codes. There should be suitably adapted storage facilities for records not in conventional format, such as maps and plans, photographs, audiovisual material and electronic records. You will need to weigh up the cost of spending a lot of money on storage of semi-current records against the possibility that the majority of them will be destroyed. Can you identify those records that are likely to contain historically valuable material (and thus likely to be selected for permanent preservation after the appraisal process)? If so, will you want to ensure that these are given a little more attention than those that are likely to be destroyed after appraisal? You may be sure that you will not be wanting to spend money on protecting those records that are transferred to the records centre with specific destruction dates. The following is a brief overview of suggested storage requirements for records in non-conventional formats:

Maps and plans

Maps and plans are best kept in plan cabinets equipped with drawers or in vertical plan cabinets equipped with hangers. If these are not available, cardboard tubes should be used. For permanent preservation, maps, plans and drawings are usually wrapped around the outside of core tubes. In a records centre it would be acceptable to roll the maps, plans or drawings inside cardboard tubes, as this tends to protect them from accidental damage during use. This practice would be especially appropriate for maps, plans or drawings that are not destined for permanent preservation.

Photographs

Photographs should be kept in acid-free folders, individually, and kept in a controlled environment. It is also important that links between photographs and other records be retained; it is often impossible to understand what a photograph depicts unless the contextual documents reveal this information.

Film

Cinematograph film also requires special storage conditions. If the film is nitrate based, it should not be accepted into the records centre under any circumstances, as it poses a significant fire risk. If the film is on safety stock it may be accepted for storage under controlled conditions. These records, like any others, should be subject to appraisal and have an action date for destruction or transfer to the archival repository.

Audio tape

Audio tape requires the same storage conditions as films. Consideration should be given to keeping equipment on which the tape can be played in the records centre.

Video tape

Video tape should be stored in conditions similar to those used for electronic records

Electronic records

Provisions for the storage of electronic records in the records centre should conform to up-to-date industry standards. In general, electronic records should be stored in areas free of dust and magnetic fields and protected from fluctuations in temperature and humidity.

EFFICIENCY AND ECONOMY

Every record held in the centre should be retrievable quickly and easily. There should be service level agreements with the provider. If the service provided by the records centre includes more than just storage and retrieval (such as review and transfer), these should be included in any such agreement.

Records management staff should be able to calculate and report reliably on the costs and benefits of the service and how these relate to possible alternatives. Consider the following factors to ensure that cost targets are met:

- The unit cost of space in a records centre is less than that in active office buildings. The records centre is itself a less expensive building than an active office site because it is designed or adapted for its specific purpose. However in some situations there may be special factors that affect these relative costs.
- Records can be stored more densely in a records centre than in an office. This density can be quantified in terms of the ratio between cubic metres of records stored per square metre of floor space.
- Records centres are organised so as to be able to identify and retrieve records efficiently, whereas offices are generally organised in support of administrative services.

IN HOUSE OR CONTRACT OUT?

Should you manage records centre operations as part of your organisation or should you contract them out to another organisation (in the private sector)?

Outsourcing (as it is generally known) has been a live issue for many years in the public sector – ever since the 1980s when pressures to reduce public expenditure were applied. It has been driven by such initiatives as market testing, competitive tendering and the reduction of administration costs. There is undoubtedly an attraction to outsourcing in that the process will provide a clear and well documented view of what the customer requires (that is users of the records management services that is provided) and of what they get. These factors stem from service level agreements and performance measurement schemes that normally accompany the process.

The reasons for and benefits of outsourcing should be based on:

- Cost (especially fixed costs)
- Quality of service
- Initiatives and innovations on the part of the supplier
- Flexibility
- Trained and/or specialist staff.

There is no generic answer to the question posed in the sub-heading. It rather depends on individual circumstances and management preferences. In setting about outsourcing, however, there are five steps to take.

Evaluation

Is there senior management support to the proposal? How effective is the current service in meeting customer needs? You should be analysing the cost benefit of outsourcing over a period of five to seven years. In considering potential suppliers you should take account of how far they understand the needs of your organisation, their track record, how flexible they are, and how committed they are to providing an efficient service. You should also consider whether any existing practices and procedures will be affected by the outsourcing (for example, appraisal and disposal).

Specification

The services you want must be clearly stated and set out. There must be no room for misunderstanding. A specification should describe in general terms the service required and then provide detailed descriptions of each part of the service – conditions of storage, packing, production and despatch, timings, security, contacts, staffing, etc. This specification will form the basis of the contract. It may be advisable to have these details checked by a legal representative.

Selection

Criteria must be agreed by the records manager with stakeholders (for example, contract staff and service users) and a plan for selecting the preferred supplier drawn up. This is likely to comprise three stages – initial sift (eliminating bidders who clearly do not meet the main criteria or where submissions are incomplete), interviews and visits to suppliers' premises.

Implementation

You will need to decide how the process is going to be managed. You might, for example, prefer to have direct control in the hands of the records manager or you may wish to hire a consultant. There are two important aspects that need to be taken into account to ensure successful implementation: 1) Management information: required by both parties to measure performance and identify trends; 2) Managing customers' expectations, especially vital where the service may differ from that provided when the service was in-house.

Consolidation

This will be based upon effective monitoring of the service and the relationship established with the provider. Indicators that show how well the service is working include customer reaction, confidence in performance and business efficiency.

STORAGE OF RECORDS

The majority of semi-current records will be destroyed. However, if your provider follows best practice with their storage, it will have invested wisely – the records will remain accessible for business purposes and the future need for conservation work on those records that will be transferred to archival storage will be lessened. It is a fine balance to make.

Environment

Unsuitable environments have damaged records more extensively than any other single factor. Careful control and observation of temperature, humidity and ventilation within storage areas and regular maintenance of heating/ventilation systems are essential. A stable environment is of paramount importance. Fluctuations in temperature and relative humidity will cause significant damage. A temperature within the range 13° to 18° C is recommended. Relative humidity should be in the range 45% to 65%. If it exceeds the latter figure, there is a significant risk of mould growth within 48 hours.

Non-paper records will require different parameters. Microform records should be stored in accordance with BS 1153 1992, *Processing and storage of silver-gelatin-type microfilm*. Sound recordings and videos should be stored in an environment of 4° to 16° C temperature and 40% to 60% relative humidity.

Environmental conditions should be monitored weekly. Thermometers are essential to check temperature readings. Hygrometers should be used to check relative humidity levels. Thermo-hygrographs provide for weekly print-outs of temperature and humidity readings. Monitoring equipment should be calibrated once a month.

LIGHTING

Lighting should provide a minimum illumination of 100 lux at floor level in order to meet health and safety requirements. A secondary automatic lighting system, independent of the normal mains supply, should be provided for use in an emergency. Other emergency lighting, such as torches in each storage area, should be available.

Windows should be fitted with filters, such as tinted film, to eliminate any harmful ultra-violet rays. High light levels should be avoided in order to minimise the fading of paper and ink.

Shelving and boxing

Semi-current records should be stored on shelves in a way that facilitates retrieval. This will not only provide for access to the records but will also make security checks more effective. There are four main ways of storing paper records:

- Reference number order
- Review date order
- Numbered boxes
- Random.

Each of these has advantages and disadvantages. For example, storing in reference number order may make retrieval easier but, depending on the nature of the series, gaps may appear as review and disposal is carried out, necessitating work in closing up or leaving wasted space. Storing in review date order will make efficient use of the space but may make retrieval protracted. Storing in numbered boxes – it is common to keep records with the same disposal date in the same box – requires an index or database of what records are in what boxes. Similarly, a random system, where the next available space in the store is used to store the next deposit, requires a detailed finding aid of what records are on what shelf.

Film should be stored in dust-free metal cans and placed horizontally on metal shelves. Microform, sound recordings and video tape should be stored in metal, cardboard or inert plastic containers, and placed vertically on metal shelving.

Records should be stored off the floor to provide some protection from flood, dampness and dust.

Large documents, such as maps, should be housed in special storage equipment to ensure that they are not damaged and are readily accessible.

The width of aisles and general layout of storage areas must conform to fire, health and safety, and similar regulations.

ELECTRONIC RECORDS

The short- to medium-term preservation period of electronic records will vary according to business needs. It is likely that increased dependence on electronic record-keeping will mean that organisations will wish to retain data for longer periods.

The British Standard BS 4783 1988, *Storage, transportation and maintenance of media for use in data processing and information storage*, recommends the following environmental conditions for data storage media:

Table 4.1 Recommended environmental conditions for data storage media

Device	Operating	Non-operating	Long term
Magnetic tape reel, 12.7mm	18 to 24° C 40 to 60% RH	5 to 32° C 20 to 80% RH	18 to 22° C 35 to 45% RH
Magnetic tape cassettes, 12.7mm	18 to 24° C 45 to 55% RH	5 to 32° C 5 to 80% RH	18 to 22° C 35 to 45% RH
Magnetic tape cartridges	10 to 45° C 20 to 80% RH	5 to 45° C 20 to 80% RH	18 to 22° C 35 to 45% RH
Magnetic tape – 4 & 8mm helical scan	5 to 45° C 20 to 80% RH	5 to 45° C 20 to 80% RH	5 to 32° C 20 to 60% RH
Optical disk cartridges (ODC)	10 to 50° C 18 to 80% RH	−10 to 50° C 5 to 90% RH	18 to 22° C 35 to 45% RH
CD-ROM	10 to 50° C 10 to 80% RH	−10 to 50° C 5 to 90% RH	18 to 22° C 35 to 45% RH

CUSTODY OF DIGITAL RECORDS

There is undoubtedly an issue concerning the custody of digital records. The rapid decline of immediate business needs for many records in the digital environment presents several challenges to their survival. The identification of secondary purposes of records will have to take place far earlier than has been the case for records in more traditional formats. Unlike paper records, which will

85

survive extended periods provided basic environmental conditions are met, active intervention is required to ensure digital records remain accessible. Media will require refreshment before it suffers fatal degradation; migration to more current or open formats may be required. Action may be required to bring valuable records held on personal or shared workspaces under the control of corporate policies.

One thing should be made clear about the retention of digital records. Although their storage is relatively and increasingly inexpensive, their management across time is likely to be costly owing to the active operations referred to above.

There is currently a great deal of investigation and consultation being undertaken in this area. Some preliminary findings and thoughts are summarised below:

- Public authorities have to take into account the requirements of freedom of information legislation when considering the storage and custody of digital material. In many cases the implementation of FOI legislation has been a driver for reaching decisions on custody of such records.
- Storing digital records for extended periods will inevitably mean that not all of them can be maintained online; offline storage may make responses to FOI requests within the statutory twenty working days difficult.
- Many organisations in the public sector do not yet have the facilities to handle semi-current or archival digital records. For many, resourcing such facilities is extremely difficult.
- Policies and procedures for the appraisal of digital records are being developed and agreed, and these need to be in place before custodial issues are resolved.
- It is envisaged that there will be a range of options to cover the needs of public sector organisations. Typically, there will be specific agreements between organisations and archival institutions on custody and transfer.
- Different working relationships are bound to evolve in respect of the custody of digital records but more particularly over questions of access and the custody of sensitive material.
- There may be scope for setting up a records centre or intermediate repository for the semi-current digital records of large parts of the public sector (for example, central government and the National Health Service).

BUSINESS RECOVERY PLANNING

The National Archives has undertaken considerable work in disaster planning and business recovery. Its guidance to central government is particularly generic and much of it is repeated here.

Protection of records against elements such as floods, fire, theft and loss through carelessness or, in the case of electronic records, disk failure and software bugs, is an essential part of the records management role. Adequate measures must be taken to safeguard all of an organisation's records. While it is important to recognise the value of preventative measures, records managers should also have in place a plan specifically designed to secure an organisation's vital records and to react effectively and efficiently in the event of a disaster. A business recovery plan should cover both prevention and reaction. It should be concerned with short to medium term measures enabling the organisation to continue its business with minimum disruption. It should not be confused with business continuity management, which is concerned with service over the longer term, such as staff shortages in specialist areas.

Business recovery planning comprises three main activities: risk assessment, identification of vital records, and the plan itself.

RISK ASSESSMENT

The process of risk assessment has three elements, detailed below.

Identification

This element falls into four main categories.

1. Flood: Water damage is the most common form of disaster to affect records. Much of this can be avoided by improving design and maintenance of buildings and expert advice in this area should be sought. However, there are a number of actions that records managers can undertake to minimise the risk of damage:

- Identify and check regularly potential internal and external hazards (for example, heating systems, water tanks and water pipes).
- Identify and regularly check potential penetration hazards (for example, windows, gutters, skylights and drains).
- Ensure that heating and air-conditioning systems are regularly checked and serviced.
- Consider the possibility of installing flood alarm systems (for example, sensors on water tanks).
- Raise bottom storage shelves five centimetres above floor level.
- Fit top storage shelves with metal covers.
- Consider boxing important series of records.
- Obtain information on local flood danger periods.
- Never put records on the floor.

It is worth noting here that it is not now considered good practice to have sprinkler systems in records stores, particularly archive stores. In the event of the system being triggered, the water will do considerably more damage to the records than the fire it is trying to extinguish. This happens mainly because it is difficult for sprinkler systems to be locally applied in the same degree that a fire would occur. The result is that large numbers of records that were not in imminent danger from the fire will be soaked. Hose reels and extinguishers, combined with an effective detection system, are usually the most efficient weapons against fire.

2. Fire: Records managers should have regular contact with fire precaution officers for their organisation. Each must be kept up to date with latest developments in their areas – the records manager needs to be satisfied that there are adequate measures (in the form of procedures, announcements, drills, etc.) that will protect the considerable asset for which they are responsible; the fire precautions officer needs to be made aware of the collections of records, where they are stored, who has access to them, and in what form they are, so that adequate measures may be taken. For example, collections of microfilm or magnetic (back-up) tapes will require different protection from paper records. In the United Kingdom the Health & Safety at Work Act 1974 and related regulations place particular obligations on organisations in respect of fire precautions. Records managers should be aware of these obligations. There are also British and International Standards relating to fire precaution. Two of the most relevant are: BS 5588, Fire precautions in the design, construction and use of buildings (various parts covering particular aspects); and BS 5839, Fire detection and alarm systems in buildings.

In identifying their own risks the following actions can be undertaken:

- Ensure that all existing fire regulations in respect of doors, extinguishers and alarm systems are enforced.
- Ensure that fire exit and other relevant signage is adequate, particularly in isolated areas such as records stores.
- Maintain a list of inflammable substances and isolate them from the building.
- Keep storage areas clean and tidy.
- Check electrical wiring regularly.

vPermit smoking only in designated, safe areas.

- Maintain liaison with local fire prevention officers.
- Ensure that staff are kept aware of procedures and means of escape in the event of fire.

3. Physical Security: Each building and each collection of records poses its own security problems. Records managers should liaise closely with security officers to minimise the risk to their holdings from loss or theft. The following actions should be undertaken:

- Caretakers/security guards should check all entrances to buildings, including ground floor windows and basements, after closing time each day and at least once every twenty-four hours during weekends and holidays.
- Buildings with no caretaker or security cover should be fitted with an automatic intruder alarm system.
- All staff members should be aware of the need for good security, for example, good key control and identification procedures. Good key control is very important. All necessary measures must be taken to prevent a compromise of key security. For example, if a key is lost, locks must be changed immediately.

4. Other. Unlikely risks to the records, such as infestation from insects and animals, and environmental pollution, should also be taken into consideration. Prevention measures, including traps and poisons, and filtering systems, should be taken.

Estimation

However many risks your organisation faces, there are relatively few effects. They might be categorised as: 1) Loss of critical systems, site or personnel; and 2) Denial of access to systems or premises.

In order to estimate potential disasters, local geographical, environmental and political factors, as well as the nature of the work of the organisation, should be taken into account. For example:

- What is the likelihood of flooding? Obtain information from local emergency services who will be able to identify vulnerable areas.
- What is the quality of the fire precautions systems? Ensure that they are checked regularly and that the local fire brigade is invited to inspect them on a regular basis.
- Is any of the work of your organisation of a sensitive nature that might attract theft or bomb threats?
- What is the volume of the identified vital records?
- What are the retrieval requirements of the identified records?
- Are special storage facilities required for all, or some, of the records, such as electronic and microfilm?

These estimations should be prioritised in order of the degree of risk. They will differ from organisation to organisation but they must be the result of an overall risk assessment programme or procedure.

The risks to electronic records may be significant. For example, electronic records could be lost through a system failure caused by internal or external factors. The risks are best avoided by having suitable storage plans and strategies. A back-up system is generally recommended. The ease with which back-ups can be rotated and protected is a key consideration in the selection of storage options. The records manager will need to liaise closely with Information and Communication Technologies (ICT) staff in order to ensure that each is aware of the other's requirements.

Evaluation

An indicator system might be used to evaluate the risks. An example is given below.

Table 4.2   Risk evaluation

Impact:		Likelihood	
1	major problem; mixture of business risks and project risks	a	high – likely to happen
		b	medium to high – could happen
2	could cause problems – mainly project risks	c	medium – might happen in right conditions
3	unlikely to cause real problems	d	low to medium – probably will not happen
		e	low – very unlikely

IDENTIFICATION OF VITAL RECORDS

Vital records are those records without which an organisation could not continue to operate. They are the records that contain information needed to re-establish the business of the organisation in the event of a disaster and that protect the assets and interests of the organisation. It is estimated that up to ten per cent of an organisation's records can be classified as vital. A distinction may be drawn between vital records and emergency records:

vital records   those whose long term preservation must be ensured to allow the organisation's functions to continue.

emergency records   those that are required for immediate access but that are not crucial in the long term.

90

The following guidance covers both these types.

The records manager needs to analyse the business and the records it produces in order to identify critical processes and functions, identify key internal and external dependencies on which these processes rely, identify external influences that may have an impact on critical processes and functions, and identify the records relating to the critical processes and functions.

Since it is expensive to make special protection arrangements for records it is important not to be tempted to include everything that *might* be vital. Key points to consider are whether the processes or functions can be re-established without the records concerned. What is the senior management view of the importance of the functions to which the records relate? For what length of time is this information required?

For the purpose of identifying vital records, all records might be classified into four groups. These are detailed, and some examples are given, in the following table.

● Vital – those records without which your organisation cannot continue to operate and which cannot easily be reproduced, if at all, from other sources
● Important – can be reproduced from original sources but only at considerable expense
● Useful – loss would cause temporary inconvenience
● Non-essential – no value beyond immediate purpose

Here are some examples of these four categories:

Table 4.3 The four categories of records

Category	Examples
1. Vital records: those without which the organisation cannot continue to operate and that cannot be easily, if at all, reproduced from other sources	Legal documents, including current contracts Corporate plans Manuals of instruction Current accounts (payable and receivable) Records identified for legal retention and other records required for evidential/legal purposes Computer software programmes and data Indexes and other finding aids to records Systems administration documentation
2. Important records: those that can be reproduced from original sources but only at considerable expense	Minutes of meetings of named committees and sub-committees Training manuals Directories File plans

3. Useful records: those whose loss would cause temporary inconvenience	Correspondence files Presentations for regular undertakings (conferences, training courses, etc. Training modules Management reports
4. Non-essential records: those with no value beyond their immediate purpose	Visitors' records Information about specific events (which have taken place) Advertisements (for example recruitment) Newsletters

When vital records have been identified they should be documented so that everyone in the organisation is aware of them. Such documentation should include:

Description	category or type of vital record
Disposal reference	cross reference to any disposal schedule pertaining to the record(s)
Format	how the vital record is protected (duplicated, dispersed, etc)
Location	where protected vital record is held (the copy, if duplicated)
Supporting documents	description of any supporting documents such as finding aids
Original or copy	whether the protected vital record is an original or copy
Box number	reference number of record's container

An example of a log of vital records is shown at the end of this chapter.

Protection

There are three options for protecting vital records:

- Duplication and dispersal (the duplicate may be in paper or alternative format, such as microform or CD).
- Use of fireproof and secure storage facilities.
- Remote storage.

The storage of records in electronic form may involve significant risks, such as technical obsolescence, but many of these can be avoided by the use of adequate storage plans and strategies. A back-up system is generally recommended. The preservation of electronic records is examined in chapter 6.

RECOVERY PLAN

The business recovery plan brings together the actions necessary at the time of an incident, details who needs to be involved, and how and when they are to be contacted. This should be coordinated with the local risk register. Your organisation should have a procedure or activity for risk assessment. Typically this will provide an estimation of the level of risk for all facets of the organisation's work, from staffing to record keeping. General risks might include an inability to recruit sufficient staff to meet the organisation's/unit's/team's objectives, the fact that staff absence has an adverse effect on targets, and response time to computer downtime is inadequate.

The risks will be laid out in a risk register that will show likelihood, impact, measures to minimise risk, etc. An example of a risk register is shown at the end of this chapter.

The recovery plan must be reviewed at least once a year and updated, if necessary. The plan should cover:

- Identification of business recovery teams
- Training and awareness programmes
- Emergency equipment
- Supplies and services
- Back-up and off-site storage arrangements
- Vital records.

Recovery Teams

Teams of three or four people should be formed to undertake salvage operations under the supervision of a Business Recovery Officer. They should be prepared to take part in the operations during or after a disaster and appropriate terms and conditions for overtime and unsocial hours work should apply. They should live within a reasonable distance of the building(s) by walking, driving or reliable public transport, and should be available on the telephone.

Training and Awareness

It is essential that all staff, especially new staff, are made aware of potential hazards, what to look out for, and what to do in the event of an emergency. This should be part of general health and safety awareness programmes or induction programmes. Information distributed to staff must be regularly updated. The records manager will need to work closely with the health and safety officer or their local representatives to ensure that both have relevant and timely information.

Staff directly involved in business recovery should make regular tours of buildings to familiarise themselves with alarm systems, fire extinguishers, shut-off points for water, gas and electricity, location of recovery equipment, and assembly points in the event of an emergency.

They should also liaise with local fire prevention officers, be familiar with the use of fire-fighting equipment, and ensure that business recovery information is kept up to date.

The Business Recovery Officer and Business Recovery Teams should undertake regular practices of the recovery plan to ensure that the procedures are still effective. This is best done by subjecting unwanted records to damage, by water or fire or some other agent, and putting the plan into effect. Such practices are very often valuable in identifying areas where the plan is susceptible to improvement.

Emergency Equipment

It is unlikely that equipment and materials to cover every emergency can be stored. However, supplies of essential equipment should be kept in different strategic areas of the building in storerooms or cupboards that are clearly marked. Small items for use in an emergency should be kept on trolleys for easy transportation. Larger items might be stored centrally or be available for loan or hire at the time of the emergency. Essential equipment should comprise:

- Buckets
- Mops
- Rubber gloves
- Floor cloths
- Hazard tape
- Torches
- Protective clothing
- Plastic sheeting
- Blotting paper
- Plastic crates
- One crate containing identification forms, large polythene bags, name tags and string, pencils and pencil sharpeners, scissors and cotton tape
- Plan of the building showing electricity cut-off, water shut-off valve, gas shut-off, sprinkler system/CO_2 system, fire extinguishers, stored chemicals and emergency equipment.

Supplies and Services

The plan must include lists of staff having specific responsibilities, with their contact details, who may need to be summoned in an emergency. In addition to the Business Recovery Officer and Business Recovery Teams, these may include key holders, building maintenance managers, first aiders, and security.

A list of services, companies and individuals, with contact details, should also be made. Those that might be needed in an emergency include:

- Gas/water/electricity authorities
- Fire/ambulance/police services
- Carpenter
- Glazier
- Locksmith
- Electrician
- Plumber
- Pest control officer
- Fire alarm service
- Legal adviser
- Conservation document salvage service
- Deep freeze facility.

The most common items likely to be needed are:

- Pumps
- Fans
- De-humidifiers
- Vans/trucks
- Additional crates.

Check to see what organisations there are locally that can provide document salvage services or deep freeze facilities. If it is likely that such a service will be required, it is advisable that they be contacted for details before an emergency occurs. By doing this it is possible to evaluate services and costs outside an emergency situation.

Storage Arrangements

In the event of an emergency it is likely that alternative provisions for storing records will be required. The recovery plan must include the location and contact details of back-up storage facilities, which may be off-site. This will require further liaison for the records manager – this time with the estates or accommodation manager.

Vital Records

The plan should include priority lists of what items should be salvaged first. The inventory of vital records (see above) could be annotated accordingly.

Model Recovery Plan
(Reproduced by kind permission of The National Archives)

REACTION PROCEDURE

1   During Working Hours

1.1   For emergencies occurring during working hours, it is essential that every member of staff be acquainted with procedures to raise the alarm.

1.2   The Head of Security [*or Estates Manager or designated person*] must be contacted. That person should be aware of maintenance or building work in progress in order to be able to assess the disaster situation effectively in so far as it affects records and information.

1.3   If the incident cannot be contained, the Business Recovery Officer must be contacted. That person will contact people from the Business Recovery Teams.

1.4   No records should be moved until the arrival of the Business Recovery Officer who will assess the damage and the help required in the first instance.

2   Out of Working Hours

2.1   Night security guards should take any action that will reduce or limit the potential damage, *if it is safe to do so*. This might include:

- turning off stopcocks
- switching off electric lights
- unplugging appliances
- closing doors and windows
- using hand-held fire extinguishers.

2.2   Even if the incident can be contained, the Estates Manager [*or designated officer*] must be informed.

2.3   If a disaster cannot be contained the emergency services must be informed and the following personnel must be contacted immediately:

		Tel. no.
• *name*	Estates Manager	xxx xxxx
• *name*	Central Services Manager	xxx xxxx
• *name*	Head of Security	xxx xxxx

[*or designated staff*]

2.4   The Estates Manager must visit the site and, after assessing the disaster, contact the Business Recovery Officer or their deputy:

	Tel. no.
● *name*	xxx xxxx
● *name*	xxx xxxx

2.5 No records must be removed until the arrival of the Business Recovery Officer who will assess the damage to the records and the help that is required in the first instance. They will:

- contact emergency services if necessary
- contact appropriate staff
- decide on the area(s) to be used for the assessment of damaged records
- allocate staff rest area(s)

2.6 If it seems that the emergency will mean the closure of the office, the Business Recovery Officer must contact the organisation's head to inform them of the situation. Emergency procedures not directly concerned with the management of records and information should then be implemented (for example, procedure in the event of a power cut).

RECOVERY PROCEDURE

ALL STAFF MUST WEAR PROTECTIVE CLOTHING BEFORE STARTING WORK

1 Instructions for Estates Manager [*or designated officer*]

1.1 When alerted about a disaster the Estates Manager must view the disaster location as soon as possible and assess the situation, in order to estimate the extent of the disaster recovery procedures and back-up facilities required.

1.2 The Estates Manager must contact the Business Recovery Officer and appraise them of the situation so that procedures to contact Business Recovery Teams can begin.

1.3 The Estates Manager must also contact facilities management personnel.

1.4 Facilities management personnel will liaise with security staff to ensure that the building and surrounding areas are secure from unauthorised access.

2 Instructions for Business Recovery Officer

2.1 When alerted about a disaster the following members of staff must be contacted before going to the disaster location. They should be put on alert for possible further action:

[*name*]   [*post*]   [*tel. no.*]

[*these staff members might be those most closely concerned with the particular records that have been damaged or senior management*]

2.2   The designated conservation document salvage service or deep freeze facility must be contacted and informed about the disaster.

2.3   On arrival at the disaster location contact must be made with the Estates Manager and, when access to the building is permitted by the Emergency Services, the damage assessed.

2.4   Air drying will be suitable for small quantities of records which have only been slightly damaged by water. Thus, if the disaster can be contained in this way, the following procedures should be followed:

- the requisite number of people from the Business Recovery Teams summoned to deal with the situation;
- use fans and de-humidifiers to assist the drying process;
- stand damp volumes upright and gently fan out the pages; interleave with blotting paper, if possible;
- books printed on coated paper and photographic prints should be interlaced with silicone release paper to prevent blocking;
- blotting paper should be placed between individual sheets of files;
- change blotting paper regularly;
- do not attempt to separate material stuck together; this is a job for expert conservators.

2.5   Small amounts of dry fragmentary material (resulting, perhaps, from fire damage) should be gathered and made available to staff of the business area to which the records belong in order that it might be identified and salvaged, if necessary.

2.6   If the disaster cannot be contained, as many members of the Business Recovery Teams as possible should be summoned. They will work under the direction of the Business Recovery Officer. When they arrive at the location of the disaster, security staff should issue them with special passes for which they must sign when entering or leaving the building. They must also be issued with protective clothing.

2.7   An assessment area must be designated to which damaged material can be taken. The major requirement for this will be enough space to lay out records and pack material for freezing.

2.8   Arrange with the facilities management staff for the installation of emergency lighting, if this is necessary.

2.9   A suitable rest area for the business recovery staff should be provided. If there is no mains water supply, the Estates Manager should be asked to arrange for a supply of drinking water and other necessary facilities. *Health and safety of the staff must be given the highest priority.*

2.10 Cupboards and doors to storerooms containing emergency equipment must be unlocked. These are located at:

xxx   xxx

2.11 Before any full-scale salvage operation is begun the Business Recovery Teams must be briefed on the following:

- location of disaster
- allocation of tasks
- location of assessment area
- location of rest area
- location of first aid room
- rotas and rest breaks.

2.12 A log of events must be kept (including photographs, if possible) and a final report on the disaster made to senior management.

2.13 Communication between teams must be maintained at all times.

2.14 Liaise with the Press Officer if the disaster attracts media attention. All requests from the media are to be referred to the Press Officer or, in their absence, to the most senior person available.

3   Instruction for Business Recovery Teams

3.1 Try to get to the location of the disaster as quickly as possible. Keep the Business Recovery Officer informed if any delay is encountered.

3.2 Having been issued with a special pass and protective clothing, report to the Business Recovery Officer.

3.3 Make sure that you have the following information:

- location of damaged records
- task assigned to
- assessment area
- rest area
- location of first aid facilities
- any areas declared out of bounds.

3.4 Any areas adjacent to the location of the disaster should be protected by plastic sheeting to prevent any further damage occurring.

3.5 When records are removed they must be labelled in the most convenient way to indicate their title/reference and location.

3.6 Damaged records must be removed from the location of the disaster to the assessment area using plastic crates and trolleys. Records should be removed from the floor first, keeping them open or closed as found. When removing records from shelves, the top shelf must be emptied first, working sequentially towards the bottom shelf. The records should be placed in polythene bags to prevent further damage before being loaded into the crates. Boxed records might be moved without having to place them in crates.

- Trolleys are to be found in [xxx].
- Crates are to be found at [xx].
- Recovery materials are kept in the emergency equipment cupboards and storerooms located at [xx].

3.7 Material slightly damaged with water can be treated by fan drying (see section 2.4).

3.8 Dry but fragmented material should be placed in a designated area ready for inspection by staff from the business areas to which the records relate. If possible, they should be sorted into those areas.

3.9 Records that have suffered bad water damage must be packed in polythene bags and packed into crates. Lists of material removed must be kept, showing the number of the crate into which each record has been packed. The crates must then be taken to a collection area for transportation to the allocated deep freeze facility. Freezing records in this way will prevent further damage while they are waiting to receive attention. Other badly damaged records should be set aside for the attention of the designated conservation document salvage service.

3.10 After records have been removed, excess water should be mopped up.

4   Restoration of the Disaster Area

4.1 The disaster area should be restored to normal use as soon as possible. The prime responsibility for this will rest with the facilities management staff.

4.2 Temperature and relative humidity readings should be taken as soon as the disaster area has been cleared.

4.3 De-humidifiers (to reduce relative humidity) and fans (to increase air circulation) should be installed, if necessary.

4.4 Walls, ceilings, floors and shelving should be washed thoroughly with a fungicide (such as sodium ortho-phenyphenol solution in water) to inhibit mould growth.

4.5 Areas can be put back to use when the temperature and relative humidity levels have stabilised at acceptable levels for a period of seven days (see the Records Management Standard: *Storage of Semi-Current Records*, RMS 3.1, PRO, 2000).

APPENDICES

1

Location of Disaster Equipment

....

2

Plans of Buildings

....

Table 4.4 Example of a Risk Register

Ref	Description	Category	Impact (1–3)	Probability (1–3)	Lack of control (1–3)	Proximity (1–3)	Risk rating	Counter measures	Owner	Contingency plans	Date entered	Up-dated	Status
2	Lack of resources – budgets		2	3	2	2	**24**	Cost modelling Resource planning Budget planning	KJS	Seek more funding. If necessary, amend scope and task timetables	29/5/06	15/1	open
3	Lack of resources – manpower, skills		3	2	2	2	**24**	Resource planning Budget planning	KJS	Seek more resources	29/5/06	15/1	open
7	Lack of coordinated communication plan		3	3	2	2	**36**	Compile plan	GG	Use process team leader forum to encourage teams to produce individual plans	19/9/06	22/1	open
9	No formal Project Manager		3	3	2	3	**54**		DB	Management Board agreed to appoint	7/7/06	16/11	closed

Table 4.5 Vital Records Log

Department/Section	Address/Location
Chief Executive's Department	Canary House, Main Street, Norwich NR32 1TU

Description	Disposal reference	Protection Format	Location	Supporting documents	Original or copy	Box number
Management Board minutes and papers, 1998/99	Sch 4/97	Duplicated record	Main Street Record Store, Norwich	Index to minutes and papers on database in Chief Executive's Office	Copy	168
Corporate Plan 2005–2009	Sch 4/97	Dispersed	IM Record Centre, London E1		Original	169

103

5 Records appraisal

AIMS

This chapter examines the evaluation of records and information for business and historical retention. Rather than undertake a philosophical examination of records appraisal, it aims to concentrate on the how and what of the process. It focuses particularly on the sampling of casepapers and disposal scheduling, and covers the physical destruction of records. The term 'appraisal' is used here to mean the process of deciding what records need to be kept for continuing business use and for historical preservation. It does not include, as is the case in some countries, the determination of what records need to be created and captured into record keeping systems.

BACKGROUND

Deciding what records should be kept and for how long is an important task for public sector bodies. A feature of government in the twentieth century has been the phenomenal growth in the quantity of records generated. The advent of the information age and electronic records has only accelerated this process.

Records and information need to be retained for three main reasons:

- For business purposes, as long as the need to consult them exists.
- For legal reasons, as evidence of title/precedence or under various statutory provisions.
- For historical value.

The retention of too many records is expensive in terms of staff, time, space and equipment. It is dangerous to think that you can keep everything in electronic form because storage is so cheap. Up to a point this is true, but what happens when systems are upgraded and you need to migrate information to new platforms or new software? Then you will find how expensive record keeping can become. Changing computer systems is the electronic equivalent of moving accommodation – time to have a clear-out – only electronically it can be much more difficult and expensive. Much better to have a system of regular disposal in the first place.

Making decisions on the continuing utility of records for an organisation's own purposes is, in effect, risk management. In other words records and information managers must weigh relative costs, such as the actual financial cost of retaining records on the off-chance that the information will again be used against the loss of effectiveness or accountability by not having the information available. This is not the same as saying that regulatory requirements, such as audit, can be ignored if there is only a small chance that particular records may be required for regulatory purposes. One of the aims of records management is to ensure that regulatory requirements are met. Any records that might be needed for audit must therefore be retained until the audit for that period has been conducted.

It is not necessary to retain records until all possibility of them being required again has ceased. Rather, retention periods should represent the point of balance between risk and continued retention.

There is no prescriptive legislation in the United Kingdom that says what information in the public sector must be kept and what must be destroyed. Records appraisal policies and procedures stem from advice and guidance from such organisations as The National Archives and professional bodies like the Records Management Society within an overall framework of enabling legislation. Some statutes, however, have an important bearing on how long records are kept; these are explored more fully in the following pages.

It is not in the interest of the public sector generally or the general public to retain records for longer than they are reasonably required to support identified needs. To attempt to preserve and maintain accessibility to all public sector records indefinitely would be prohibitively expensive and impractical to manage – even in the electronic environment. In addition, there are certain types of records, such as those containing personal information, which the public expects will be disposed of when they are no longer required for the purpose for which they were created or for related administrative purposes and where there are no other overriding factors requiring their retention; in the United Kingdom such parameters are governed by the Data Protection Act 1998.

All records are created for an identifiable business or administrative purpose and the majority of these records can be disposed of by destruction once that purpose has been fulfilled and all legal and accountability requirements for their retention have been met. In essence organisations need to ask themselves: 'Do we need this record any longer for the conduct of our current business?' If the answer is 'no', the record can be destroyed, subject (of course) to any possible historical value, because there are some types of records that, because of the purpose for which they were created, the activity they document and the information they contain, have enduring value to government or to the general public. These records are identified and kept as archives. In central government records are usually kept for permanent preservation for two main reasons: 1) As a record of the administration of government – often called 'The Nation's Memory' and 2) To provide material for historical research.

The first of these is paramount. It is the primary reason for the existence of a national archives. It explains why the majority of records in archives have not been consulted by researchers – but they will be, eventually.

In other parts of the public sector the emphasis is more towards research. Local authorities in the United Kingdom, for example, do not enjoy well-established connections with local archive repositories and the identification of local cultural heritage and history is almost non-existent from their point of view. Rather, the activity is in the other direction. Local record and archive respositories are collecting institutions and often rely on personal connections to identify potentially historical material. Ad hoc arrangements are often made to appraise this and transfer it to the archive. Records and information managers in local authorities and other parts of the public sector outside central government should consider establishing more formal arrangements with local archivists. The latter can provide valuable advice and guidance on the appraisal and disposal of records that will help organisations to achieve greater business efficiency.

The process of appraisal is important to ensure that the records that should be kept are kept for as long as they are required – either for finite, identified periods or as archives – and that disposal decisions are properly justified and documented (as required, in the United Kingdom and an increasing number of other countries, by Freedom of Information legislation).

A planned and sytematic approach to the appraisal of records in the United Kingdom central government was first introduced in 1954 as a result of the report of the Grigg Committee (Committee on Departmental Records, Cmd 9163, 1954). Before then the destruction of records and the identification of national archives was characterised by ad hoc decision-making and cumbersome procedures. The Grigg Report provided a new framework for the appraisal and review of public records. Overall the report formed the basis of the legislation under which The National Archives still operates – the Public Records Act 1958.

As mentioned above there is no systematic approach to appraisal in the United Kingdom outside central government. There have been significant moves in this direction, however, over the last few years (encouraged, no doubt, by the need for better records management in a Freedom of Information environment) but there is still a long way to go.

The theory of appraisal in many countries is based upon the writings of

Theodore Schellenberg, particularly his *The Appraisal of Modern Public Records* (1956) (excerpts also published in *A Modern Archives Reader*, National Archives and Records Administration, USA, 1984). Since then many new approaches have been adopted but the basic theory of primary/secondary and evidential/ informational values still hold good.

It almost seems too obvious to say that it is necessary that records are neither disposed of too late nor too early in their life cycle. If disposed of too early, records with continuing utility or enduring value may be destroyed. If disposed of too late, resources are wasted in storing and maintaining unneeded records.

ELECTRONIC RECORDS

Nearly all of what is said in the following pages on this subject is applicable to all records in whatever format they may be. Appraisal is about evaluating the inform- ation in the record not the format. However, there will be exceptions. In most cases it should be obvious where descriptions and advice pertain only to paper records or only to electronic records (or only to records in any other format for that matter). Where this is not the case, particular attention has been drawn to statements.

One important aspect about the appraisal of electronic records is that they have to be appraised at an early stage in their lives. Traditionally historical appraisal, particularly, has been perceived to gain more validity by taking a view over time. Evaluation has typically taken place 25–30 years after the record's creation. We cannot, of course, afford that luxury with electronic records. Almost certainly, after that time span, the technology – both hardware and software – will have become obsolete. Practitioners will often recommend that electronic records be appraised at creation – making greater use, for example, of disposal schedules. Where this may not be possible, the maximum period up to which to undertake appraisal should be five years.

KEY TERMS

Let's understand the key terms in the appraisal process before we go any further. Different words and phrases are used by different people in the profession but, for the purposes of this book, the following have been adopted:

Appraisal   The process of evaluating an organisation's activities to determine what records should be kept, and for how long, to meet the needs of the organisation, the requirements of government or other accountability, and the expectations of researchers and other users of the records.

Disposal	The implementation of apprasial and review decisions. These comprise the destruction of records and the transfer of custody of records (including the transfer of selected records to an archival institution). They may also include the movement of records from one system to another (for example, paper to electronic).
Disposal schedule	A list of collection/series of records for which pre-determined periods of retention have been agreed between the business manager and the records manager.
Retention	The continued storage and maintenance of records for as long as they are required by the creating or holding organisation until their disposal.
Review	The examination of records to determine whether they should be destroyed, retained for a further period, transferred to an archival institution or presented to a third party.

KEY PROCESSES

Appraisal is not just the process of determining the medium- to long-term value of a record. It also involves determining what the records are (or what they will be once they are created), who creates them and why, how they relate to the creating agency's functions and to other records, how, when and by whom they are used. Once all this information is known, the continuing utility or enduring value of the records can be assessed. The appreciation and analysis of the context of a record is a vital part of the overall process of appraisal.

The appraisal and disposal of records are two distinct activities, but they are inextricably linked. They need not be undertaken together; indeed they are usually separated by a prescribed period of retention. However, appraisal that is not followed in due course by disposal is pointless; and disposal without prior appraisal is an unsound practice and may even be unlawful.

DESTROY NOW OR REVIEW LATER?

At the creation of certain categories of records, such as minutes of a top-level committee, it is possible to predict how long those records are likely to be needed by their creators and users. It is also possible to predict that the records will have an enduring value because the evidence they contain will have a permanent value for the purposes of evidence or historical research. For many other categories of records, however, it is not always possible to predict at the point of their creation how long their usefulness or value will last. For example, no matter how precisely the contents of a series of operational files has been defined, it will not be possible to determine in advance whether the whole series will have an enduring value or whether the whole series may be destroyed at a future date. For this reason, review at a later date will be necessary for some categories of records. However, the aim should always be to determine a future action at the time the records are created, whether that is to destroy the records after a certain period (up to which they may have reference use even though thay may have passed out of day-to-day use), transfer them to an archival institution or review them at a particular date.

APPRAISAL PROCEDURES

Records appraisal must not be an ad hoc exercise. It should not be undertaken in a hurry when the quantity of records has outgrown the storage space available or when an organisation has to move to new accommodation. If it is done in such an unplanned, non-systematic manner, the wholesale, uncritical destruction of records may take place. Similarly it is often the case that records are examined item-by-item in order to separate current, semi-current records and non-current records – a very time-consuming exercise. Some of the non-current records may then be offered to an archival institution for appraisal to determine whether any of the records have historical value. The archival institution then has to review these records without the necessary contextual information about their origins or purpose. All of these scenarios are extremely wasteful of resources.

Several different systems of appraisal have been formulated over the years. Debates still rage over the various methodologies. There seems to be overlap between some of them. It is not the intention here to play the advocate for a particular approach. Have a look at the three main methodologies below and decide which one or combination of them best fits the particular situation in which you find yourself. At the end of the day the objective of appraisal ought to be three-fold. From a business point of view, to idientify those records of continuing use to the functions and activities of the organisation. From a historical perspective, to aid the selection of records that document the history of the organisation/sector (it's 'memory'), and the provision of records for historical research (as far as is practicably possible, giving the users what they want).

FILE-BY-FILE REVIEW (CENTRAL GOVERNMENT: THE GRIGG SYSTEM)

In the United Kingdom the report of the Grigg Committee in 1954 recommended a process of First and Second Review for public records (essentially the records of central government). This featured only paper records (electronic records did not exist at that time) and evolved as shown in the following table:

Table 5.1   Standard procedure for handling the appraisal of public records

	Action	Time	Period
A	Record opened	0	0
B	Record closed	5	5
C	First Review	B + 5	10
D	Second Review	A + 25	25
E	Opened to the public	B + 30	35

Key:
Action A – the record is created (at nil years in time, after nil years have passed)
Action B – it was recommended that government departments and agencies close their records (files, folders, units) when they became five years old *or* when they became too thick. This rider of thickness, while sounding pedantic, was based on good reasoning (which took on added importance under Freedom of Information legislation). Experience had shown that information and data was being lost or damaged because files and folders were being over-used in an attempt to maintain all papers relating to a case or process on the same physical unit. Organisations were encouraged to open new parts to a file when the papers exceeded the width or gusset of a standard file cover. This over-filing was not often policed effectively; it was felt that scarce resources were better employed in more important areas – after all, once these records had ceased to be active, they were consigned to basements and storerooms, and forgotten about until they reached their assigned disposal period. They were not accessible to the public generally (the general rule of access to public records was from thirty years) and were rarely required for reference. With the introduction of Freedom of Information, however, the possible need to access the records increased; the thirty year rule was abolished and this 'closed' information was suddenly accessible to those who wanted to see it. It made sense, therefore, to ensure that none of this information was damaged or destroyed through poor record keeping.
Action C – Five years after closure of the record it is given a first review. This is the administrative or business review. The main decision is whether the record is of further use for the conduct of current business. If not, it can be destroyed. If, however, it is considered to have possible historical value, it is set aside for a further (second) review. A period of five to ten years (depending on when the record was closed) will have elapsed.
Action D – Those records that survive the first review are given a second review when they are twenty-five years old. This is the historical review – is the record worthy of permanent preservation in an archives because it has historical value?
Action E – Under the Grigg system the selected records were then made available to the public (as a general rule – there were some exceptions permitted under the legislation) when they became thirty years old.

The First Review was mainly the provenance of the records manager of the organisation which held the records. In the UK central government records managers were called 'departmental record officers' (DRO) – all public record bodies were required to appoint a DRO as part of the introduction of the Public Records Act 1958. The National Archives (known, until April 2003, as the Public

Record Office) supervised the process. Thus knowledge and expertise of the functions covered by the records was brought to bear – a sensible, if obvious, approach since the main decision centred round business or administrative requirements; it also meant, of course, that those undertaking the review were very likely to have been in the organisation at the time the records were created and thus have direct knowledge of their content.

The Second Review was a joint operation between the DRO and staff of The National Archives (currently having the title 'Client Managers'). Thus a historical expertise was brought to bear on the records. The role of the Client Managers included background analysis and investigation of the records under review – the contextual requirement mentioned above. In practice, especially in large organisations, reviewers employed by the government departments undertook the work under DRO and Client Manager supervision. These reviewers were (and are) often former employees of the department and are recruited for their knowledge and experience of the organisation's functions.

No matter how knowledgeable the records manager (DRO) or archivist might be, it is not possible to find enough time to deal with all the records of a modern government department in this two-stage way. Appraising all of its records, file-by-file, item-by-item, is beyond the human and financial resources of any organisation. Overall in the UK government, if this were the case, the amount of records that would currently be considered for second review would amount to over 100 miles of shelving. The aim of an appraisal process should always be to reduce it to a routine whenever possible, so that it becomes part of the regular activities of the records professional and the administration.

Outside central government

In many countries local authority and similar records (although not often records from schools and universities) are integrated, as far as policy, procedures and legislation are concerned, with the records of central government. In the United Kingdom this is not the case. Local authorities rarely have a tradition or understanding of the value of records outside the business environment. In addition, procedurally, they often operate in silos so that different records systems operate in different units of the authority. This approach is a recipe for disaster in that it promotes widespread duplication, decision-making is impaired and the efficacy of business procedures is thrown into doubt.

How can these authorities learn from the systems that have been well-established in central government? As might be expected there is no easy answer to this question. The search for a solution is examined, as far as possible, in chapter 8, *Roles and Responsibilities*. It involves trying to ensure that the records management function is recognised as an important and corporate function in the organisation. It is much easier to say this than do it, especially with the strain on resources that many public sector organisations experience. But what is the alternative? Unless something is done, records and archives management will become moribund in such areas.

In the context of appraisal the lessons learnt must first embrace the principles of appraisal. When managers and operational staff understand that the implementation of such principles are beneficial to them and their business, they can go on to take the practical steps necessary to achieve the better management and accessibility of their records and information. This sounds easy and somewhat presumptious but organisations without accepted procedures for disposing of unwanted records effectively cannot go on as they are for much longer. As digital records become the norm over the coming years, they will find their recordkeeping problems magnified by the accompanying technical issues.

For a number of reasons, file-by-file appraisal (or values-based appraisal as it is sometimes called) does not identify the best records of enduring value. These reasons include the following:

- No matter how objective or informed the appraiser, it is impossible to predict all the potential users and uses of records.
- The quantity of records in the second half of the twentieth century is too great.
- The approach tends to downplay the importance of the provenance of the records (the organisational and functional context of their creation) in favour of the subject of the records.
- There is too great a potential for the interests and biases of the appraiser to determine what records should be preserved on a long-term or permanent basis, to the detriment of research by those with different interests.

MACRO APPRAISAL

Having said that there will be no advocacy for a particular system of appraisal, it has to be said that the dual review procedure is impossible to apply to electronic records. By the time such records are twenty-five years old, we would have to pay a visit to the local science museum to find equipment and software to look at the records. Electronic records will not have been 'pruned' by a business review at an early stage and set aside for a second review later on to determine long-term value. Their transient nature does not allow us to do this. Some other method has to be found.

Macro appraisal methodologies have gained greater prominence with the increased creation and use of electronic information. Far more records are created in an electronic environment than in the paper world. Our work patterns have changed over the years and we have an unquenchable thirst for more information. Electronic systems will often create this information automatically –

it does not have to be entered in the form we want to use it. This mass of information cannot be appraised in the same way as paper records. A higher level evaluation needs to take place. This may mean losing some information that might normally have been selected in paper methodologies or even selecting some information that would normally have been discarded with traditional methodologies. The electronic records manager needs to strike a balance between this possible loss and losing all the information by not appraising in time. The macro approach involves:

- Examining the background to the organisation – the legislation under which it operates and its administrative history.
- Analysing the organisation's structure to establish what it did, how it did i,t and why it did it; also what it does now and how it does it.
- Identifying relationships with other organisations and with stakeholders.

The focus of this process is the structure of records and information. It can be defined as assessing the value of records at an organisational, departmental or unit level rather than at an individual document or file level. The methodology requires the examination of an organisation's structure, what it did, how it did it, why it did it, what it does now and how it does it. The focus is on identifying what parts of the organisation (and following from that what parts of its file plan) contain information that is likely to be of long-term value. The analysis is often accompanied by a breakdown of the organisation along the following lines: committee structure, policy areas, operational work, what is published, databases, special records for consideration (for example, scientific information), and internal administration records.

A key to the analysis is to understand the position of file prefixes, units or departments in the wider organisational context. The aim is to alert appraisers to key documents so that they can target selection accordingly.

The results of the analysis should be documented, in the form of a report, so that they can be referred to in future appraisals. The analysis will help in the development of disposal schedules and will serve as a useful guide to future development of file plans.

When folders in the file plan that contain information fitting the selection criteria are identified they will be selected and transferred accordingly.

Table 5.2 Example file plan

Function	Activity	Task
Shared Services	Strategic Services Operational Services	
Corporate Governance	Audit	External audit Internal audit
	Boards	Executive Board Non-Executive Board
	Chairman's Office Chief Executive	
	Compliance	Data Protection Freedom of Information Human Rights Public Records
	Directors' Portfolios Environmental management Environmental Futures Guidance	
	Local management/policy	Advice Advocacy Consultation Joint ventures Liaison Research
	Natural England vesting Performance management Policy management/development Project management Quality management	
	Regional management/policy	Advice Advocacy Consultation Joint ventures Liaison Research Region 1 Region 2 Region 3 Region 4 Region 5 Region 6 Region 7 Region 8 Region 9
	Risk management	
	Strategic planning	National Programme Organisational development

Human Resource Management	Agency staff	
	Attendance management	Flexitime
		Leave
		Overtime
		Sickness recording
		Timekeeping
	Conditions of service	
	Discipline	
	Employee relations	
	Manpower planning and organisation	
	Performance management	
	Pensions administration	
	Policy and strategy	
	Recruitment	Advertising
		External
		Internal
		Interviewing
		Job descriptions
		Transfers
		Vacancies
	Staff Files/Folders	Individually named case folders
	Training	Course administration
		Development programmes
		Executive Leadership
		Handbook
		Induction
		Staff Handbook
	Welfare	
	Work experience	
Financial Management	Accounting	Audit
		Consolidated Fund
		Contingency Fund
		Guidance
		Invoices
		Payments processing
		Receipts processing
		Refunds
		Reports
		Systems development
	Asset management	Additions
		Asset audit
		Asset register
		Capitalisation
		Compliance
		Cost centres
		Current assets
		Current liabilities
		Depreciation
		Disposals
		Locations

	Budget management	Final budgets
		Fund raising
		Planning
		Public Expenditure Survey (PES)
		Reconciliation
		Reports
		Requests
	Commercial support	
	Contracting	
	Credit management	
	Income Generation	
	Insurance	
	Investments	
	Pay	
	Pensions	
	Planning and Strategy	
	Procurement	
	Tax management	
ICT Management	Infrastructure	Disposal
		Fault reporting
		Licensing
		Help Desk
		Information security
		Network maintenance
		Server maintenance
		Spatial data management
		Storage
		Strategy
		Web development
Knowledge and Information Management	Access to information	
	Archives	
	Knowledge management	
	Records Management	Compliance
		Forms development
		Image capture
		Disposal scheduling
		Tracking
Estates and Facilities Management	Acquisition and Disposal	
	Buildings maintenance	Works programmes
		Building 1
		Building 2
	Catering	
	Cleaning	
	Copying	
	Environmental monitoring	
	Equipment	
	Grounds maintenance	
	Incidents	
	Lifts	

117

	Mechanical and Electrical Services	
	Outsourcing	
	Pest control	
	Planning and Development	
	Postal services	
	Reception facilities	
	Relocation	
	Security	Advice and guidance
		Bomb control
		Equipment
		Inspections
		Reporting
		Reviews
	Transport	Car Hire
		Rail travel
Occupational Health	Health and Safety	Community safety
		Compliance
		Emergency planning
		Monitoring
		Risk management
Communication	Campaigns	
	Education	
	Events	
	Press and Public Relations	
	Publicity	Internal
		External
Stakeholders	UK	
	International	
Legal Services	Advice	
	Land registration	
	Litigation	
	Management of legal activities	
	Planning controls	
Designated Areas	National Parks	
	Areas of Outstanding Natural Beauty	
	National Nature Reserves	
	Sites of Special Scientific Interest	
Conservation		
Land Use		
Funding		
Research, Science, Evidence		

Based upon an analysis of the organisation, its functions, its priorities, what it did, how it did it, and so on, the shaded functions, activities and tasks might be considered as the most important. These will be the target files and folders for the appraiser. All the documents in these files/folders may be selected or there may be a closer examination and only certain sub-files/folders selected.

FUNCTIONAL APPRAISAL

Functional appraisal may be seen as a subset of macro appraisal. Its central argument is that records do not have intrinsic value but take their value from the importance of the function that produces them. Assessment of the value of functions is seen as a more objective approach than trying to assess the possible future research value of a subject. In functional appraisal, therefore, it is necessary to focus on organisations and what they do. The main aspect of this approach is to understand the context in which the records were created – a functional analysis. This is very similar to the work undertaken in developing a functional file plan (see Chapter 4) in that it involves identifying an organisation's aims and objectives that come from three levels of business operations:

Functions	The main areas of responsibility through which an organisation achieves its goals; these are usually stated in statutes and annual reports.
Activities	Major areas of work that need to be done to carry out the function; these can be obtained from an analysis of the functions or from documentary sources such as annual reports, organisation charts and manuals.
Transactions	Specific actions necessary to ensure that the activity is made operational. It is at this level that most records are created.

A more detailed approach to analysing the business of an organisation forms part of the DIRKS methodology (Designing and Implementing Record Keeping Systems) developed by the National Archives of Australia. It is based on the function – activity – transaction analysis and includes the development of a business classification scheme. The main activities of this part of DIRKS are:

● Collection of information from documentary sources and interviews.
● Identification and documentation of each business function, activity and transaction: assigning terms to functions and activities, defining the scope of functions and activities, and assigning dates to functions and activities.
● Development of a business classification scheme.
● Linking stakeholders to to functions and activities.
● Assessment of risk.

- Recording findings.
- Validation.

Another way of analysing business activities is to examine processes. These usually cut across functions, are results oriented, have inputs and outputs, and relate to clients and their needs. They cut across the vertical line running from function to activity to transaction.

Once functions, activities and transactions have been described and charted, it is possible to assign values to records for business and historical needs on the basis of the relative importance of the function, activity or transaction.

A substantial proportion of non-current records relate to common administrative functions (estates, health and safety, personnel, finance, etc.). Such functions fit very well within the scope of functional appraisal. The methodology could be applied to such functions across particular sectors or sub-sectors, thereby saving considerable time and effort.

Case files are not easily fitted into functional appraisal because several activities may be carried out in one file. The appraisal of case files is examined separately below.

CASE FILES

This type of record is generally defined as 'large collections or series of records, whose component files contain similar information about a specific group of people, organisations, places, etc.' From an appraisal point of view each individual document is unlikely to be important but taken together (or by way of a sample) they enable broad conclusions of historical, economical or social trends to be drawn. The size of these collections present significant appraisal and storage problems and are often considered separately from other appraisal methodologies.

There are three broad types of case files:

- Simple – such as returns on a printed form or standard questionnaire. Inputs and outputs are standard and the files record simple transactions. It is the type of information that is now usually entered into a dataset.
- Complex – although the files of this type are generated by the same piece of legislation or the same procedure, each file may become different from others in the series. For example, property files have a common theme but each may contain different information relating to tenants, changes in structure, value, etc. It often happens that such files begin to take on the characteristics of a policy file as, for example, the development of a particular case may involve the reconsideration or reinterpretation of existing policies.
- Project – files covering work which is project based. Each project might be viewed as a case but some may contain standardised information while others

may be complex. Scientific and technical research records are typical examples of such files.

Because series of case files or papers are usually bulky, they can rarely be preserved in their entirety. However, by their very nature, they may contain valuable information that can be useful for research, particularly by statistical analysis. Moreover, some case file series may contain individual records of enduring value (for example, about an event or person of historical significance), but the value of such records will often not be known when they are created. Some case record series, such as personnel files, will have to be retained for long periods before they are destroyed or transferred to the archival institution because the evidence they contain is required over a very long period (such as the working life or lifetime of the subject) for administrative purposes. Other case files may have an enduring value as specimens because of the processes and procedures that they document.

Sampling

Where bulk precludes the selection and preservation of the whole of a series of case papers, sampling may be an alternative procedure. It will only be appropriate when the records contain significant quantities of information that can be analysed statistically. Sampling is not an appraisal option to be used indiscriminately to evade responsibility for the destruction of a series of records. Rather, it is a positive appraisal decision to be used in specific instances, when the outcome will be of benefit to future users. Moreover, it is an option that may be costly both in terms of the need to take advice from outside consultants, the time required to implement the decisions and the continuing expense of storing and maintaining the sample.

The types of file series suitable for sampling are case files where the information contained is mostly routine and voluminous in nature. The greater the variety in the nature of the files' contents, the less suitable they are for sampling. To some extent this can be addressed by varying the type of sample taken (for example a stratified random sample instead of a pure random sample), or by taking a larger sample size, but highly varied case files may not be suitable for sampling.

The table below gives a summary of the most appropriate sampling methods for particular series structures. It is not exhaustive and combinations of different methods may be required to derive the most suitable sample.

If only a portion of a file series is to be selected, this should be representative of the series as a whole.

Before sampling it is important to know the contents of the records, the structure of the records, the type of use to which the sample will be put, for

Table 5.3 Different sampling methods

Type of sample required	Structure of files series	Appropriate sampling techniques
Non-random	Homogeneous, internal structure may be present	Convenience selection Exemplary selection Exceptional selection
	Heterogeneous groups	Quota sample (whilst quota sampling is in theory a form of random sampling, in practice it is rarely random as the selection of files is subjective)
Random	Homogeneous, no internal structure	Simple random sampling Systematic sampling
	Homogeneous groups	Cluster sampling
	Heterogeneous groups	Stratified random sampling Multi-Stage sampling

Note:
Homogeneous – where parts/files/folders of the group/structure/series etc. are similar throughout.
Heterogeneous – where parts/folders/files of the group/structure/series are dissimilar and cannote be compared.

example for longitudinal studies, and the way in which we wish it to be representative.

This will determine the type of sample that is most appropriate for each situation.

When a file series is still accruing it is difficult to determine how many files belong to the series or whether they are homogeneous or otherwise. In order to obtain a sample, the file series can be 'artificially closed' every few years. However there is no guarantee that separate samples taken at different time periods will add up to one taken of the eventual whole series. Each sample must be treated as representative of the time period in which it was drawn and not used to make inferences from the whole series.

The sampling techniques set out in the table above are described below.

Non-random sampling

Convenience Selection

Suitable for   Homogeneous file series

Example	Files of benefit claims
Method	Select the most convenient sample to hand, for example the first 20 files, the middle shelf etc.
Pros	Simple to carry out
Cons	No statistical validity unless we know the files are in a random order

Exemplary Selection

Suitable for	File series where a particular grouping of files are thought to be representative of the whole series and there is homogeneity both within and between groups
Example	Files such as benefit claims where a convenient grouping could be all those dealt with by a particular person or office, or all files opened within a defined time period. The group would be chosen because it is seen to be representative of the series as a whole
Method	Select a grouping of case files
Pros	Simple to carry out, may appear less biased then convenience sampling
Cons	The common characteristic by which a group of files is selected must be chosen with care, no statistical validity

Exceptional Selection

Suitable for	Mostly homogeneousgenous file series with a few interesting cases
Example	Death duties where files concerning persons of note are deemed worthy of preservation
Method	Select the individual cases judged to have value using pre-determined criteria such as precedent-setting cases or cases which attracted national press interest. The 'fat' file selection procedure is of this type since the fattest files are selected because they relate to cases that generate more correspondence and which are, therefore, likely to be more interesting. Similarly files could be selected that have a high number of movements, as this shows they have been consulted frequently
Pros	Simple to carry out, preserves interesting cases
Cons	No statistical validity as it over-represents the 'interesting' cases compared to the routine work

Quota Sampling

Suitable for	File series organised into internally homogeneous groups where the identity of the groups and their proportions within the whole series are known. The aim is to ensure proportional representation of these groups
Example	This is most often used in surveys such as opinion polls where the identification of the sampling units is crucial to obtain reliable results
Method	Identify the groupings of special interest, predetermine the numbers to take from each group, take a simple random sample from each group of interest
Pros	This method can provide an efficient mechanism to ensure all groups are represented if used with care
Cons	It is not really random. Attempts to mimic stratified random sampling often fail because random selection is not used, often just the first few files are selected or some other such convenient selection. Results are very often unreliable, for example, many general election forecasts obtained from such sampling are widely inaccurate. This approach relies much more on subjective judgement than other approaches.

Random sampling

The aim of sampling is to preserve the main features of the population so that inferences can be made about the characteristics of the whole population by examining a small proportion of it. To do this with statistical validity, it is essential that a *random* sample is taken in order to avoid bias.

An important issue is sample size – how large a sample we need to be able to reconstruct the characteristics of the whole file series with confidence. The statistical validity depends on the size of the sample as well as on its being randomly chosen. There is a trade-off between resources required in terms of effort and storage and precision/size. The greater the variability a file series displays, the greater the sample size required.

A percentage sample size should be avoided because it will often give too large or too small a number. The accepted maximum sample size is 1400 files regardless of the size of the file series. An industry adopted standard, developed by Bell Laboratories, which takes into account the variability of file series follows:

Table 5.4 An industry adopted standard for sample size

Population Total number of items sampled from	Sample Size Low sample sizes are taken for files which are very similar in terms of content and subject matter; high sample sizes are needed for more diverse series		
	Low	Medium	High
51–90	5	13	20
91–150	8	20	32
151–280	13	32	50
281–500	20	50	80
501–1,200	32	80	125
1,201–3,200	50	125	200
3,201–10,000	80	200	315
10,001–35,000	125	315	500
35,001–150,000	200	500	800

Simple Random Sampling

Suitable for   This is the most appropriate technique to use if a file series is largely homogeneous with no meaningful internal structure. With simple random sampling, every file has an equal chance of being selected. This method of selection is only really practicable if there is a convenient listing of records, otherwise the allocation of random numbers and identification of files can be extremely time consuming

Example   Papers such as tax claims

Method   In principle a simple random sample is straightforward to achieve: 1) Establish how many files are in the series; 2) Decide the sample size required; 3) Generate n random numbers between 1 and the total number of files; 4) If a duplicate number is generated, generate another number; 5) Select the files which correspond to the random numbers generated. For example, to obtain a sample of size n=100 from a file series of 1000 files, generate 100 random numbers between 1 and 1000. If the numbers generated are {71, 263, ...,106}, select the files with the corresponding positions in the list, that is the 71st, 263rd, ...106th files

Pros   The ideal form of sample from a statistical point of view. It is completely random – every file in the series has an equal chance of being picked

Cons   Simple random sampling can be very hard to achieve in practice because all the files in the files series must be clearly identified and accessible with an equal chance of being selected. The allocation of random numbers can be time-consuming unless the records or a catalogue of the records is held on computer. A randomly selected sample might not include small, but important, sub-groups, in which case a stratified random sample would be more appropriate

Systematic Sampling

Suitable for   Sufficiently large file series with no internal structure
Example   Large volumes of papers such as claim forms
Method   ● Establish the number of files in the series
               ● Decide the sample size
               ● Divide the total number of files by the required sample size to obtain a number, n
               ● Select every nth file
               ● The first file in the sample should be a randomly chosen number between 1 and n
               For example: if we have a series of 10,000 files and desire a sample of 200, then we take every 10,000/200=50th file. A random number between 1 and 50 is generated to determine the first file
Pros   Easier to implement than simple random sampling
Cons   Not statistically valid as the method is open to bias if files are systematically arranged. The sample might not include small, but important, subgroups

Cluster Sampling

Suitable for   Record series that fall into convenient groupings (clusters). The records are broadly alike both between and within the clusters
Example   Benefit claims made to different offices. The different offices can be considered as clusters. Since the claims are broadly similar, it is more efficient to randomly choose a few offices and select all their records than to randomly select files regardless of the office
Method   Use simple random sampling to choose whole clusters. Every record within a selected cluster is preserved as part of the sample
Pros   Relatively simple and efficient to carry out. Statistically valid if carried out carefully.
Cons   There must be little between-cluster variation, otherwise the sample becomes a convenience sample with no valid statistical properties

Stratified Random Sampling

Suitable for	Records series that have a meaningful internal structure and fall into distinct groups (strata). Records within each strata are largely homogeneous, but the strata are heterogeneous. This method ensures that the representative sample has a proportional number of files from each strata
Example	A series of case records where the records could be classified according to land usage, for example northern industrial region, southern industrial region, northern rural region, etc.
Method	Identify the strata to which each file belongs. Use either simple random or systematic sampling to draw a sample from each strata. It is usual to have proportionally representative samples from each strata to avoid bias in the resulting complete sample. However, some strata may be too small for this to be possible. In this case either select the whole of the strata concerned or amalgamate it with similar strata. The identity of the files concerned should be high-lighted in the accompanying documentation so that subsequent analyses can be adjusted to allow for this bias in selection
Pros	Guarantees representation of each strata, regardless of size. In some circumstances this means it produces a more meaningful sample than simple random sampling or systematic sampling. For example, if a series of 10,000 files includes a strata of 500 files, a 10% simple random sample has a probability of slightly less than 6% of actually including a 10% sample (50 files) of this particular strata. A stratified sample can ensure exact proportional representation. Statistically valid when carried out properly
Cons	Requires prior identification of all strata

Multi-Stage Sampling

Suitable for	File series with a complex internal structure consisting of a combination of clusters and strata
Example	Where a cluster sample may give too many records, we can use simple random sampling to further reduce the files selected within the cluster. In the benefits office example each office may still produce a large amount of records despite only a few offices being selected. Random sampling may be used to reduce the volume to a manageable number
Method	A combination of the above methods can be used to form samples. The structure of the records will dictate which are the most appropriate sampling techniques to use

Pros   May be more efficient because it makes use of the internal series structure

Cons   Can be complicated to carry out. Requires the identification of suitable groupings of files

DISPOSAL SCHEDULING

Disposal schedules are the most important element of any records management system. If you do nothing else in the coming year than introduce disposal schedules in your organisation, you will have achieved a great deal. They will give you better control over your records and will promote a more efficient record keeping system.

The schedules cover series or collections of records for which a retention period can be determined for the whole series/collection and agreed between an organisation's business manager (for the area in which the records were created or are held) and the records manager. The schedules identify and describe each record collection or series and not the individual records they contain. If possible, all the records of an organisation should be covered by disposal schedules. They have far-reaching benefits:

- Faster retrieval of important records from systems due to the early elimination of records of no further value.
- Clear instructions on what happens to records when they are no longer needed to support the organisation's business (so that everyone knows what to do with them).
- Definitive periods of time for which records should be kept and remain accessible (enabling better planning of storage, services, etc.).
- Consistency in retention of records across the organisation.
- Compliance with legal and regulatory requirements.
- Evidence of what records were created but destroyed (for example, for freedom of information compliance).
- Highlighting of records that require special handling due to sensitivity.
- Identification of historically important records at an early stage.
- Elimination of duplicate records at the earliest possible opportunity.

A disposal schedule, an example of which is shown at the end of the chapter, should contain the following elements:

- The name of the department/operational area or unit.
- A schedule reference number.
- Reference numbers (if applicable) of the records.

- Descriptions of the record series/collections.
- Disposal action/retention period.
- Date of the schedule.
- Signatures of the Records Manager and Business Manager.

There may also be space on the schedule to record such information as medium and format, master or copy, comments and how long the record should be kept in office accommodation or on a main server.

The Records Manager should maintain a master set of all schedules and amendments/additions must be agreed with them before updated versions are issued.

Timetables for the disposal of records is usually expressed in years but this should not prevent citing the destruction of records after months if this is the period for which they are required.

Disposal action will either be destroy or select for permanent preservation (in an archives). For a very few records the action might be review but this should be used as sparingly as possible as a disposal action because all it really does is postpone the disposal action. It might be valid, however, for records resulting from new functions or for complicated series where only a portion of the records should be kept.

The action is usually accompanied by a point in time that is commonly called a trigger. For example: 7 years *after the file is closed* (this is the most common and the trigger is often omitted and left understood); 10 *after the end of the project*; 3 years *after the end of the contract*; or 100 years *after the date of birth of the individual*.

Once finalised the schedule can be implemented. This should be carried out once a year by the business manager (or person designated by them). Make sure this action is actually carried out. It almost goes without saying that it is pointless drawing up schedules if they are not going to be implemented – and, considering their importance and value to effective records management, it would be a crime if they were not implemented.

Having examined the process of appraisal and its various methodologies, you can see that the greater use of disposal schedules make that time-consuming process redundant. It may not be possible to include all records on disposal schedules and for those to which this applies the appraisal methodologies described will need to be used.

Schedules should also be reviewed regularly to ensure that they are up to date, for example that newly created record series are added to it (if appropriate) and record series no longer existing (that is after the last record in it has been disposed of) are removed from it. Disposal actions, retention periods and triggers should also be reviewed to see if they are still appropriate. This review would normally be carried out by the business manager but the records manager should be in a position to give advice and guidance, and undertake some overall monitoring of disposal policy.

There are many types of records which all organisations create. These are commonly called generic or housekeeping records. These probably account for as much as 50% of an organisation's records and cover the following areas:

- Estates and buildings
- Personnel (human resources)
- Finance
- Health and safety
- Contracts
- Complaints
- Project management
- Press and public relations
- Records and information management
- Audit
- ICT.

The National Archives have published guidance on these records, which include model schedules. This list may not be comprehensive as far as the whole of the public sector is concerned. Sections of the sector (for example, schools, local government) have created their own guidance on generic records, often under the auspices of professional organisations such as the Records Management Society.

FOR HOW LONG SHOULD RECORDS BE KEPT?

There are three important considerations to be taken into account when deciding retention periods for records: business needs, legal and regulatory requirements, and historical value.

BUSINESS NEEDS

Your organisation should be retaining only those records that it needs for the undertaking of current operations. When that need expires, the records should be disposed of. Only the business area itself can decide how long this retention period should be. However, experience shows that there is often a great reluctance to destroy records under this heading – thoughts of 'it might come in useful', '…just in case', 'what if we get an enquiry?', etc. often prevail. Just consider how often you refer to closed records. What really are the consequences if you have to turn down a request for information because the record has been destroyed? Keeping records that you do not need wastes space, time and energy. They take up valuable and expensive accommodation, accessibility is slowed, and those that are not needed get in the way of those that are – the important information. The following breakdown of the use of records after they cease to be of current use (that is, they are closed) is based on experience in the UK government:

- 1st year – most active
- 2nd year – 1 in 5 used
- 3rd year – 1 in 20 used
- 4th year on …
- Therefore, 19 out of 20 files are never used again.

A robust disposal policy is at the heart of good records management and good business. You should always set aside time to destroy worthless information.

An organisation's requirements for retaining records must be based on an analysis of its functions, activities and transactions, and the relative importance of them:

- What are core function(s) of the organisation?
- What does the organisation primarily exist to do?
- Which functions, activities and transactions are vital to the organisation?
- Which functions, activities and transactions are neither core nor vital to the organisation?
- Which functions, activities and transactions are facilitative, and which play a support function?

Records that relate to the core and vital functions, activities and transactions will be of greater overall value to an organisation than records that do not. However, for any organisation, the activities and operations carried out at a number of levels are likely to become less important as the work flows downwards, from the general to the specific and the varied to the routine.

Every organisation uses information to make decisions, consider options, execute its programmes and plan for the future. This information may come from records created by the organisation itself or from other sources of information. It is important to know where it comes from and what contribution it makes to the organisation's ability to conduct its business. For example, if information such as employment statistics, vacancy returns or economic indicators is received entirely from an external source, it is likely to be of short-term value. In any case it should continue to be available elsewhere. The organisation's copies of this information may therefore be destroyed after a relatively short period.

A further factor in determining records' business needs is the role of records in the organisation's operations: Is the value of the records evidential – do they provide evidence of the organisation's organisation, policies and procedures? Or is the value of the records purely informational – do they contain information that relates purely to individuals, organisations, and events with which the organisation deals in the course of its routine business?

Records likely to have continuing utility to an organisation are those that relate to the development of policy, methodology and procedure. Records unlikely to have ongoing value are those that deal with the routine application and implementation of established policy.

LEGAL AND REGULATORY REQUIREMENTS

Primary legislation (enacted by Parliament) and secondary legislation (regulations or instruments etc. issued under Acts of Parliament) may establish policy that will determine or influence the period during which records must be retained.

In the United Kingdom the Limitation Act 1980 prescribes a time limit on the period within which a party can commence legal proceedings or (in some circumstances) to require notice of a claim to be given to the other party to potential legal proceedings (many other countries have similar legislation). This has an important effect on the retention of records since organisations have to manage the risk of actions arising from contracts and duties of care to employees, citizens and others. The retention of records plays an important part in this. The period in the Limitation Act needs to be validated against other needs before being assumed to match the retention period of relevant records. In many cases, where records have more than one business purpose, the one specified in the Act will be longer but this should be checked.

Table 5.5   Key periods in the Limitation Act 1980

Cause	Period	Comment
Negligence	Within 6 years of the negligent act or omission	
Latent damage	3 years from the date of knowledge	Negligent latent damage is barred by way of long stop after 15 years from the negligent act or omission
Contract	Within 12 years of the breach of contract	
Contract under seal	Within 12 years of the breach of contract or deed	

Recovery of land	Within 12 years of the right accruing	After 12 years the title of the person is extinguished
Personal injury or death	3 years	
Recovery of goods	6 years	
Sums recoverable by statute	6 years	
Rent recovery	6 years	

Note: This does not constitute legal advice and, in all cases, organisations should check with their legal departments.

You will need to ensure that disposal schedules are consistent with the fair processing principles of the Data Protection Act 1998. The Act requires the disposal of information (personal data) in a timely, orderly manner and not to retain it without good reason. Such information is invariably an integral part of the record and will have to be managed as part of it, meaning that the disposal of the record will have to take account of the processing of the personal data. However, personal data occurring within individual records cannot be altered or removed without undermining the integrity of the records – so this should never be done. There is one exception – research, statistics and historical processing may justify continued retention of personal data beyond the original purpose.

There are a number of specific statutory obligations on public bodies to retain, withhold or release records. Many statute bars on disclosure were removed as part of the implementation of the Freedom of Information Act 2000 in the United Kingdom. As with all legal matters of this nature, records managers should confirm their actions with formal legal advice.

HISTORICAL VALUE

WHAT TO SELECT FOR PERMANENT PRESERVATION

In arriving at appraisal decisions, it is firstly necessary to determine whether information contained in records is unique or exists elsewhere. The information in the records may be wholly or substantially available in a variety of other sources and forms. For example, the same information may be found in: records in other formats (maps and plans) or other media (microforms, electronic systems); other records of the organisation, such as regional and local offices; the records of other organisations; or published works.

Primary and Secondary Values

The American archivist Theodore Schellenberg set out an appraisal model in the 1950s in which he argued that the value of records could be divided into two basic categories: primary value and secondary value. *Primary Value* – the continuing utility of records for the transaction of the business that gave rise to their creation. *Secondary Value* – the continuing utility of records for purposes other than the transaction of the business that gave rise to their creation (typically historical)

Schellenberg's model of 'primary value' remains useful today for determining which records are of continuing utility to an organisation for business purposes. In the model primary value is further subdivided into operational value (the primary value of records for the continuance of the administration of operations of an organisation or as evidence thereof), financial value (the primary value of records for the continuance of the financial or fiscal business of an organisation or as evidence thereof), and legal value (the primary value of records for the continuance of the legal business of an organisation or the protection of its legal rights or those of its employees or third parties).

The period of continuing utility may be as short as one year or less, or it may be as long as thirty years or more. However, it is always finite. In determining the end, the appraiser needs to consider the operational, financial and legal value of the records to the organisation.

The secondary value of the records needs to be considered when deciding what should be selected for permanent preservation. Secondary value can be further divided into evidential, informational and intrinsic value.

Evidential value

The value that derives from evidence of how organisations conducted their core functions – their strategies, policies and procedures. Records of long-term value that are likely to be selected under this heading would include:

- records that must be preserved under any statutory provision;
- records documenting continuing rights or obligations of the state, the agency or third parties under national or international law;
- legal instruments, such as land titles, leases, endowments, agreements and contracts;
- records relating to the formulation of legislation and policy arising from the core functions of the agency; and
- records documenting precedent.

Informational value

This is the value for reference and research deriving from the information contained in the records (and often incidental to their original purpose). Criteria for measuring information value should be: the uniqueness of the information; the form of the information and of the records; and the importance of the information to a significant number of actual or potential users,

The following types of records may be identified as having informational value:

- records that relate to notable events or persons and that add significantly to what is already known about them;
- records that relate to major developments or trends in political, legal, social, economic or cultural history;
- records that relate to significant scientific, technological, ecological or medical research and development;
- records that document significant regional or local events, personalities or conditions, where these are not reflected adequately in other records;
- records that are suitable for statistical and quantitative analysis for demographic, medical, social, cultural and economic history and historical geography;
- control documentation that continues to serve as a means of reference to records of enduring value or to provide a useful overview of the activities that resulted in records that are not themselves of enduring value. The following types of control documentation are particularly likely to have long-term value: a copy of each version of the organisation's file classification and coding scheme, and disposal schedules; file plans for series that are to be retained in whole or in part; registers that continue to be the only or main means of reference to records that have been scheduled for retention; software manuals and other systems documentation essential to the continued use of electronic records scheduled for retention; and indexs to any of these types of documentation.

Intrinsic value

This is the value by reason of age, historical association, physical form or features, aesthetic or artistic quality or monetary value. With intrinsic value, it is the uniqueness of the association or form of the record rather than the uniqueness of the information that is the determining factor. For example, the constitution of a newly independent country may be widely available in print, but the original, signed at independence, will clearly have intrinsic value. Similarly, an ephemeral document bearing the autograph of a head of state may have intrinsic value, whereas the same kind of document signed by other persons would not.

Acquisition and Selection Policies

Every organisation should have a policy on what records and information it will earmark for permanent preservation because of their historical value. Such a policy will set out the values that guide the selection of such records. It should be drawn up after consultation with appropriate stakeholders and should be published.

There is no doubt that, over the past twenty years or so, research into archives has diversified. Records of national, local and other archives establishments have attracted attention from a broader range of disciplines. Historians themselves now choose to study a much wider range of subjects. In numerical terms the most striking change has been the increase in researchers studying the history of their families or their localities. In common with an increasing number of other users of records and archives, genealogists are not necessarily interested in what the records show us about the government's own policies and processes. Their focus is more on the individuals and communities with which the government had dealings. It is important, therefore, that any acquisition or selection policy should keep pace with current research trends and draw upon a value system that is relevant to contemporary studies and research. Consequently, such a policy should be flexible and fluid.

An acquisition policy represents a statement of the overall objectives of the acquisition of records for permanent preservation and is the reference point for work on the selection of records. It is put into practice through the development of selection policies, which are detailed statements of appraisal plans as they apply to particular organisations or to specific categories of records that are found in more than one organisation in the sector. An example of a policy statement is given in the following table.

Table 5.6 The National Archives acquisition policy statement

1. Strategic objectives

Our objectives are to record the principal policies and actions of the UK central government and to document the state's interactions with its citizens and with the physical environment. In doing so, we will seek to provide a research resource for our generation and for future generations.

2. Collection themes

Our collection themes are grouped under two headings: (1) the state's own administrative and policy processes and (2) the state's interaction with individuals, communities and organisations outside the state's formal boundaries and its impact on the physical environment. The number of themes and their order are not significant: they do not suggest the volume of records which will be collected under each theme. If our collections are to be intelligible, we must document the administrative context of policy and case material. In particular, it is necessary to document major reforms of the state's organisational structure. But the documentation of administrative context should not be an end in itself: structures and processes are to be documented so that the state's activities may be understood.

2.1 Policy and administrative processes of the state
- 2.1.1 Formulation of policy and management of public resources by the core executive
- 2.1.2 Management of the economy
- 2.1.3 External relations and defence policy
- 2.1.4 Administration of justice and the maintenance of security
- 2.1.5 Formulation and delivery of social policies
- 2.1.6 Cultural policy

2.2 Interaction of the state with its citizens and its impact on the physical environment
- 2.2.1 The economic, social and demographic condition of the UK, as documented by the state's dealings with individuals, communities and organisations outside its own formal boundaries
- 2.2.2 Impact of the state on the physical environment

3. Collection policies

3.1 At each formal review of the policy and in the development of certain of the operational selection policies, we will consult with the research communities and other interested parties.

3.2 The policy will be reviewed first in 2002/03 and thereafter on a ten year cycle, but the policy is a working tool and this pattern of formal reviews will not prevent improvements from being made in the interim.

3.3 We intend to develop operational selection policies across government. It is through these more detailed policies that the collection themes will be applied to the records of individual departments and agencies.

3.4 We must operate within available resources. The cost of selection and of storage must therefore be an explicit element in appraisal decisions and, as part of this, the rate at which The National Archives acquires records must be carefully controlled.

One way of implementing acquisition policies such as this is to support them with operational selection policies. These focus on the records of particular sectoral functions. Such policies for central government functions can be seen on The National Archives website at www.nationalarchives.gov.uk/recordsmanagement/selection.

Two examples of collection policies for local record offices in the United Kingdom are shown at the end of this chapter. In the UK local authority sector the collection policies themselves are usually sufficient when it comes to implementing appraisal policies. There is generally no need for the kind of detailed operational selection policies used in large central government departments.

REVIEWING PARTS OF FILES AND SUB-FILES

Though part-files and sub-files could be judged on their individual merits, their contribution to the wider picture arising from their shared context and sequence may often justify retention when their individual content is of marginal value. There needs to be a common sense approach here; clearly a part file that is empty or has ephemeral material in it will not be selected for preservation. As a general rule, all the parts of a file should be selected for preservation or earmarked for destruction on the basis of the appraisal of the whole file as a single unit. For long-running files, this appraisal may have to be done when the first part of the file is reviewed.

STRIPPING OR WEEDING

Many files selected for retention will include duplicate, routine or other ephemeral material that appears to contain no significant unique information. However, stripping or weeding of such material is rarely cost-effective. Furthermore, there is always a risk that the removal of documents of no apparent value will destroy important evidence of context and sequence. The practice should be avoided. A file should always be treated as a unit and be retained or preserved in its entirety or not at all. Exercising discipline in filing to exclude rough drafts, duplicates and ephemera from the outset will facilitate the good management of records.

DESTRUCTION

Duplicate records should be destroyed. Where information has been regularly shared between departments/units, only the original records should be retained in accordance with agreed guidance. But be careful – make sure that seemingly duplicate records have not been annotated. Only one copy of each document should be kept as the corporate record.

The method of destruction of unwanted records will depend on their sensitivity (often indicated by a protective marking system – typically something like 'Restricted', 'Staff in Confidence', 'Personal' or even 'Secret'). Protectively marked waste, before destruction, should be clearly identified and kept separate from other waste.

NON-SENSITIVE (NO PROTECTIVE MARKING)

Ordinary rubbish bins may be used for material already in the public domain. Records which otherwise would not be made available to the public should be torn into small pieces and placed in a rubbish bag for collection by an approved firm.

SENSITIVE

Sensitive records should be disposed of in different ways depending on its definition.

- Restricted – waste should be strip-shredded and placed in paper rubbish sacks for collection by an approved firm.
- Confidential – waste should be placed in paper rubbish sacks for collection by an approved firm (it should be designated for shredding). The material should be pulped or burnt.
- Secret – waste should be cross-shredded or disintegrated using a grille size no larger than 6 mm and placed in paper rubbish sacks for collection by an approved firm. The material should be burnt.

When destroying electronic records, it is important to realise that just removing an electronic file from a directory does not mean the file has been destroyed. Reuse by overwriting is an option for magnetic media (computer tapes and disks, audiotapes and videotapes), but if the media contain sensitive information, total erasure or destruction may be necessary. When destroying restricted documents, especially those that are security classified, it is usually necessary to erase the entire disk or tape, in order to ensure that the file in question cannot be recovered.

There are a few websites covering the destruction of records. Among the most useful is the website of the British Security Industry Association, at www.bsia.co.uk.

DOCUMENTING APPRAISAL

It is important to document the reasoning behind appraisal decisions, for a number of reasons:

- Organisations need to maintain an audit trail of important decisions. In the case of public authorities in the United Kingdom, this is specified in the *Code of Practice on the Management of Records under section 46 of the Freedom of Information Act 2000* (2002).
- The archives institution must also be accountable for decisions about the permanent preservation of records that provide the historical accountability of the organisation.
- It may be policy (either now or in the future) to re-examine appraisal decisions to determine if a more appropriate decision can be made. Access to the reasoning behind the original decision is essential.
- The research and analysis required to arrive at an appraisal decision can be of use for other purposes. In archival description, the documentation of appraisal

decisions can provide vital information about the provenance of the records and may also help in the preparation of administrative histories and finding aids.

In essence the documentation of destruction of records must provide evidence that destruction has taken place in accordance with established policies and schedules. The kinds of documentation that might be kept are acquisition policies, selection policies, disposal schedules, record transfer lists and receipts, record transfer or presentation agreements, lists of records destroyed, and certificates of destruction.

SMALL ORGANISATIONS AND APPRAISAL

The appraisal methodologies described above have developed over the years for organisations that have well-established practices and a well-defined records management or archival dimension. Many small organisations do not enjoy such luxury and often struggle to clear backlogs of records that should either have been destroyed or preserved years before. The problem has often been that the resources or expertise to judge what should be kept and what need not be kept (either for business purposes or historical reasons) have not been present. The inevitable result is that everything is kept, often based on the 'just in case' theory. Is there an option here for buying in expertise? There are several consultants who are in a position to help such organisations. These may come from the public or private sector. When hiring consultants on any job, you need to be satisfied that the required expertise and experience are present. For example, undertaking appraisal to identify material that needs to be retained for business reasons obviously requires a good understanding of the business of the organisation, of its legal obligations and its role in its particular sector. Undertaking appraisal for historical selection requires experience of the process, knowledge of the historical context and an understanding of the collection or acquisition policies of the archive to which the selected records will be transferred.

There is one area where small organisations will benefit greatly from the relative small investment they will need to put in – disposal scheduling. Disposal schedules are the most important element of an effective records management system. They promote control of the records and information resource of the organisation. Valuable material is identified and properly managed, and worthless material is eliminated as soon as it is no longer required. So, if you are struggling in your organisation with poor records management, make the introduction of disposal schedules a priority. They will serve you and the organisation well.

THE WIDER CONTEXT OF APPRAISAL

The appraisal process is about research and reflection to understand an organisation and its role in the sector to which it belongs, whether that is central government, local government, the National Health Service, or wherever. Evaluation should be based on the documentation of sectoral functions and research value. These are the two premises under which all records appraisal should be undertaken.

Records appraisal should also be transparent. This has not always been the case but the passing of the Freedom of Information Act in 2000 has been a catalyst to making acquision and collection policies more available to consultation and comment. Many policies are now published on organisations' websites. Copies of two are provided at the end of this chapter.

Department:	Administration		Ref:	2 of 2005
Ref	**Description**	**Disposal**	**Comments**	
	Finance:			
FIN 2	deductions ledger	7 years		
FIN 3/1	payroll	7 years		
FIN 3/2	accounts	7 years		
FIN 8	administrative	2 years		
	Human resources:			
	personal files	7 years after leaving		
P1 to P9	administrative	2 years		
	database	Archive		
	Business processes:			
	purchasing records	7 years		
	administrative	2 years		
	contacts	7 years		
Signed _____ (Records manager)				
_____ (Business Manager)				
Date _____				

Figure 5.1   Example layout for a disposal schedule

141

EXAMPLES OF COLLECTION POLICIES

BEDFORDSHIRE COUNTY COUNCIL

What Bedfordshire and Luton Archives and Records Service Does

Bedfordshire and Luton Archives and Records Service exists to preserve local records, to make them available for use and to promote the study of the county's past. It exercises statutory functions in respect of certain classes of public and ecclesiastical records and also accepts and preserves private and business archives relating to Bedfordshire. In brief, Bedfordshire and Luton Archives and Records Service collects two main category of record:

- documents relating to the topography, ownership, occupation and use of land in Bedfordshire;
- documents recording or illustrating all aspects of human activity in Bedfordshire.

What We Collect

- Documents of sufficient evidential and/or informational value to merit permanent preservation.
- Documents of any date – deposit of important material created today is positively encouraged.
- Documents in any physical form or media, provided Bedfordshire and Luton Archives and Records Service has suitable facilities for storage and access.
- Local topographical prints, drawings, photographs etc.
- Archive copies of local newspapers.
- Microform and facsimile copies of Bedfordshire material held in other repositories or private ownership.

What We Do Not Collect

- Three dimensional artefacts and specimens falling within the collecting policies of local museums.
- Frames, tin trunks, deed chests and other containers, which will be returned to the owner or destroyed.
- Film and sound archives, since we do not currently have suitable storage or access facilities.
- Literary manuscripts unless associated with other archive material falling within our collecting criteria.
- Works of art of primarily visual interest and appeal.
- Printed or published books, pamphlets or documents falling more within the

scope of the public library service, unless the material is suitable for our searchroom reference library.

- Duplicates of documents already held unless they are in better condition or are gifts and duplicate material on loan.

NORFOLK RECORD OFFICE
ARCHIVE COLLECTING POLICY

1. This policy statement relates to the Norfolk Record Office, The Archive Centre, Martineau Lane, Norwich NR1 2DQ.

2. The Norfolk Record Office is part of Norfolk County Council's Department of Cultural Services, which also encompasses the Norfolk Library and Information Service, Norfolk Museums and Archaeology Service, Norfolk Arts Service, Norfolk Adult Education Service, and Norfolk Guidance Service. It is a joint service of the County Council and the councils of the City of Norwich, the boroughs and the districts in Norfolk, all of which are represented on the Norfolk Records Committee, *via* which the Record Office is democratically accountable. Other stakeholders, with non-voting representatives on the Records Committee, are the Bishop of Norwich, the Norfolk Record Society and the *Custos Rotulorum*, together with three co-opted members and an observer, who represent a wide range of interests within the county.

3. The Norfolk Record Office is the only public archive service in the county of Norfolk. It collects and preserves records of historical significance relating to the county of Norfolk and makes them available to as many people as possible.

4. The Museums, Libraries and Archives Council has 'Designated' the Norfolk Record Office's collection in its entirety as being of outstanding international importance. The Norfolk Record Office is rated by The National Archives as a three-star archive service (the highest category).

5. The Record Office seeks to abide by all relevant archive legislation, including the following:
   - The Public Records Act, 1958, Section 4.
   - The Manorial Documents Rules, 1959 and 1967.
   - The Tithe Rules, 1960 and 1963.
   - The Local Government (Records) Act, 1962.
   - Sections 224–9 of the Local Government Act, 1972.
   - The Parochial Registers and Records Measure, 1978 and 1993.
   - The Local Government (Access to Information) Act, 1985.
   - The Data Protection Act, 1998.
   - The Freedom of Information Act, 2000.

6.   The Norfolk Record Office is appointed by the Lord Chancellor as a place of deposit for public records and is recognised by The National Archives: Historical Manuscripts Commission in respect of tithe and manorial records.

7.   The Norfolk Record Office is designated by the Bishop of Norwich as the Norwich Diocesan Record Office in respect of diocesan and parochial records (including Lothingland deanery in Suffolk) and by the Bishop of Ely as the Diocesan Record Office in respect of diocesan tithe maps for Norfolk parishes in the Diocese of Ely and parochial records from parishes in the deaneries of Feltwell and Fincham.

8.   'Records' are documents of any date created or accumulated by organisations or individuals during the conduct of their affairs. They may include manuscript, printed, typescript and computer-generated text, musical and other notation, maps, plans, drawings and photographs, and documents in digital formats.

9.   The Record Office will acquire and preserve records of any date assessed as being worthy of permanent preservation, including those of the following:

- Norfolk County Council and its predecessors.
- Local authorities in respect of which the County Council is the statutory archive authority.
- Statutory bodies operating within Norfolk.
- Public records offered to the Norfolk Record Office under the Public Records Acts.
- Manorial and tithe records.
- The Diocese of Norwich.
- Ecclesiastical parishes in respect of which the Record Office is the Diocesan Record Office.
- Organisations, businesses, families and individuals.
- Sound recordings and related material, in connection with the Norfolk Sound Archive (which has its own Collecting Policy).

10. The Record Office recognizes that people from many different cultural backgrounds have played a significant role in the history and culture of Norfolk and will bear this in mind when collecting material.

11. Records will be accepted by transfer from the constituent authorities of the joint records service and by donation, deposit or purchase. Priority in acquiring records will be given to those which are at risk of loss, destruction or damage.

12. Records relating to places which, during the period when the records were created or accumulated, were not in the county of Norfolk nor created by bodies or individuals based in Norfolk will only be acquired if they are part of

an archive group which does relate to such a place, body or individual. The Record Office recognises that the integrity of archival groups should be preserved as far as practicable, and will consult, where appropriate, with other record repositories in respect of archives which relate partly to other counties, in seeking to ensure that they are housed in the most appropriate repository.

13. Records are acquired with the intention that they shall be preserved permanently, but, exceptionally, they may be reviewed at a later date: for example, in relation to subsequent accessions of or relating to the same body or individual. No deposited records will be destroyed or transferred to another repository without the permission of the owner or depositor.

14. It is a condition of acceptance that records will be available for public access (subject to their being fit for production) either immediately or from a specified date, which may be at the end of a statutory period of closure or agreed in respect of non-official records between the County Archivist and the depositor.

15. The Record Office does not actively seek to acquire copies or transcripts of documents, historical and genealogical notes and pedigrees. It may, however, accept such material as part of a larger archival group or if it complements another archive held by or likely to be acquired by the Record Office. Copies or transcripts may also be accepted if the original is unavailable or is believed to be at risk.

16. The Record Office does not seek to acquire photographs, paintings, prints, engravings, newspapers, published material including ephemera or films, but will accept such material if it was created or collected by an archive-creating body or individual, usually, though not exclusively, as part of a larger archival group.

17. The Record Office will not normally acquire records in a format or language which require for their preservation, consultation or interpretation, storage conditions or specialist skills or equipment which the Record Office does not, or does not plan to, provide. If such records are at risk of loss or destruction, however, they may be accepted on a temporary basis until a suitable repository for them can be identified.

18. When assessing potential donations or deposits, the Record Office will, when appropriate, advise owners and custodians of other record repositories and of museums and libraries with relevant collecting policies. In particular, films will be referred to the East Anglian Film Archive, published material and purely photographic collections to Norfolk Library and Information Service, and paintings and objects to Norfolk Museums and Archaeology Service.

145

19. This policy statement was approved by the Norfolk Records Committee on 19 January 2007. It will be reviewed as necessary and not later than five years from this date.

6 Archiving

AIMS

This chapter briefly examines the management of inactive records – from a records manager's point of view rather than an archivist's point of view. It also examines questions relating to digital preservation.

FUNCTIONS

The functions for which archivists are mainly responsible emerge at the end of the life-cycle, at that time when records have ceased to be useful for supporting the business activities of an organisation and have been selected for permanent preservation because they have been judged to have a continuing (usually historical) value. In a sense, archives are a sub-set of records. The functions include the following.

ACQUISITION

The process of taking archives into an archival repository, whether by transfer from the creating body, or by donation or on loan as a collecting repository is known as acquisition.

ACCESSION

Accession refers to the activity of logging each new archival acquisition. The following details are usually recorded:

- date received
- depositing person or organisation

- their location or address
- a brief description of the contents
- its extent or quantity and condition
- the terms under which it has been transferred or deposited (for example, access provisions)
- archival reference.

ARRANGEMENT AND DESCRIPTION

If the archives are transferred from an organisation with an established records management system, there will be an existing arrangement and description of the material that may be re-worked to cater for archival access and other requirements. If a deposit is received from an organisation without such a system, it will be arranged and described from scratch

PRESERVATION

An overarching function aimed at securing the long-term survival of archives is preservation. It encompasses physical and environmental storage, handling practices, reformatting of fragile series (by microfilm, digitisation etc.), conversion and migration (electronic records), and the physical repair of individual items (conservation). Digital preservation is the subject of much debate and continuing development; this is examined more fully on page 157.

ACCESS

Archives should be made physically and intellectually accessible, as legal requirements permit (see chapter 7).

OUTREACH

Outreach is a programme that advocates archives to the outside world, and raises the profile of the organisation internally and externally. It is implemented through planned outreach activities such as exhibitions, media involvement, talks, presentations and publications.

CONTEXT

While it is essential to establish and maintain good recordkeeping practices in an organisation, it is impossible to administer a fully functional records management programme unless it has an archival dimension, which safeguards and makes accessible those records that have been deemed worthy of permanent preservation.

Archives are those records that are worthy of permanent retention because of their enduring value as evidence or for research. Archives are an elite body of records. They provide a reliable and authentic knowledge base, enabling the past to be reconstructed and understood. Without archives, the past would remain largely unknown. By documenting the significant decisions, transactions and events of political, social and economic life, archives serve as the essential link in the chain of human history. In the government context they are 'The Nation's Memory'.

Archives are preserved in and managed by specialist archival repositories where they are safeguarded and made available for use. Records and archives are a research resource, and archival repositories are the specialist facilities in which historical and related research is concentrated. It is the function of archival repositories to manage the raw material of history for the benefit of society as a whole. The archival repository also ought to have a distinct character that marks it out from the management of current records and gives it a cultural dimension.

In addition to acquiring records through appraisal methodologies (see previous chapter), many archival repositories are in the business of taking in collections of records which, for one reason or another, have lost ownership – the organisation previously responsible may have been abolished or they may have taken the decision that they can no longer hold the records in question. In this context the archivist is 'rescuing' records that may or may not have long-term value but, invariably, they have been maintained for many years and will continue to be so by the archives establishment.

ARCHIVAL SERVICES

An archival service should operate under the provisions of specific legislation or regulations and policies authorised by such legislation. These should include the following:

- Establishment of an archival facility as a public institution – covering powers and duties, jurisdiction of the institution over records generated in the public sector or particular part of it, or over any other records of importance that are included in its remit.
- Public right of access to the holdings of the archival repository – policy on the regular opening of records and policies/procedures for sensitivity review and declassification (in accordance with freedom of information legislation, if that exists).

149

- Protection for the rights of individuals and organisations that may have provided information held in the records, under terms of confidentiality – often governed by privacy and copyright legislation.
- Provision for public scrutiny of the archival repository and its success in achieving its targets.

ACCESSIONING RECORDS

No records should be accessioned into an archival repository unless they have been prepared in accordance with appropriate regulations or policies. By their very nature archives are irreplaceable. If they are looked after properly from the outset, they will last longer. Provisions should cover the following:

- Arrangement – placing files, volumes, bundles, papers etc. into an intelligible order that facilitates retrieval.
- Packing – making sure that the records are tidy and properly packed in their folders or containers which should be acid-free. All ferrous clips and tags should be removed and plastic or brass tags and clips used to replace them.
- Cataloguing – transfers to an archival repository should be accompanied by transfer lists. These may be full descriptions that will eventually be made available for public consultation or brief listings that will be developed into a standard archival catalogue.
- In all cases the transferring organisation and the archival repository must record exactly what has been transferred so that physical custody is established and known.

ARRANGEMENT AND REFERENCING

When archives are accessioned, their original order and origins should be kept – commonly known as maintaining provenance. Archival referencing varies between countries but the most common is the combination of letters and numbers as described below. The levels of arrangement and referencing should include:

- The creating organisation – referenced by letter, often an abbreviation of the organisation (for example, ADM in the figure below).
- The class or series – bringing together those records that relate to the same function or activity or have a common form or some other relationship arising from their creation. A number is allocated to each separate class or series.
- The item or unit – the basic unit (file, map, etc.) that will be produced to the user. A number is allocated to each unit.

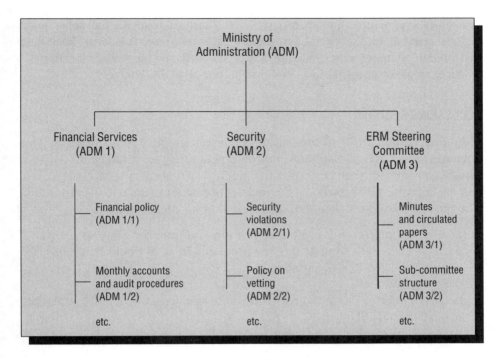

Figure 6.1   Example arrangement

The parallels with file plan arrangements are irresistible (see chapter 3).

ACCESSIONS FORM

All transfers of records to the archival repository should be recorded. One essential part of this record is the accessions or transfer form. This document has legal value and must be kept securely as a vital record. It should be completed by the transferring organisation and signed by their authorised representative (usually the records manager). The form should be sent to the archival repository with the records it covers. There should be an accessions form for each transfer. This might be one or several units but each form should be restricted to units in the same group or series. Before records are transferred, archives staff should be able to decide the group/series number and unit numbers and inform the transferring organisation accordingly. The full archival reference codes should be entered on the accessions form.

As soon as the archival repository receives the form an authorised representative should sign it. At that stage the institution assumes responsibility for the custody, preservation and use of the records, which must then be treated in accordance with the provisions of relevant archival legislation and the

151

repository's regulations and procedures. In the archival repository all subsequent actions relating to the accession should be entered on the form (including distribution of the relevant catalogue, any repair work and the storage location).

An example of a transfer form is shown at the end of this chapter.

ACCESSIONS REGISTER

The other essential part of the transfer record is the accessions register. This document also has legal value and must be kept securely as a vital record. This is a formal document that records the archival repository's acceptance of responsibility for the records and the transfer of custody of them to the repository. The accessions register should contain the following information:

- accession number – this is often in the form year/number, starting again at '1' each January (for example, the first accession in 1998 would be 1998/1, the second would be 1998/2 and so on)
- date received
- details of transfer (series number, title or description, covering dates, number of boxes or quantity
- source – transferring organisation or depositor
- archival references
- remarks (for example, variations to the statutory closure period)
- date accessioning action completed.

A sample page is shown at the end of this chapter.

DESCRIPTION

The international standard commonly used for description is the General International Standard Archival Description (ISAD(G)), published by the International Council on Archives in 1994. ISAD(G) is a set of general rules for archival description that will:

- ensure the creation of consistent, appropriate and self-explanatory descriptions within individual archival repositories;
- facilitate the retrieval and exchange of information about archival materials
- enable the sharing of authority data;
- make possible the integration of descriptions from different archival repositories into a unified information system.

As general rules they are intended to be broadly applicable to descriptions of archival materials regardless of medium and format or of the level and size of the unit of description.

PRESERVATION

Preservation is the term used to describe the measures necessary to ensure that records are stored, handled and managed so that their physical state, as well as the information they contain, is protected for as long as they are needed. This may be for posterity, or it may be for a fairly short retention period. All who work with records are involved in preservation, because virtually every record function has a preservation aspect. See chapter 4 on records maintenance.

The proper preservation of records and archives enables access to current and historical information, facilitates accountability, and promotes the corporate memory.

A very important standard to follow in the matter of archival preservation is BS 5454 – *Recommendations for the storage and exhibition of archival documents.*

ELECTRONIC RECORDS: DIGITAL PRESERVATION ISSUES

In the increasing world of digital information it is vital that steps are taken to ensure that in years to come you still have access to this information (if you need it), and that it is complete and intact and has not been altered in any way. Unlike traditional media, preservation is an issue from the outset in the management of electronic records. If it is not taken into consideration at the point of creation, problems of technological obsolescence, storage media fragility and authenticity will render them valueless. A further difficulty might be the matter of proprietary technology where some software producers place limits on what can be done to specific data formats, thus reducing the capacity for updating them by others.

The concern of digital preservation programmes is therefore to maintain the usability of records so that they can be read by future, as well as current technologies. Very specific measures can be taken to ensure that the original content, the bit stream, is preserved in an open (non proprietary) preservation format that will enable it to be modified without constraint. Open-source technology (software that can be downloaded from the Internet free of charge and used without a specific licence) gives users freedom to modify products to suit their changing needs.

There are a number of issues that ought to be considered by the creators and managers of electronic records when selecting file formats for use. Choice of file format should always be determined by the functional requirements of the record-creating process. However, record creators should be aware that long-term sustainability might be a requirement, both for ongoing business processes and archival preservation. Sustainability costs are inevitably minimised when these factors are taken into account prior to data creation – attempts to bring electronic records into a managed and sustainable regime after the fact tend to be expensive, complex and, generally, less successful.

File formats encode information into a form that can only be processed and rendered comprehensible by very specific combinations of hardware and software. The accessibility of that information is therefore highly vulnerable in today's rapidly evolving technological environment. This issue is not solely the concern of digital archivists, but of all those responsible for managing and sustaining access to electronic records over even relatively short timescales.

The practicality of managing any large collection of electronic records, whether in a business or archival context, is greatly simplified by minimising the number of separate formats involved. It is therefore highly desirable to identify the minimum set of formats that meet both the active business needs and sustainability requirements, and restrict data creation to these formats.

There has been much debate about the use of the PDF format for the preservation of electronic information. This has been followed in a number of different contexts, such as the digitisation or scanning of information to save space from having to store it in paper form and also in making available redacted information in electronic form as a result of a freedom of information request. The debate is ongoing and you may well want to pursue this if it is an issue in your current operations. It will certainly become an issue in the not too distant future. In the meantime it is worth pointing out that there is an international standard on this subject, ISO 19005, *Document management – Electronic document file format for long-term preservation – Part 1: Use of PDF 1.4 (PDF/A-1)*.

It might be useful to say a word here about metadata in electronic systems. It should be noted that metadata itself, which is critical to electronic records retaining their characteristics of content, context and structure, is also electronic. It is therefore subject to the same issues that affect other digital data – it is technology dependent and created on technology that is subject to upgrades and that may have been recreated on software that is no longer supported by its manufacturer. It therefore requires careful management in order to ensure that it survives along with the records to which it is to lend reliability and authenticity.

SOME PRESERVATION SOLUTIONS

Migration

Migration is designed to achieve the periodic transfer of digital materials from one hardware/software configuration to another or from one generation of computer technology to a subsequent generation. It aims to retain the ability to display, retrieve, manipulate and use digital information in the face of constantly changing technology. It involves changing its configuration and format and there may be

154

some loss of the original representation. Upgrading systems in this way is normally only done on current records, not on semi-current records or archives. In some cases there is a danger that records may never be migrated and, in effect, written off. If this is carried out in an unmanaged way, valuable records could be lost forever.

Replication

This is a technique of migration that refreshes digital information by copying it onto new media. It generates a complete reproduction of both content and the formal elements of the records so that the records that result can be viewed as a faithful copy of the original. The problem with replication is that it can only be carried out as long as the information is encoded in a format that is independent of the particular hardware and software needed to use it and as long as there exists software to manipulate the format in current use.

Emulation

A method whereby the development of archive emulators of software and operating systems would allow the contents of digital information to be carried forward and used in its original form.

Digital preservation is a complex and fast developing subject. Some of the best advice and guidance can be found from the Digital Preservation Coalition (http://www.dpconline.org/graphics/index.html) and from the Digital Preservation Department of The National Archives (http://www. nationalarchives.gov.uk/preservation/digital.htm).

STANDARDS

BS 5454: RECOMMENDATIONS FOR THE STORAGE AND EXHIBITION OF ARCHIVAL DOCUMENTS

BS 5454 is the foremost British Standard relating to archival records. It is wide-ranging, covering sites for archival buildings, building structure and material, custody and security, fire precautions, lighting, environment, storage and archive materials. Although the standard has been revised over the years, it remains the cornerstone of archival storage best practice. At the heart of the standard are the recommendations for environmental monitoring and control. Unsuitable environments have damaged records more than any other single factor. The two key factors – temperature and relative humidity – should be in the following ranges: temperature, 13°C to 16°C; relative humidity, 45% to 65%.

While the ranges are significant it is often stability that promotes longer survival of records. Fluctuations, even within the ranges specified, can be damaging.

Practical steps to improve the environment of archival buildings begin with basic measures such as sealing the building to reduce air infiltration (and thus the danger of pollutants entering the internal atmosphere), ingress of pests and rodents, heat loss and gain, and moisture (which will affect the levels of relative humidity). Thus those steps with which we are familiar in domestic dwellings – draught excluders, securely fitted windows, good air circulation, insulation, etc. – have their role in archival storage.

ISAD(G): THE GENERAL INTERNATIONAL STANDARD ON ARCHIVAL DESCRIPTION

ISAD(G) was first issued in 1996. A second edition was published (by the International Council on Archives) in 1999. The standard provides general guidance for the preparation of archival descriptions, whose purpose is described as 'to identify and explain the context and content of archival material in order to promote its accessibility'.[1] It contains general rules for archival description that may be applied irrespective of the form or medium of the archival material. Its intention is for it to be used in conjunction with existing national standards or as the basis for the development of national standards. For details about ISAD(G) see the website of the International Council on Archives, http://www.ica.org/biblio.php?pdocid=1.

ISO 19005:1: DOCUMENT MANAGEMENT – ELECTRONIC DOCUMENT FILE FORMAT FOR PRESERVATION (PART 1)

This international standard specifies how to use Portable Document Format for the long-term preservation of electronic documents. This is becoming a key area, especially in the United Kingdom in the context of the release of information under the Freedom of Information Act 2000. Electronic documents often need to be redacted prior to information being released and the PDF format has usually been considered a secure vehicle for such release. This is a fast-moving and fast-changing area, however, and you should look at the subject of digital preservation in some detail before deciding what route(s) to take. Have a look at the work undertaken by the Digital Preservation Coalition, which provides a wealth of advice and guidance – http://www.dpconline.org/graphics/index.html.

STANDARD FOR RECORD REPOSITORIES

The standard was published in 2004 and is aimed at archivists and governing

---

[1] ISAD(G) 1999, Introduction, p. 7.

bodies of record offices, libraries, museums and other institutions holding records which are available to the public for research. It covers matters of constitution and finance, staff, acquisition, access, storage and preservation. It includes recommendations on the preservation of electronic records. The full text of the standard is available on The National Archives website at http://www. nationalarchives.gov.uk/documents/standard2005.pdf.

Proposal to transfer records selected for permanent preservation

Transferring organisation Reference: ....

Organisation proposing transfer:	
Series Title	

Letter Code and Series Number		References of records to be transferred	

Covering Dates			Number of pieces or extracts		Is the series accruing? Yes or No	

FOI/Access: Are the records open on transfer? If NO, what variations are proposed?
Note references, FOI exemptions and Schedule numbers below

Reference	Item reference (if relevant)	Closure period	FOI schedule number

Documents retained:
Note reference numbers below and the authority for retention

Piece number	Item reference (if relevant)	Authority

Documents missing at transfer: Note reference numbers and any numbers not used

Missing:

Not used:

Should access be denied to list description of documents? If YES note piece numbers and FOI exemptions	Name any other organisation which may also requisition these documents:

Physical type of records (insert 'YES' into relevant boxes)			
Files		Seals	
Booklets		Artefacts	
Volumes		Audiovisual	
Rolled or flat maps		Electronic	
Bundles		Microform	
Photographs		Other (describe)	

Number of boxes:		Dimensions of boxes:	

Physical Condition: State *Good*, *Satisfactory*, *Poor*, *Very Poor*, or *Insect/Mould Damage*	

Note here the reference numbers of any documents that may need inspection by conservation specialists	

Special Items: Note here any records that include maps, plans, photographs or other non-standard items	Reference:	Description:

Any further information:	

Name of Records Manager ....

Date ....

Name of Accepting Officer (Archival Repository) ....

Date ....

Figure 6.2   Example transfer form

Accession Number	Date Received	Details of Records Received	Source of Depositor	Archival References	Remarks	Initials of Person Receiving and Date
268	4/1/94	Minutes and papers of the Housing Policy Committee, 1981–1985	Norfolk County Council	NCC 8/6–10	Files	
269	10/1/94	Cemetery registration books, 1760–1850	Aylsham Parish Council	AY 26/1–21	Volumes; pieces 18 and 19 unfit – require conservation	
270	10/1/94	Official Guide to Norfolk, changes, 1910	Norfolk County Council	NCC 1/59	Volume	

Figure 6.3   Archives Accession Register

7 Access to records

AIMS

This chapter examines the background of access to records in the public sector in the United Kingdom, and focuses on the requirements of Freedom of Information legislation – the introduction of which in many parts of the world has radically changed access to records and information, and indeed has changed the whole profile of records management.

'Access' generally includes both the legal right of access and the means of arrangement and description whereby users can achieve access to the records. This chapter covers the first of these meanings.

BACKGROUND

The legal right of access must cover the time at which material will be made available to the public, together with any exceptions to it. These are most likely to include categories of material withheld for periods longer than the norm. 'Withheld' may mean closed but it may simply mean retained by the creator. The implications of this need to be clarified – for example, the grounds on which such exceptions are made should be spelt out; certain types of records may be available even though they are retained by the creator; some records may be available in the creator's organisation before the normal opening date (legislation should clarify that these remain open on transfer to an archives repository even if this takes place before the normal access date).

Other aspects of access that need to be made clear include specifying the authority that is responsible for sanctioning variations to the normal access period, any appeals procedure, and whether there are any arrangements for privileged access to certain categories of records.

Table 7.1   Summary of UK legislation and regulations impacting upon access to records in the public sector

Title and date	Coverage on Access
Public Records Act 1958 (s.5)	Public records open to inspection when 50 years old, unless special considerations dictate a different period of closure Also makes clear that certain classes of public records contain information which, by the terms of the statute under which the information is collected, may not be disclosed for purposes other than those set out in the statute (commonly called 'statute-barred records')
Public Records Act 1967	Reduced the period at which public records are normally open to public inspection to 30 years
Local Government Act 1972 (s.228)	Access by certain categories of user to certain categories of local authority records
Rehabilitation of Offenders Act 1974	Non-disclosure of spent convictions except in prescribed circumstances
Data Protection Act 1984	Rights granted to individuals to see information about themselves held on computers
Local Government (Access to Information) Act 1985	Local council meetings, reports and papers
Access to Personal Files Act 1987	Manually held social work and housing records
Access to Medical Records Act 1988	Reports produced by a doctor for an employer or insurance company
Environment and Safety Information Act 1988	Enforcement notices when organisations breach laws dealing with environmental protection and safety
Land Registration Act 1988	Access to the Land Register
Environmental Protection Act 1990	Access to various pollution registers
Access to Health Records Act 1990	Information in medical records
Environmental Information Regulations 1992	Environmental information

Public Interest Disclosure Act 1998	Protection of individuals who make certain disclosures of information in the public interest (and connected purposes)
Local Government Act 2000	Requirement on local authorities to: • Issue monthly forward plans showing forthcoming decisions and listing related documents • Give a minimum of three days prior access to reports, agenda and background papers for decisions • Ensure that meetings at which 'key decisions' are to be discussed or taken are open to the public • Produce a record of such decisions and the reasoning behind them
Local Authorities (Executive Arrangements) (Access to Information) (England) Regulations 2000	Access to local government information

CODES OF PRACTICE

The United Kingdom introduced several codes of practice during the 1990s – a useful non-statutory device – which impacted upon the accessibility of records in the public sector.

The White Paper *Open Government* – published in July 1993 – set out proposals for new legislation and for a *Code of Practice on Access to Government Information*. The Code was introduced in 1994, and revised in 1997, but the accompanying legislation never saw the light of day. In subsequent years similar codes of practice were introduced for the Welsh Assembly, Scottish Executive and the National Health Service. These codes of practice – which remained in force until the Freedom of Information Act 2000 was fully implemented – all had the same basic premise, stated in their introductions, albeit in slightly different ways:

> This Code of Practice sets out the basic principles underlying public access to information about the NHS. It reflects the Government's intention to ensure greater access by the public to information about public services and complements the Code of Access to Information which applies to the Department of Health, including the NHS Executive. [...] The aims of the Code are to ensure that people:
>
> • have access to available information about the services provided by the NHS, the cost of those services, quality standards and performance against targets;
> • are provided with explanations about proposed service changes and have an opportunity to influence decisions on such changes;

163

- are aware of the reasons for decisions and actions affecting their own treatment;
- know what information is available and where they can get it.

(Code of Practice on Openness in the NHS, 1995)

All the codes contained various exemption provisions and reference to a public interest test. In the case of the Welsh Assembly code the standard for the test for what was contrary to the public interest was higher than the other codes. While all the codes recognised the need for exemptions, there was some difficulty in achieving a balance. It was generally accepted that the exemptions contained in the Government code, for example, were very broad. This meant that government departments and agencies were frequently criticised for looking at opportunities to refuse requests for information.

The *Code of Practice on Access to Government Information* came into effect on 4 April 1994 and included five commitments, to:

- supply facts and analysis of the facts which the government considers relevant and important in framing major policy proposals and decisions;
- open up internal guidelines about government departments' dealings with the public;
- supply reasons for administrative decisions;
- provide information under the Citizen's Charter about public services, what they cost, targets, performance, complaints and redress;
- respond to requests for information relating to policies, actions and decisions.

The *National Assembly for Wales: Code of Practice on Public Access to Information* went further than any other in providing rights of access to information. It was a reflection of the Assembly's desire to be at the forefront of promoting open government and included commitment to the following principles:

- Maximising openness in its business.
- Presenting National Assembly business in clear language, in line with its bilingual policy and taking account of different needs.
- Using the Internet as a means of publishing National Assembly information.
- Maintaining a register of documents published by the National Assembly.
- Respecting personal privacy, commercial confidentiality, the duty of confidence and all laws governing the release of information.
- Providing a prompt and comprehensive response to requests for information (15 days is the time limit set by the code).
- Providing a right of complaint where a member of the public is not satisfied with the response received.
- Providing information free of charge where possible.

The *Code of Practice on Openness in the NHS* built on the progress made by the Patient's Charter[1] which set out the rights of people to information about the NHS:

> Because the NHS is a public service, it should be open about its activities and plans. So, information about how it is run, who is in charge and how it performs should be widely available. Greater sharing of information will also help foster mutual confidence between the NHS and the public.

GENERAL PRINCIPLES OF ACCESS

Public access to the records of government is a fundamental right in a democratic society. In general access principles should focus on ensuring that the users of records and archives are clear about their rights and responsibilities. The National Archives Council and its research arm, the Public Service Quality Group, have undertaken a considerable amount of work in recent years on access policy and principles. The final edition of an access standard was published in 2006. It sets out a series of clear guidelines and best practice principles on access to archive collections and repositories. It does not create new rights of access but sets out the conditions necessary to ensure that rights of access are meaningful in the practical business of archives. See the website http://www.ncaonline.org.uk/research_and_development/access_standard/.

THE THIRTY YEAR RULE

The general rule of access followed by much of the public sector in the United Kingdom – thirty years after the last date of the record (which may come in the form of a file, folder or volume) – was effectively abolished by the Freedom of Information Act 2000. This repealed sections 5(1), 5(2) and 5(4) and amended 5(3) and 5(5) – section 5 being the principal section of that act relating to access.

> The Public Records Act 1958 standardised arrangements for the transfer of records to the Public Record Office (now The National Archives) and specified that they should be opened to the public after the expiry of fifty years. The Public Records Act 1967 reduced this period to thirty years.

There is no statutory authority in Scotland and Northern Ireland relating to access to public records. They adopt this UK practice.

In almost all areas of the UK, public sector organisations followed the thirty-year rule until the introduction of Freedom of Information legislation from 2005.

---

[1] Now superseded by *Your Guide to the NHS: Getting the most from your National Health Service* (Department of Health 2001).

In other countries the same rule has been common, although some have twenty year periods and others forty year periods.

EXTENDED CLOSURE

Sections 5(1) and 5(2) of the Public Records Act 1958 allowed a variation of the thirty-year period for which records ordinarily remain closed. The former provided that a class of records remains closed for thirty years or a longer period prescribed by the Lord Chancellor, with the approval or at the request of the minister. Section 5(2) provided that, where selected records contain information obtained from the public under such conditions that their opening would constitute a breach of good faith on the part of the government, those records will not be available for public inspection except in such circumstances as approved by the Lord Chancellor and the person/organisation transferring the records.

Both these provisions required the concurrence of the minister of the relevant department and the Lord Chancellor. The Act was silent as to the outcome if the Lord Chancellor and the minister did not agree, either in relation to closure generally under section 5(1) or the period of extended closure or appropriate conditions under section 5(2). The Wilson Committee report *(Modern Public Records, Selection and Access,* 1981, Cmnd 8204) suggested that the matter be raised at Cabinet level for agreement to be reached but this appears never to have been necessary. The provisions of section 5(1) were so wide that, for the purposes of extended closure, section 5(2) was not generally invoked. Section 5(2) was, however, the provision that provided the power to allow conditional access to closed records.

Under the Freedom of Information Act 2000 sections 5(1) and 5(2) of the Public Records Act 1958 were repealed.

FREEDOM OF INFORMATION (FOI)

In the United Kingdom, prior to the 1997 General Election, the Labour Party included in its manifesto a promise to introduce a 'Freedom of Information Act leading to more open government'. When it was elected to office it quickly published the White Paper *Your Right to Know: The Government's proposals for a Freedom of Information Act* (Cm 3818, December 1997). A draft Freedom of Information Bill was published on 24 May 1999 (Cmnd 4355). After minor amendments during its passage through Parliament the Bill became law on 1 December 2000.

RIGHT OF ACCESS UNDER FOI

One of the most significant parts of the Freedom of Information Act for records managers is that relating to the timing of the provision of information.

Responding to requests for information

> ... a public authority must comply ... promptly and in any event not later than the twentieth working day following the date of receipt.

This provision is really at the heart of the legislation. From it stems many of the important requirements in complying with the legislation, such as good records management, an infrastructure to handle requests quickly and efficiently, a system for logging requests, and training and awareness of authorities' staff.

In simple terms a clock starts ticking the moment a request is received. A public authority must confirm or deny that they have the information requested and provide it before the end of twenty working days from the date of receipt of the request. The twenty working day limit applies irrespective of the geographical location of the applicant. The clock will only stop for the authority in the following circumstances:

- When a request for payment is sent to the applicant. It will start again (from where it stopped, not back to the beginning of the twenty days) when the appropriate fee is received.
- When a request for information is transferred to another public authority (rather than stopping the clock, this is more the completion of the request as far as the original public authority is concerned, since it has to inform the applicant that the request has been transferred).

Note that where a public authority decides that it has to consult another authority rather than transfer a request to it, the clock does not stop for the request.

Refusing a request for information

A request can be refused on five grounds. These are where:

- an exemption applies;
- the public authority has asked the requester for further information;
- the request is vexatious;
- the request is repeated;
- the cost of complying exceeds the appropriate limit set out in regulations issued under the Act.

The Act requires a public authority to give the applicant notice of refusal to answer a request for information. This notice has to be given within the twenty working day time limit for complying with requests. In the case of exempt information the authority must specify the exemption or exemptions in question. The notice must state:

- the fact of the refusal;
- the exemption in question;
- why the exemption applies (if that is not otherwise apparent) but not if this would involve the disclosure of information which would itself be exempt.

When the public authority needs to apply the public interest test (see below) and has not yet reached a decision whether to confirm, deny, refuse or disclose, the notice must state that no decision has been reached and give an estimate of the date by which the public authority expects to make the decision. When, or if, a decision has been made, the notice must state that the public interest in maintaining the exemption or in not confirming or denying that the information is held outweighs the public interest in disclosing whether the public authority holds the information or in disclosing it.

All notices refusing a request must also contain or include:

- details of the right for applicants to apply to the Information Commissioner for a decision notice;
- details of the authority's procedures for dealing with complaints about the handling of requests for information, or;
- a statement that the public authority has no such complaints procedure.

This information might take the form of a general leaflet on handling FOI requests which would include the details for complaining and appealing against the Information Commissioner's decisions.

If the request is judged to be vexatious or repeated, the authority does not have to give the notice of refusal where such a notice has already been given and it is unreasonable to expect another to be issued.

The cost of complying with a request might include circumstances where a record (more usually one that has been archived) is not in a suitable condition to be copied or handled. This is usually termed 'unfit for production'. A public authority could undertake to repair the relevant documentation, providing the applicant with an estimate of the time taken to undertake the work. It may decide to include the cost of repair in its charges, in giving effect to any preference expressed by the applicant over the means of providing the information. Alternatively the public authority might decide that such a charge would not be reasonable under the Act. Alternatively the authority might make the document available under supervision. Care has to be taken that exempt information, which may be part of the same document, is not inadvertently made available.

EXEMPTIONS

Under Freedom of Information there is a presumption of openness, irrespective of the date of the information, unless an exemption applies. The balance between being more transparent and open, and protecting information so that business can continue effectively was the subject of much debate during the framing of the legislation. It is bound to continue to be so. Maintaining the balance is not an easy process for public authorities. It is not surprising, therefore, that the application of the exemptions is a complex issue. Case law and good practice will continue to inform this area of the legislation for some time to come.

For public authorities outside central government there will be some exemptions that will not apply. These are the exemptions that are relevant only to the interests of the government as a whole and to the state, such as those relating to national security, international relations and defence.

It is generally accepted that there are twenty-three exemptions but a few of these cover more than one facet. There are two categories of exemptions:

- 'Public interest' – those in which the public authority seeking to rely on the exemption has to establish that the public interest in maintaining the exemption outweighs the public interest in disclosing the information.
- 'Absolute' – where no public interest test is required

Some exemptions automatically cease to apply after a pre-defined period. In the case of those exemptions without such a period, the information remains exempt for as long as the criteria for the exemption lasts.

The table below describes the exemptions. It arranges them in *Class* or *Prejudice* categories: 'Class' being where the exemption relates solely to the type of information, and 'Prejudice' being where a test of prejudice needs to be applied.

Table 7.2 Exemptions under Freedom of Information

1. CLASS:			
Exemption	**Description**	**Absolute or Public Interest**	**Section of the Act + Duration**
Already accessible	Reasonably accessible to the applicant by other means (such as by virtue of other legislation or in a publication scheme), even if only on payment. For example: • Certificates of birth, marriage and death (available under other legislation)	Absolute	21 30 years

	● Books, pamphlets and leaflets (published).		
Intended for future publication	Information intended for publication where it is reasonable that it should not be disclosed until the intended date of publication. Normally the publication scheme will cover this; where it does not, authorities must tell the applicant when publication is planned. For example: ● Minutes and papers of regular (for example monthly) meetings ● Results of research projects	Public Interest	22 30 years
Supplied by, or relating to, bodies dealing with security matters	The following bodies are specified: ● Security Service. ● Secret Intelligence Service. ● Government Communications Headquarters (GCHQ). ● Special Forces. ● Tribunals established under: s.65 Regulation of Investigatory Powers Act 2000; s.7 Interception of Communications Act 1985; s.5 Security Service Act 1989; s.9 Intelligence Services Act 1994. ● Security Vetting Appeals Panel ● Security Commission ● National Criminal Intelligence Service ● Service Authority for the National Criminal Intelligence Service.	Absolute	23 No specified limit
International relations (1)	Confidential information obtained from a state other than the UK or from an international organisation or international court.	Public Interest	27 No specified limit
Investigations and proceedings conducted by public authorities	Information held by a public authority for the purposes of a criminal investigation or criminal proceedings, or information obtained from confidential sources by the public authority for the purposes of criminal investigations, criminal proceedings, other specified investigations, or civil proceedings arising from such investigations.	Public interest	30 30 years (but no specified limit for information relating to civil or criminal proceedings which use confidential sources)

170

Court records	Information contained in: • Any document filed with a court for the purpose of proceedings in a particular cause or matter • Any document served on, or by, a public authority for the purposes of proceedings in a particular cause or matter • Any document created by a court or member of the administrative staff of a court for the purpose of proceedings in a particular cause or matter • Any document placed in the custody of a person conducting an enquiry or arbitration for the purposes of that enquiry or arbitration • Any document created by a person conducting an enquiry or arbitration for the purposes of that enquiry or arbitration.	Absolute	32 30 years
Formulation of government policy	Information relating to: • Formulation or development of government policy • Ministerial communications • Request for and provision of advice by Law Officers • Operation of Ministerial private offices.	Public Interest	35 30 years
Communications with her Majesty and honours	Information relating to communications with the Royal Family or Royal Household or to the conferring of any honour or dignity by the Crown.	Public Interest	37 30 years (Royal Family etc.) 60 years (Honours)
Environmental information	Information relating to the environment as defined in the Environment Information Regulations (EIR) 2004.	Public interest	39 No specified period
Personal information (1)	Information which constitutes 'personal data' as defined by the Data Protection Act 1998. This may be data that relates to the applicant (the data subject) – in which case it is covered by the Data Protection Act.	Absolute	40 Lifetime of the data subject

Commercial interests (1)	Trade secrets.	Public Interest	43
			30 years
Prohibitions on disclosure	Prohibited by or under any enactment incompatible with any European Community obligation would constitute or be punishable as a contempt of court.	Absolute	44
			No specified period

2. PREJUDICE

National security	Information required for the purpose of safeguarding national security.	Public Interest	24
			No specified limit
Defence	If the information would, or would be likely to, prejudice the defence of the British Islands or of any colony, or the capability, effectiveness or security of the armed forces of the Crown and any forces cooperating with those forces.	Public Interest	26
			No specified limit
International	If the information would, or would be likely to, prejudice: • Relations between UK and any other state; • Relations between UK and any international organisation or international court; • Interests of UK abroad; • Promotion or protection by UK of its interests abroad.	Public Interest	27
			No specified limit
Relations within the United Kingdom	If the information would, or would be likely to, prejudice relations between any two administrations in the UK (that is Government of the UK, Scottish Administration, Executive Committee of the Northern Ireland Assembly, National Assembly for Wales).	Public Interest	28
			30 years
The economy	If the information would, or would be likely to, prejudice the economic interests of the UK or the financial interests of any UK administration.	Public Interest	29
			No specified limit

Law enforcement	If the information would, or would be likely to, predice: • prevention or detection of crime; • apprehension or prosecution of offenders; • administration of justice; • Assessment or collection of any tax or duty or any imposition of a similar nature • Operation of immigration controls • Maintenance of good security and good order in prisons or other institutions where people are lawfully detained; • Civil proceedings brought by or on behalf of the public authority; • Exercise of public authority functions for: ascertaining whether any person has failed to comply with the law, ascertaining whether anyone is responsible for any conduct which is improper, ascertaining whether circumstances exist or may exist which would justify regulatory action, ascertaining whether a person is fit or competent in relation to the management of corporate bodies, ascertaining the cause of an accident, protecting charities against misconduct or mismanagement, or securing the health, safety and welfare of persons at work	Public Interest	31 100 years
Audit functions	If the information would, or would be likely to, prejudice the audit of public accounts or the examination of the economy, efficiency and effectiveness with which other public authorities use their resources in discharging their functions.	Public Interest	33 30 years
Parliamentary privilege	Information required for the purpose of avoiding an infringement of the privileges of the Houses of Parliament.	Absolute	34 No specified period
Prejudice to effective conduct of public affairs	Including information which would, or would be likely to, predudice: • maintenance of the convention of the collective responsibility of Ministers,	Public Interest, except for information held by the Houses of	36 30 years

	• Work of the Executive Committee of the Northern Ireland Assembly, • Work of the executive committee of the National Assembly for Wales. Or would, or would be likely to, inhibit: • Free and frank provision of advice, • Free and frank exchange of views for the purpose of deliberation.	Parliament (which is absolute)	
Health and safety	Information which would, or would be likely to, endanger the physical or mental health or the safety of any individual.	Public Interest	38 No specified period
Personal information (2)	Information which constitutes 'personal data' as defined by the Data Protection Act 1998. This may be data which relates to an identifiable individual other than the applicant, and: • Disclosure would contravene any of the data protection principles. • If the person to whom it relates would not have a right to know about it or a right of access to it under the DPA. • Disclosure would affect an individual's right to prevent processing that might cause damage or distress under the DPA.	Absolute	40 Lifetime of the data subject
Information provided in confidence	Information obtained from any other person the disclosure of which would constitute a breach of confidence actionable by any person.	Absolute	41 No specified period
Legal professional	Information in respect of which a claim to legal professional privilege (in Scotland to confidentiality of communications) can be maintained.	Public Interest	42 30 years
Commercial interests (2)	Information which would, or would be likely to, prejudice the commercial interests of any person.	Public Interest	43 30 years

Public Interest

> ... the public interest in maintaining the exclusion of the duty to confirm or deny outweighs the public interest in disclosing whether the public authority holds the information, ...

> ... If ... the public interest in maintaining the exemption outweighs the public interest in disclosing the information.

When a request for information is received and the public authority decides that an exemption applies to some or all of the information requested, there are six instances when this is the end of the matter (except where the applicant might appeal against non-disclosure). These are the six absolute exemptions:

- already accessible;
- supplied by, or relating to, bodies dealing with security matters;
- court records;
- parliamentary privilege;
- information provided in confidence;
- prohibitions on disclosure.

In addition two other exemptions are partly absolute:

- personal information;
- prejudice to the effective conduct of public affairs (information held by the Houses of Parliament).

The rest of the exemptions are subject to the 'public interest test' – where the public authority needs to balance the public interest in withholding the information against the public interest in making it available. This task does not fall within the twenty working day deadline but public authorities are expected to inform applicants of the likely date for decision and to take that decision within a reasonable time.

The 'public interest' is not defined by the Act. A case-by-case assessment will be required. This is the first aspect of the Act that is likely to be tested in law and it will no doubt be a prominent subject in the related case law. Among the aspects that will have to be taken into consideration are:

- The amount of damage to a particular interest (the greater such damage, the greater the weight of public interest there will have to be).
- Timing (for example, releasing information before a trial may well prejudice the outcome of the proceedings).
- The importance of openness and transparency (for example, the expenditure of public funds).
- The public's need to be better informed (for example, so that they can better participate in public affairs or be more aware of any danger to public health).
- Reasons for decisions.

175

If it would involve the disclosure of information which would itself be exempt information, a public authority does not have to state why an exemption applies, having applied the public interest test, or why it has decided not to disclose or to refuse to confirm or deny.

DATA PROTECTION

The Information Commissioner is responsible for supervising the implementation of both data protection and freedom of information legislation. At first sight this appears to be a conflict of interest, and there is no doubt that there is a certain tension between the two Acts (Data Protection Act 1998 and Freedom of Information Act 2000). However, the FOI Act counters this quite effectively by making most applications for personal data exempt under section 40. When the freedom of information legislation was being drafted and debated, many argued that, if any conflict between privacy and openness were to arise, then let it be resolved by one person.

DEFINITION OF PERSONAL DATA

The Data Protection Act 1998 defines data as:

> … information which -
> (a) is being processed by means of equipment operating automatically in response to instructions given for that purpose,
> (b) is recorded with the intention that it should be processed by means of such equipment,
> (c) is recorded as part of a relevant filing system or with the intention that it should form part of a relevant filing system, or
> (d) does not fall within paragraph (a), (b) or (c) but forms part of an accessible record as defined by section 68;[2]

and personal data as:

> ….. data which relate to a living individual who can be identified -
> (a) from those data, or
> (b) from those data and other information which is in the possession of, or is likely to come into the possession of, the data controller,
> and includes any expressions of opinion about the individual and any indication of the intentions of the data controller or any other person in respect of the individual;

---

[2] Section 68 defines an accessible record as a health record, an educational record or an accessible public record. These are defined in great detail in the Data Protection Act 1998.

A relevant filing system is regarded under the Data Protection Act as any set of information relating to individuals that is structured by reference to individuals or by reference to criteria relating to individuals, in such a way that information relating to a particular individual is readily accessible. It includes information processed automatically (that is by computer) and manually (that is paper and other systems).

The Freedom of Information Act 2000 extends the definition of personal data to include all information – not just that in a relevant filing system – in relation to organisations which are public authorities under the Act. This may have significant implications for managers in particular. Where they have kept loose information on their staff to help them in, for example, annual assessments, such information may now be accessed by the individuals. However, not all the data subject's rights are applicable to this extended category of data. They can see the data and request any inaccuracies to be amended, but they cannot prevent use of the data for the purposes of direct marketing and retention of the data for longer than is necessary for a specific purpose. In addition there are some procedural requirements for accessing unstructured data.

In essence the right of access to information about third parties under the Freedom of Information Act is subject to three main conditions:

- Disclosure should not contravene the eight Data Protection Principles: 1) fair and lawful processing, 2) processing for a specified and lawful purpose, 3) data not to be excessive, 4) accuracy of the data, 5) data not to be kept longer than necessary, 6) data subject rights, 7) security, and 8) transfer outside the EU.
- Information would be disclosed to the data subject (of the information) if they applied under the Data Protection Act 1998 provisions.
- The data subject(s) have not exercised their rights to prevent processing likely to cause damage or distress.

While private personal data (home address, marital status, personal life, etc.) would not be disclosed under the new arrangements, it is likely that some information about public servants in connection with their work will be accessible, for example work telephone number and address, role and responsibilities and grade.

The use and making available of personal data under the Data Protection Act 1998 is a very complex area, and strictly not within the scope of this work. For freedom of information purposes the main point is that requests for personal information by the subject of that data must be dealt with under the data protection legislation. Similar requests from a third party must be dealt with under the freedom of information legislation. The flow chart on the next page will help public authorities to deal with requests for personal information.

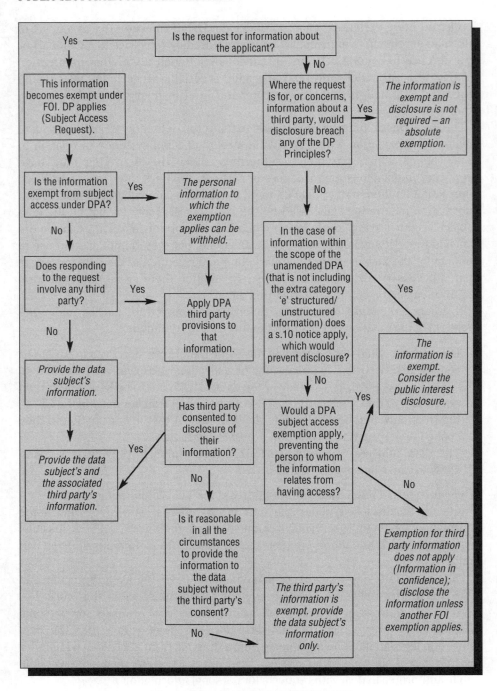

Figure 7.1   Access to personal information

REHABILITATION OF OFFENDERS

The Rehabilitation of Offenders Act 1974 provides that, for the less serious offences, a person's criminal convictions are not held against them forever. After a particular length of time, which is longer the more severe the sentence, a person is said to be rehabilitated. The conviction is then referred to as 'spent' and it may not be disclosed, except in prescribed circumstances although it remains on the Police National Computer. Custodial sentences of more than two and half years can never become spent. The sentences detailed in Table 7.3 become spent after fixed periods from the date of conviction.

Table 7.3 Rehabilitation periods for different sentences

Sentence	Rehabilitation period Age 18 or over when convicted	Rehabilitation period Age 17 or under when convicted
Prison sentences of 6 months or less, including suspended sentences, youth custody (abolished in 1988) and detention in a young offender institution	7 years	3 and a half years
Prison sentences of more than 6 months to 2 and a half years, including suspended sentences, youth custody (abolished in 1988) and detention in a young offender institution	10 years	5 years
Borstal (abolished in 1983)	7 years	7 years
Detention Centres (abolished in 1988)	3 years	3 years
Fines (even if subsequently imprisoned for fine default), compensation, probation (for convictions on or after 3 February 1995), community service, combination, action plan, curfew, drug treatment and testing and reparation orders	5 years	2 and a half years
Absolute discharge	6 months	6 months

With some sentences, the rehabilitation period varies.

Table 7.4 Variable rehabilitation periods

Sentence	Rehabilitation period
Conditional discharge or bind-over, probation (for convictions before 3 February 1995), supervision, care-orders	1 year or until the order expires (whichever is longer)
Attendance centre orders	1 year after the order expires
Hospital orders (with or without a restriction order)	5 years or 2 years after the order expires (whichever is longer)
Referral order	Once the order expires

HUMAN RIGHTS

All public authorities, including those which for one reason or another are not subject to the Freedom of Information Act 2000 and those bodies which have a mixture of private and public functions, are public authorities under the Human Rights Act 1998. This Act makes it unlawful for any public authority to act in a way that is incompatible with the European Convention on Human Rights.

There are five articles of the Convention which, when it was introduced, were felt to have a bearing on access to records and information:

● *Article 2: Right to life* – the provision of information relating to health and safety may affect this protection of the right to life.
● *Article 5: Right to liberty and security* – the right to access to information may be necessary in providing an individual with the right of access to a court to test the lawfulness of detention under this article.
● *Article 6: Right to a fair trial* – defendants in criminal cases may be able to argue that it is in the public interest for information on the investigation to be disclosed.
● *Article 8: Respect for private and family life* – as well as private and family life, this includes the individual's home and correspondence. Thus there may be a request for access to information that contravenes this article.
● *Article 10: Freedom of expression* – the right also includes freedom to receive and impart information.

In practice the impact has been less than expected. It is as well to remember, however, that, where the European Convention on Human Rights allows the release of information, it will be unlawful for a public authority to withhold that information. The Information Commissioner will be able to interpret the Act in such a way that the public interest test can be applied in such circumstances.

ISSUES WITH PARTICULAR RECORDS

ENVIRONMENTAL INFORMATION

A right of access to information relating to the environment held by public authorities has been provided by the Environmental Information Regulations 1992 and by the Environmental Information (Amendment) Regulations 1998. These regulations require public authorities to make available information about the condition of the environment, anything that has a negative effect upon it, and what measures are being taken to counter the negative effects. From a practical point of view these regulations:

● apply to a wider range of public authorities than the freedom of information act;
● apply to all requests for environmental information (not just written requests);
● have fewer potential grounds for refusal;
● override domestic information regimes.

A description of the regulations can be found in Chapter 3.

Table 7.5 Freedom of Information Act (FOI) and Environmental Information Regulations (EIRs): key differences between the regimes[3]

FOI regime	EIR regime
1 FOI concerns all recorded information held by public authorities.	EIRs concern all recorded environmental information held by public authorities. The definition of public authorities in this context might also include private sector organisations that provide public services or exercise public functions under the control of a public body.
2 FOI requests must be made in writing.	EIR requests can be made in writing but do not have to be. They can also be made orally – in person or over the telephone.
3 The term used under FOI for information that is not releasable under the Act is 'exemption'.	Exemptions in the EIRs are called exceptions.

[3] Reproduced with kind permission of Public Partners.

4 A FOI request can be refused if an exemption applies. However, with many (but not all) exemptions, there is a further requirement to consider whether the public interest in disclosing exempt information is greater than the public interest in withholding it.	An EIR request can be refused if an exception applies. EIR exceptions cover the same ground as FOI exemptions but there are two key differences: ● Under the EIRs the public interest test applies to all exceptions including statute bars. ● An exception cannot usually be claimed if the information is about emissions.
5 There is a charge limit below which information is provided free of charge.	No cost limit is specified in the EIRs and cost is not a sufficient reason for refusing to find and provide the information.
6 Public authorities have 20 working days to answer a FOI request. Where the information is exempt and a public interest test is required, there is a further unspecified period in which to do this. The initial reply to the applicant (within the 20 working days) must say how long the public interest test will take.	A 20 working day deadline is specified in the EIRs for straightforward requests for environmental information and the public interest test must be done within this period. However, a further 20 working days is allowed to answer very complicated or high volume queries, although an initial reply must be sent within 20 working days.

SOCIAL SERVICES RECORDS

Information on social services is kept in a variety of ways, such as log books, paper files, or computer. These records will usually be kept at local Adult Social Care and Health Department offices or at day centres or residential units. These records are covered by the Data Protection Act 1998.

HEALTH AND MEDICAL RECORDS

A health record is defined in the Data Protection Act 1998 as a record consisting of information about the physical or mental health or condition of an identifiable individual made by or on behalf of a health professional in connection with the care of that individual. A health record can be recorded in electronic form or in manual form or a mixture of both. Health records may include such things as: hand-written clinical notes, letters to and from other health professionals, laboratory reports, radiographs and other imaging records for example X-rays and not just X-ray reports, printouts from monitoring equipment, photographs, videos and tape-recordings of telephone conversations.

Access to the health records of living patients is governed by the Data Protection Act 1998.

Access to the health records of a deceased person is governed by the Access to Health Records Act 1990. Health records relating to deceased people do not carry a common law duty of confidentiality. However, it seems to be Department of

Health and General Medical Council policy that records relating to deceased people should be treated with the same level of confidentiality as those relating to living people. Under this legislation when a patient has died, their personal representative or executor or administrator or anyone having a claim resulting from the death (this could be a relative or another person), has the right to apply for access to the deceased's health records.

Access to medical records is governed by The Access to Medical Reports Act 1988. This Act was passed 'to establish a right of access by individuals to reports relating to themselves provided by medical practitioners for employment or insurance purposes and to make provision for related matters.' It came into force on 1 January 1989 and was not retrospective. It does not extend to Northern Ireland and relates only to employment and insurance reports.

The aim of the Act is to allow individuals to see medical reports written about them, for employment or insurance purposes, by a doctor who they usually see in a normal doctor/patient capacity. This right can be exercised either before or after that report is sent. A patient who chooses not to see the report before it is sent may apply for a copy of the report within 6 months of it having been supplied. The individual patient/client then has the right to signal any disagreement with matters of fact recorded in that report, and to append their disagreement to the report, or to withhold the report wholly, effectively by withdrawing consent to the release of information.

An applicant (for example, an insurance company) must not apply to a medical practitioner for a medical report relating to an individual, until he has notified the individual that he proposes to make the application and that the individual has notified the applicant that he consents to the making of the application. In general before any medical report can be written – whether for insurance, pre-employment or for any other purpose – the doctor must be content that the individual has genuinely consented to the release of that information.

In keeping with the subject access provisions of the Data Protection Act the doctor has the right to withhold from the patient any information the release of which would cause serious harm to the mental or physical health of the patient. In the context of employment or insurance reports this is likely to be an exceptionally rare occurrence. In the same way, the patient has no right of access to any information where disclosure would be likely to reveal information about another person or reveal the identity of someone other than a health professional acting in their professional capacity, who has supplied information to the doctor about the individual.

Caldicott Guardians

In December 1997 a report by the Caldicott Committee (set up in 1996 to 'review all patient-identifiable information which passes from NHS organisations to other NHS or non-NHS bodies for purposes other than direct care, medical research or where there is a statutory requirement for information') made a number of recommendations aimed at improving the way the National Health Service handles and protects patient information. These included the establishment of a network of Caldicott Guardians to oversee access to patient-identifiable information. Their role includes:

- agreeing and reviewing internal protocols governing the protection and use of patient-identifiable information by the staff of their organisation;
- agreeing and reviewing protocols governing the disclosure of patient information across organisational boundaries;
- ensuring that protocols address the requirements of national policy and guidance, and the prevailing law;
- developing security and confidential policy.

8   Roles and responsibilities

AIMS

This chapter examines the roles and responsibilities of the staff who will be required to manage an organisation's records and information. It provides an overview of organisational responsibilities, gives a detailed framework of the skills and knowledge required by records staff, and suggests three types of training programme. At the heart of the chapter is the competency framework, developed by the author and colleagues at The National Archives. It has proved useful over the years and is a workable tool generally in the public sector.

COMPETENCIES

Competencies describe what people do in the workplace at various levels and specify the standards for each of those levels; they identify the characteristics, knowledge and skills possessed or required by individuals that enable them to undertake their duties and responsibilities effectively and thus to achieve professional quality standards in their work; and they should cover all aspects of records management performance – particular skills and knowledge, attitudes, communication, application and development. Three kinds of competence are used in this framework:

- *Core Competencies* – these are competencies relating to a records management organisation's strategic priorities and values. They will be applicable to all records management staff.
- *Functional Competencies* – these describe the role-specific abilities required and usually relate to professional or technical skills.
- *Managerial Competencies* – these competencies reflect the managerial activity and performance required in certain records management roles.

ORGANISATIONAL RESPONSIBILITY

In the United Kingdom the code of practice under section 46 of the Freedom of Information Act 2000 (in Scotland section 61 of the Freedom of Information (Scotland) Act 2002) requires all public authorities to have a records manager. Not all countries are so lucky to have such a formal directive. However, with the increasing recognition of the importance of the role of records management in an organisation, the allocation of responsibility for the function has also become important. The *records manager* is the person responsible for providing advice and guidance on the management of the organisation's records from the moment they are created until the time of their destruction or preservation in an archive. They must be aware of and control all records created and received within the organisation, whether these are part of a formal structure of files or unstructured folders, photographs, films, videos, sound recordings, electronic material, etc.

It also seems clear that in many organisations it would be desirable for the records manager to include in their competencies an archival function. This is particularly the case where there is no central source of archival advice upon which organisations can call. In the United Kingdom local authority sector, for example, advice and guidance is often not available within an authority, perhaps not even from the local record office, and guidelines issued by The National Archives, while having some generic relevance, are naturally aimed at public record (central government) bodies.

Organisations today are creating electronic and paper records in greater and greater quantities. In order to ensure records are to retain their administrative use and archival value, records managers must be significantly involved with the record-creating process itself, rather than be passive recipients of records that may no longer be authentic or reliable. Records managers must also become more involved with and understand the processes that lead to the creation of records. It is not sufficient to study the record and its physical nature and characteristics. Records professionals must understand the business functions, activities and working practices that cause documents to be made, used and maintained. For example, it is no use designing a classification scheme that does not match the business processes that give rise to the records to be classified. This is yet another reason illustrating the need for records management to be recognised as a specific corporate function within an organisation.

The records manager's role will be more effective and the corporate identity of records management will be enhanced if at functional levels of the organisation (groups, directorates, divisions or similar units) a person is nominated to serve as the formal contact for that unit with the records manager. Depending on the size and complexity of the organisation, this may be a full time post or included with other duties of the post holder. The development of such a network of *records officers* in the organisation is vital for good communications and for ensuring that standard corporate policies and procedures are developed and implemented.

All staff of the organisation are responsible for recording the actions and decisions that they take in accordance with their official duties, and the safeguarding of that information until it passes out of active operational involvement. Advice and guidance on general record keeping practices is provided by the records manager and records officers. The increasing use of and reliance on electronic records and information, the higher expectations of people seeking and using information and the immediacy of freedom of information processes have meant that all staff in an organisation need to be more aware of good record keeping practices.

An *archive repository* is responsible for preserving and making available those records of constituent organisations that have been selected for permanent preservation because of their historical value. The records manager should maintain regular contact with the archive repository so that those records which have historical and research value are properly earmarked and selected for preservation. In addition the archive repository will give general advice and guidance on the preservation of archival records.

Records do not just materialise on desks, in filing cabinets or on computer drives and servers; people create them and put them there and people have to manage them in such a way that when the information in them is required, they will be available at the right time. The management of records requires a professional approach on the part of the staff of any organisation. Until about ten years ago the person responsible for records was the junior office clerk with low pay, overburdened and under qualified, or perhaps an older member of staff who was tucked away in the records area waiting for retirement. In most countries this is no longer the case; in many others the situation is changing rapidly as politicians and senior management recognise the importance of good records management and the accessibility of information. In today's office environment the records officer is required to be a professional. He or she has to have the knowledge, skill and expertise to advise on and control the records and information required by other professionals in the organisation – information that is vital in decision making and policy formulation. The increasing professionalism of records staff has been a strong factor in promoting confidence and trust in record keeping systems by users.

Chapter 1 examined the drivers behind records management – business efficiency, access to information legislation, and electronic ways of working. These drivers are organisation-wide. They affect the organisation as a corporate body, not just its individual staff. Records management programmes and systems need to embrace the whole of the organisation and every participant must prioritise the needs of the organisation as a whole when creating and managing information. Records are not individual property. They are created for and on behalf of the corporate body. They sit in corporate filing cabinets or on corporate desks or in corporate electronic systems. They must be available to everyone in the organisation (subject to any security restrictions) whenever they are required – including those periods when the creator, custodian or user is absent.

Records management must therefore be seen as a specific corporate programme within an organisation. Subjects such as human resources, finance, health and safety, security and accommodation are seen as corporate responsibilities and services. Records management should be no different. It affects everybody in just the same way as those areas, which we have long regarded as corporate without thinking twice about it. In yearly business plans and strategies there ought to be something about the organisation's management of its information. Targets and objectives will be informed by monitoring programmes through which improvements and changes can be identified.

STAFFING

Staff appointed to undertake records work are generally regarded as part of the staff of the organisation in which they serve. In some countries their professional development is controlled by a central body (usually the National Archives) and a professional cadre is formed. This is often accompanied by a scheme of service formulated and monitored by a central civil service organisation. Whatever the degree of involvement from central bodies, there must be one official source of advice and guidance for the profession. National archives establishments are usually best placed to provide this service.

The records staff will consist of a number of grades at different levels. Not all of these grades will be used in every organisation or location. The grading structure in any organisation can vary according to the needs of the work to be carried out. Post holders undertaking similar work will not necessarily be graded at the same level if the range and complexity of the duties are of a different scale. For example, the manager responsible for appraisal and review in a headquarters may be at a higher grade than his or her equivalent in a regional office where the content of the records may be less complex and their scope more limited, or the manager with responsibility for the whole range of records of a large agency with many branches may be at a higher grade than his or her equivalent in a small agency with only one or no branches.

The work of records staff will cover a great variety of specific tasks falling within broad groups of records management work. The main types of work undertaken are:

- creation and maintenance of records in all formats;
- control of the receipt and registration of records;
- maintenance of control records and registers;
- classification and filing of records;
- safeguarding, control and issue of records;
- preparation of indexes and other finding aids to facilitate retrieval of information and records;
- identification and retrieval of information held within records;
- management of subordinate staff;
- development and implementation of agreed appraisal and review policies and procedures;
- preparation and implementation of record disposal schedules;
- rehabilitation, repair, conservation and reproduction of records;
- archiving and preservation; and
- design and implementation of appropriate records management systems and procedures.

Three types of skill are required for this work:

- Core skills for all staff.
- Functional skills that need to be applied to particular activities or groups of activities.
- Management skills for staff in supervisory and managerial positions.

There may be a mix of skills associated with particular posts. The framework set out in the following pages will allow senior staff to develop a profile of the skills required for specific posts. This profile can be translated into pay and grading terms with the help of human resource specialists.

COMPETENCY FRAMEWORK

The competency framework, which can be a powerful tool in helping government supported initiatives such as Investors in People, Citizen's Charter, etc., has been developed to help define the 'people capability' required in records management organisations. The competencies are set in a framework of four descriptive levels that relate closely to the grouping of work in records management units. The competencies themselves, however, may be utilised in various ways when applied to an organisation, depending on a number of factors: its functions, its size, information and corporate strategies, and the level of information technology it uses. The levels do not correspond to grading; for example, a senior member of staff may have a low requirement for some of the functional competencies but a very high requirement for the managerial competencies.

The following framework has purposely been kept as simple as possible while trying to cover all the skills and knowledge that we would expect to be required in the records management profession. In trying to cope with the rapidly changing world of information management, many governments are developing complex frameworks for professional skills. These have a vital role to play in the changing environment but have some way to go to maturity. For the time being this simplified version has been felt to be more in keeping with the overall aim of this book.

LEVELS OF KNOWLEDGE/EXPERTISE

The framework uses four levels of knowledge and expertise:

- *Learner* – requires some support; just beginning to need to demonstrate the competence.
- *Threshold* – able to perform most aspects of a competence without supervision.
- *Excellent* – consistently demonstrates very good performance in most aspects of the competence; coaching others in the competence is an important part of this level.
- *Expert* – demonstrates outstanding performance in a competence at a complex level; viewed as superior by others (within the organisation and outside it); creates the environment in which others can succeed in the competence.

FRAMEWORK

The framework is prefaced by a list of the competencies in the three categories of core, functional and managerial. Each one of these competencies is then described at the four levels of learner, threshold, excellent and expert. The descriptions for each level are examples of the skills or knowledge that should be reached before qualifying for the particular level. In the case of the core and managerial competencies these descriptions might be considered as relatively standard across a particular part of the public sector. The functional competencies, however, may be dependent on the strategic objectives and organisational management of particular organisations.

APPLICATION OF THE FRAMEWORK

Each role in a records management unit can be described in terms of a 'competence profile' that indicates the competencies required in the job (selected from the framework), and the level of competence which must be demonstrated in that job.

The framework is a tool that organisations can use or adapt to draw up their own role profiles. It can also be used to identify training and development needs, by assessing staff against role profiles, and to define the competencies required when recruiting new staff. Competence frameworks and role profiles work best when they are tailored to a particular organisation. In this respect the framework offered here should serve as an effective starting point.

A senior member of staff should take responsibility for the framework and ensure that it is maintained and kept up to date in the light of experience and developments in records management. It is suggested that revisions should be considered at least annually.

Table 8.1   List of competencies

Core Competencies

- Knowledge and History of the Organisation
- Knowledge of the [sectoral] Environment
- Professionalism
- Communication and Promoting Records Management
- Team working
- Planning and Time Management
- IT Literacy
- Flexibility
- Customer Care/Client Focus

Functional Competencies

- Information Policy
- Information Management
- Information Technology
- Records Management and Archival Practice
- Administration
- Specialist Knowledge

Managerial Competencies

- Coaching and Development
- Influencing
- Manage Performance
- Maintaining Standards
- Manage People
- Manage Proejcts

Table 8.2   Core competencies

Level	Description
	Knowledge and History of the Organisation
1	• Has a basic understanding of the function and role of the organisation, both past and present, and can explain this to others.
	• Is familiar with the structure of the organisation.
2	• Understands the remit afforded to the organisation by legislation, both past and present.
	• Understands the different record keeping and referencing systems used by the organisation over the past 25 years or more and can explain them to others.
	• Is aware of the high-profile subjects covered by the organisation and their implications on records work.
3	• Understands and acts on implications of past and present processes in the department, including the review and selection of records.
	• Explains and advises on the changes in the organisation's role and responsibilities over the past few years and the documentary evidence supporting them.
4	• Envisions future role of records within the organisation.
	• Coaches colleagues in developing their knowledge and understanding of the organisation both past and present.
	Knowledge of the Government[1] Environment
1	• Understands how the department fits into the government framework.
2	• Understands how the policy process works.
	• Is aware of the implications of government information policy on records work and can explain this to others.
	• Demonstrates own knowledge of government environment in decision making.
	• Demonstrates a knowledge of modern British history.
3	• Is able to identify records implications of new government policy.
	• Actively improves own understanding of the machinery of government and the decision making process.
4	• Understands changes in status and structure of government, government departments and social factors, and analyses impact on the department.
	• Is able to influence the policy process outside the department.
	• Is seen by others as an expert source of advice within the department on the machinery of government and modern British administrative history.
	• Coaches colleagues to generate greater insight into government roles and organisation.
	Professionalism
1	• Creates a positive impression of the section with clients.
	• Is delivery focused.
	• Responds promptly to requests for advice.
	• Refers questions to experts and ensures that action is taken to resolve issues.
2	• Provides objective professional advice to clients.
	• Communicates records policy consistently to clients and colleagues.
	• Has a confident approach in the application of records management.
	• Seeks to maintain current level of expertise.

[1] Government used as an example of a particular sector.

3
- Demonstrates relevant expertise and applies this consistently in records work.
- Is up-to-date with developments in own field of expertise and applies this in own work.
- Takes ownership of client issues and ensures their successful resolution.
- Deals confidently with senior managers in other divisions.
- Coaches others in developing more professional standards.

4
- Initiates records policy.
- Informs records policy with best practice approach.
- Role models standards to colleagues.

Communication and Promoting Records Management

1
- Is clear and precise in written and oral communication.
- Can make simple presentations.
- Makes best use of available means of communication.

2
- Communicates effectively to different audiences.
- Generates interest and enthusiasm in others.
- Translates technical terms into formats appropriate for their audience.

3
- Develops opportunities for raising the profile of records management.
- Produces effective communication and marketing plans.
- Can assimilate and disseminate complex information.
- Is able to interpret a brief, and create and deliver an effective presentation to large groups.

4
- Is an effective and inspirational speaker.
- Is persuasive and influential when conversing with others.
- Enhances communication and marketing through the development and implementation of communication and marketing strategies.

Team working

1
- Provides support for colleagues on own initiative.
- Understands own and others roles within the team.
- Recognises the need for teamwork.

2
- Energetically pursues team targets.
- Willingly undertakes different team roles.
- Forms good working relationships with other teams.

3
- Builds team effectiveness.
- Sets and communicates direction for a team.
- Generates enthusiasm for team and individual goals.

4
- Able to select team members according to business needs and individual development requirements.
- Role models team working.
- Identifies and manages the collective responsibility of the team.
- Aims to develop the team's collective ability.

Planning and Time Management

1
- Completes tasks allocated on time.
- Understands the scarcity of the time resource and the requirement to manage it.
- Prioritises according to organisational policy.
- Manages conflicting priorities in own work.

2
- Plans and manages own workload to ensure completion.
- Monitors progress against targets and takes corrective action when required.
- Accurately plans out activities according to workload requirements.
- Works methodically.

3
- Ensures that resources within a project or task are best deployed to meet targets.
- Delegates tasks effectively to others and ensures that they have the skills to succeed.

4
- Uses past experience to inform project planning and work allocation.
- Resolves priority conflicts for team members.
- Allocates assignments in the most efficient way.
- Recognises the importance of making personal time available for individual person management.
- Generates options to address resource issues.
- Is solutions-focused.

IT Literacy

1
- Demonstrates basic knowledge of relevant IT packages and systems.*
- Uses this knowledge to perform own work efficiently.

2
- Demonstrates good knowledge of relevant IT packages and systems.*
- Actively seeks to extend competence in information systems.

3
- Able to use relevant specialist software in the organisation.
- Able to use records management software packages.
- Coaches colleagues in the use of software and hardware.

4
- Identifies requirements for new, or new versions of, software applications.
- Maintains a good level of knowledge of IT developments.
- Advises colleagues on IT issues.

* *relevant IT packages and systems cover word processing, spreadsheets, databases, e-mail, Internet.*

Flexibility

1
- Willing to accept changes to job content.
- Adapts personal schedule to meet critical demands and to support colleagues.
- Is responsive to client and/or client needs.

2
- Moves willingly between different jobs.
- Works easily with different people.
- Displays ability to apply policy flexibly.
- Works effectively in a changing environment.

3
- Initiates and manages change.
- Is professionally innovative.
- Demonstrates ability to alter management style to suit different situations.
- Is results orientated.

4
- Role models and encourages flexibility in others.
- Creates a flexible culture for others.
- Seeks to improve performance and the working environment through change and innovation.

Customer Care/Client Focus

1
- Understands the importance of ongoing customer care.
- Adjusts personal style to deal with different customers.
- Recognises the importance of service levels.

2
- Builds relationships at a number of different levels in a customer's organisation.
- Understands clients' needs.
- Has systematic contact with customers on a regular basis.
- Formulates and manages service level agreements with customers.

3
- Actively solicits feedback from customers.
- Ensures continuity of service levels through mentoring and coaching.
- Makes every effort to ensure that customers have the necessary resources to meet required records management standards.

4	• Monitors service levels for a number of customers and deals with conflicting demands.
	• Provides expertise and coaches others in customer care.
	• Develops policies for achieving close and effective relationships with customers.
	• Actively develops relations with customers at a senior level.
	• Seeks and uses feedback from customers to improve customer care.

Table 8.3 Functional competencies

Information Management

1	• Recognises and understands the differences between various types of electronic records and the systems which produce them.
2	• Is able to supervise the inventory and audit of electronic records assemblies.
	• Is able to provide advice on the development and application of procedures for managing electronic records.
3	• Advises colleagues on mapping the information flows between different systems, putting the information in a business context, and assesses the implications of new systems development on electronic and paper records.
	• Actively encourages colleagues to use and manage records as information assets.
	• Contributes to the development of corporate records policies.
4	• Develops an understanding of information policy and its implications for electronic records.
	• Develops and maintains outside contacts to keep abreast of information management issues and techniques.
	• Generates new and innovative approaches to tackling information management issues.

Information Technology

1	• Has a basic knowledge of software and hardware applications and their usage in the organisation.
2	• Has practical experience of software/systems design and the provision of ongoing support.
	• Is able to generate solutions to ensure the continuing integrity of data held by the organisation.
3	• Is able to develop an IT strategy for records and to contribute to organisation-wide IT strategies.
	• Demonstrates an awareness of leading edge developments in IT.
	• Is able to implement an electronic document management system.
	• Understands the implications of related office systems, such as workflow and image processing, for records management systems.
	• Liaises with relevant IT specialists in government and industry.
4	• Generates approaches to electronic records management issues emerging from IT strategies.
	• Challenges and develops other's knowledge of IT systems and developments.

Information Policy

1	• Understands and can explain to others the implications of the organisation's information policy.
	• Continuously develops own understanding of the information policy.
2	• Facilitates liaison with other information professionals Demonstrates awareness of issues relating to the management of current information.
	• Understands the implications of Data Protection and Freedom of Information legislation and can interpret and apply relevant guidelines.

3
- Contributes to the development of responses to changes in information policy.
- Ensures that own reports understand changes in information policy.

4
- Is consulted as an expert on information policy.
- Provides guidance and advice on the implications of Data Protection and Freedom of Information.
- Develops organisational information policy and expertise.

Records Management and Archival Practice

1
- Is aware of different records media and associated records management implications.
- Has a basic knowledge of document preservation and repair techniques.
- Demonstrates knowledge of packaging, transfer and storage techniques.

2
- Is able to interpret and apply guidelines on the management of conventional and electronic records.
- Follows best practice principles in managing records.
- Demonstrates knowledge of records legislation.

3
- Seeks to think creatively about the records management and archival process.
- Has a knowledge of other records repositories and their specialisms.
- Applies records management standards and best practice guidelines in storing, appraising and selecting appropriate records.

4
- Develops records management policies which reflect best practice and legislative environment.
- Is seen as an expert on records management and archives administration within the organisation and by external bodies.
- Uses experience and knowledge to coach others in records management.
- Is involved with external bodies in the further development of best practice in records management and archives administration.

Administration

1
- Administers simple tasks successfully and learns from mistakes.
- Follows procedures.
- Able to use basic office equipment.
- Respects and maintains the confidential nature of records and information entrusted to them.
- Pays attention to detail.

2
- Checks for accuracy in other people's work.
- Creates and administers simple budgets.
- Administers complex tasks successfully.
- Maintains an effective filing system.
- Works within agreed procedures.

3
- Initiates invoices.
- Demonstrates a basic working knowledge of procurement and contract management.
- Works within and monitors procedures.

4
- Allocates administrative tasks across team members.
- Monitors the administration of a number of complex tasks.

Specialist Knowledge[2]

1
- Demonstrates a basic knowledge of the subject.
- Is able to access sources for more information/greater detail.

---

[2] Specialist knowledge might include: understanding of statistical research and sampling techniques; knowledge of particular types of records; specialist IT knowledge.

2	• Demonstrates a good knowledge of subject, both in theory and application.
	• Is able to apply knowledge to current working environment.
3	• Demonstrates an in-depth subject knowledge.
	• Provides relevant and helpful advice to others.
	• Shares knowledge willingly.
4	• Demonstrates a subject knowledge in breadth and depth.
	• Is seen as an expert and consulted by others regularly.

Table 8.4   Managerial competencies

Coaching and Development

1	• Takes personal responsibility for own development.
	• Continuously improves personal competence in line with requirements of own job and career aspiration.
	• Regularly seeks feedback on personal performance.
2	• Regularly discusses training and development needs with staff, linking them with individual and team business targets.
	• Identifies and agrees training and development needs and ensures that they are met.
	• Actively supports staff throughout the training process, by briefing and debriefing, and provides information about available training.
3	• Identifies potential and expertise in others.
	• Measures and evaluates impact of training and development initiatives.
	• Ensures individuals' knowledge is shared and captured.
4	• Creates and encourages a culture of knowledge sharing within the organisation.
	• Creates opportunities to enhance learning and knowledge across the organisation.
	• Identifies and implements career development opportunities for staff.

Influencing

1	• Is able to identify the benefits of records management policies.
	• Is assertive with others in ensuring understanding of key information.
	• Understands and can apply own influencing styles.
2	• Is able to describe to others the benefits of changing records management practices.
	• Is able to utilise a range of persuasion techniques.
	• Understands how to influence others.
	• Recognises when to be assertive to achieve results.
3	• Is able to change existing records management behaviours.
	• Is able to moderate personal style with others to maximise outcomes.
	• Is able to create change in records management policies throughout the organisation.
4	• Facilitates inter-departmental debates on records management best practice.
	• Coaches others in developing their influencing skills.
	• Works to ensure that the records section is closely involved in the departmental decision making process.

Manage Performance

1	• Contributes to the achievement of individual and team targets.
	• Monitors own performance on a regular basis.
2	• Identifies potential risks to performance achievement and responds promptly.
	• Sets clear and achievable team targets and objectives, and manages their successful achievement.

3
- Understands how processes underlie performance.
- Uses resources to maximise cost effectiveness of service provision.
- Consistently delivers targets within budget and provides accurate management information.
- Is able to develop corporate and business plans with useful measures of performance.

4
- Manages collective performance to achieve business priorities and objectives.
- Allocates and manages resources to ensure the achievement of business priorities and objectives.
- Manages risk in order to maintain performance levels.
- Encourages others to initiate change to improve performance.

Maintaining Standards

1
- Understands and communicates the need for quality standards.
- Able to identify and implement ideas for improved quality of service in own work.
- Consistently applies records management standards.

2
- Implements changes to quality standards.
- Able to identify and implement ideas for improved quality of performance.
- Recognises resource constraints in achieving quality standards.

3
- Generates standards to meet organisational needs.
- Promotes quality improvement throughout the organisation.
- Seeks feedback on overall quality of service.
- Monitors standards and provides management information as required.

4
- Promotes quality improvements in records management.
- Creates a culture that promotes the need for standards.
- Ensures availability of accurate quality information for management reporting.

Manage People

1
- Manages self and others in the completion of a task.
- Represents the needs of colleagues to superiors.
- Understands the performance management system and ensures that own contribution is valid.
- Demonstrates commitment to personal development.

2
- Recognises and rewards good performance both formally and informally.
- Reviews individual and team performance and provides feedback.
- Forms effective working relationships.
- Delegates effectively to others.

3
- Creates and communicates direction in a clear and consistent way.
- Enhances productive working relationships.
- Consults and communicates with others in areas of joint interest.
- Provides effective change management.

4
- Creates an environment in which people are motivated and inspired.
- Creates a culture where individuals and teams own the impact of their actions.
- Provides leadership and direction during change.

Manage Projects

1
- Can plan and deliver simple projects.
- Monitors progress against objectives.
- Understands basic project management techniques.

2
- Identifies project objectives, risks and success factors.
- Delivers projects according to time, cost and quality targets.
- Takes action where progress is not in line with objectives.
- Understands and can apply a range of project management techniques.
- Manages suppliers on a day-to-day basis.

3	• Manages complex or multiple projects.
	• Manages contracts with external suppliers.
	• Identifies in advance potential risks and their solutions.
	• Creates, develops and manages project teams.
	• Is able to negotiate satisfactory contracts with suppliers.
4	• Is seen by others as an expert in project management.
	• Generates, communicates and maintains a best practice project management model.
	• Ensures deliverables are in line with business strategies.

Records Manager:

Role: develop and manage an organisation-wide records management programme designed to ensure that records practices are effectively meeting the organisation's objectives

Competence	Level
Core	
Knowledge and History of the Organisation	3
Knowledge of the [sectoral] Environment	3
Professionalism	3
Communication and Marketing	3
Team working	2
Planning and Time Management	3
IT Literacy	2
Flexibility	3
Customer Care	3
Score:	25
Functional	
Administration	2
Information Management	2
Information Technology	1
Information Policy	3
Records Management and Archival Practice	3
Specialist Knowledge	3
Score:	14
Managerial	
Coaching and Development	3
Influencing	3
Advice and Guidance	3
Manage Performance	3
Manage People	2
Manage Projects	3
Maintaining Standards	3
Score:	20
Total score:	59

Figure 8.1 Example of a profile

199

In conjunction with human resource specialists the scoring may be translated into appropriate pay and grading levels.

ROLE TYPES

Roles in records management may be said to be of four main types (the descriptors may vary).

Director of Information Services

This is the post that oversees the information management function in an organisation, usually including IT and information management responsibility; their main role is the formulation of policy and contribution to the achievement of the organisation's corporate objectives by ensuring that it raises the standard of records and information management, including electronic records.

Records Manager/Departmental Record Officer

This post has direct managerial responsibility for the records management function, including the management and appraisal of electronic records.

Records Executive

Typically the records executive or records supervisor will take charge of specific areas of records management within the overall management of an organisation's records and information. For example, they may be responsible for all matters concerning the management of active records – file classification systems, inspection of file management units, or liaison with nominated officers throughout the organisation. They may take charge of an organisation's intermediate records and be responsible for the operation of an appraisal system.

Records Assistant

The post of records assistant may be used in a number of ways, for example, preparing records for transfer to an archive, retrieving and replacing records for the organisation's own staff, compiling lists and other finding aids to selected records.

JOB AND PERSON SPECIFICATIONS

Job descriptions, or specifications, should be drawn up for each post. This should also include a person specification which can be used principally to aid managers in the recruitment of suitable staff to records management units. Both can also be used as a basis for performance management plans with staff at the beginning of each business year and, in conjunction with performance assessments, may be used to identify training and development requirements.

Job Specifications

A job specification should comprise two main elements: 1) job purpose, and 2) job description.

The *job purpose* consists of a short statement outlining the main components of a particular role. These will underpin the job holder's performance management plan and contribute to departmental and corporate objectives. The following are examples of such statements for four different jobs:

1. Responsible for the management and use of departmental information and administrative services, including strategic planning and information technology.
2. Develop and manage an organisation-wide records management programme designed to ensure that records practices are effectively meeting the organisation's needs.
3. Oversee all activities pertaining to the management of non-current records, including receipt, storage, retrieval, review and disposal.
4. Assist in the provision of an efficient records management system and mail processing system to service the whole of the organisation's operations.

The *job description* lists the particular duties and responsibilities of the role. The following are examples corresponding to the four examples of job purpose above:

1a. Create, manage, control and direct the records and information management programme for the whole Department;
1b. direct the development of records and information policies and procedures;
1c. undertake the role of information strategist, determining staffing, equipment and other resources required to meet corporate objectives;
1d. responsible for financial planning of records and information services.

2a. Establish procedures and direct the implementation of the records management programme;
2b. monitor compliance with legislative and other recordkeeping requirements;
2c. develop recordkeeping and records management standards and rules, including those for electronic recordkeeping;
2d. provide technical support and co-ordination of personnel resources necessary for the successful operation of the programme;
2e. provide technical training to business unit records personnel as required;
2f. responsible for addressing and resolving issues within the records management areas;

2g. responsible to the Information Services Director for the records management budget and cost control;

2h. establish procedures for the evaluation, development and review of manual and automated records systems;

2i. design and implement effective records disposal schemes;

2j. advise on and implement effective strategies for storage of active records (electronic and paper); manage an off-site storage programme for inactive records;

2k. prepare periodic reports for the Information Services Director with respect to the records management operations.

3a. Supervise and co-ordinate the work of the records centre staff;

3b. develop and supervise training programmes for records centre staff and for user departments to ensure consistency and standardisation;

3c. develop and implement policies and procedures for the records centre;

3d. undertake special research requests from user departments;

3e. ensure the application of disposal schedules;

3f. ensure efficient utilisation of storage space;

3g. ensure security and preservation of the records in the records centre;

3h. ensure that records are produced to user departments when requested and within agreed timescales;

3i. liaise with the PRO Client Manager on review procedures;

3j. prepare reports on the maintenance, use and disposal of non-current records.

4a. Account for the accurate recording of file data and movement of files throughout the organisation;

4b. make files available on demand;

4c. circulate files to officers in accordance with established procedures;

4d. provide assistance and information on status of files;

4e. collect and distribute outward mail;

4f. process inward mail;

4g. establish and maintain property series files under the direction of the Records Manager;

4h. assist with co-ordination of copier maintenance;

4i. assist with file courier service as required.

Person Specifications

The *person specification* draws directly on the competence framework. It specifies those skills required for the job and the level at which they should be pitched. For example, the role described in 1 above might require the following person specification:

- *qualifications* – honours degree, or at least five years experience in senior management;
- *experience* – an understanding of organisational structures and policy-making processes; an awareness of records management principles and practices;
- *skills* – high level of interpersonal skills; ability to work as part of a team; initiative; decisiveness; consistency.

The role described in 2 above might have the following person specification:

- *qualifications* – tertiary qualification in records management;
- *experience* – five years records management experience, ideally in a supervisory role; experience in implementing and maintaining a computer-based records system is desirable;
- *specialist skills and knowledge* – computer keyboard skills; knowledge of activities and operations of government; understanding of archives legislation;
- *management skills* – ability to work within specified timescales to achieve set objectives;
- *interpersonal skills* – ability to liaise with staff at all levels and assist them in records and research functions; essential to work in a team environment to achieve a team objective.

TRAINING AND DEVELOPMENT

The issues surrounding the demand for more efficient and reliable management of information and the automation of business give rise to training and development needs. The competence framework detailed above and the job and person specifications linked to it provide the means to identify those needs.

Training and development in records management require commitment on the part of organisations, particularly in planning the development of employees on the basis of competence assessment and action to implement the plans. This would be followed by an evaluation of the results of the training in order to assess achievement and improve future effectiveness. The following chapter examines this subject in more detail.

9 Training and development

AIMS

This chapter provides some ideas and suggestions about training and development framework. It sets out some opportunities currently available and looks at the subject of mentoring. It also examines some of the changes that are affecting records management as the profession develops and concludes with some suggestions for measuring performance in records management.

INTRODUCTION

It's no use producing the most comprehensive manual or guidance on records management subjects if there is no training and development framework in which to set it. Many people can learn theories and procedures from written advice and guidance but the practice is best learnt by interacting with fellow professionals and by hands on training. In an environment of decreasing resources it may be difficult to embark upon a comprehensive programme and records managers may well have to focus on one or a few areas at a time. There is no doubt, however, that time and money spent wisely on training and development is a good investment.

There are two aspects to records management training and development – one to cover the organisation as a whole and one for those whose main job is in records and information management (in smaller organisations this is often a part of wider, but related, responsibilities). After the detailed description of these aspects below there follows a tabular summary.

ORGANISATION-WIDE

There are three levels to records and information management training in the organisation as a whole, aimed at:

- Senior managers – those responsible for corporate strategy and policy;
- Operational staff – including line managers;
- Records liaison staff.

SENIOR MANAGERS

Senior staff in organisations need to be aware of developments in records and information management without being burdened with the detail of procedures and practices. They need to acquire an understanding of the wider issues involved with, for example, the introduction of electronic records management systems or changes in access to information provisions so that they can take decisions on strategy and resources.

One of the most effective ways of keeping senior management in touch with records and information management issues is for the records manager to make a contribution within existing governance frameworks. Typically this might be making a short presentation at regular meetings of management boards or executive teams. In some cases this might be on a monthly basis or, more likely, quarterly. These presentations need not be formal and can be kept relatively short – 15 minutes is common. The important point is to keep records and information management firmly on the governance agenda. Support from senior management is vital if resources are to be forthcoming.

A less effective, but sometimes rewarding, way to get senior management on board is to invite them to seminars, workshops, open days and other records management events that might be arranged. It is not always possible for all such managers to attend but for some it can be an enlightening experience. In some cases the invitation might include them giving an introductory presentation to the event.

OPERATIONAL STAFF

The introduction of access to information legislation in many areas of the world has meant that records and information management has become a more immediate issue for operational staff than has hitherto been the case. Before such legislation records were created, used and disposed of – in many cases sent to a file store to be dealt with by specialist records staff. The operational staff were primarily concerned with discharging their responsibilities and not unduly concerned with what happened to the records afterwards. The records themselves often languished in storerooms or basements, frequently ill-kept and abandoned, until they reached their disposal date and were destroyed. This changed with the introduction of freedom of information. Those records that were forgotten about until disposal schedules came into play might now be the subject of access requests. They therefore needed to be looked after a little better than before. This placed added responsibilities upon operational staff. They needed to be more aware of record keeping policies and procedures so that they could ensure that information was filed away where it could be easily and quickly retrieved if required. They needed to ensure that closed records remained accessible and in good order for as long as disposal schedules required.

Records and information management training for operational staff in the organisation therefore needs to be in the nature of awareness rather than an exposition of detailed procedures. They need to be aware of the need to create records and information that adequately documents the decisions and processes that they undertake as part of their duties. They need to be familiar with the file plan or file classification scheme, and aware of the importance of good filing practices (such as the use of naming conventions) so that information can be quickly retrieved. They need to know who to approach or where to look if they are uncertain of what to do in the area of records management. They need to be familiar with good records maintenance procedures, including the use of email systems.

It is often impossible to gather operational staff together for face-to-face training. The most effective way to get messages across to them is often achieved by using in-house newsletters, the organisation's intranet or circulars on particular subjects. In this respect line managers have an important role to play. They can be targeted and required to cascade information down to their teams and units.

RECORDS LIAISON STAFF

A vital aspect of the framework of records and information management in an organisation is to establish and maintain a network of staff in the various business areas who have local responsibility for records. In very large organisations these staff might be full-time and be engaged in appraising and reviewing records in their business areas or be responsible for administering local file classification schemes. More often than not, however, they will have other responsibilities. Such staff will not be under the direct command of the records manager.

The training of records liaison staff should be of three kinds:

- Introductory – a half day introduction to records and information management in the organisation aimed at new staff. This might include the legislative background to records management, the organisation's policy and procedures, the interaction of records and information management with all parts of the organisation, and latest developments. It should be delivered by the records manager.

- Specialist training – one or half day courses/workshops on particular issues. This might be necessary, for example, with the introduction of an electronic records management system or with a change in policy or procedure. Such specialist training could be delivered by a member of the records management team or the services of a specialist consultant might be used.
- Annual event – it is often very useful to hold an annual conference of records liaison staff. This provides them (and the records management team) with an opportunity to reflect on developments over the previous year and to make plans for the future. The networking opportunities provided by such an event cannot be overstated.

RECORDS AND INFORMATION MANAGEMENT STAFF

There are three levels of training for records and information management staff: introductory, vocational, and advanced.

See the end of the chapter for some examples of what these levels might comprise.

INTRODUCTORY

This should be aimed at staff new to records and information management and might comprise a combination of hands-on training (working directly with colleagues for a short period), directed reading and courses on basic records management procedures and practices. In the United Kingdom The National Archives provides an introduction to the public records system, aimed at central government staff but relevant to the wider public sector, which covers the following areas:

- Background to record keeping in the UK;
- Legislative background;
- Role of The National Archives;
- Appraisal and disposal;
- Access;
- Electronic records;
- Future developments.

This half day course is followed by a tour of The National Archives facilities.

The aim of introductory training must be to put the newcomer's role into context. What is their role? How does it fit into the organisation? How does it interact with outside organisations? An important part of this should be to provide the trainee with access to sources that they might need and with names of people whom they might need to contact in the course of their work.

VOCATIONAL

After the introductory phase of their careers, which may last anything up to a year, staff will need access to more specialist and focussed training and education. It needs to be directly relevant to their work – hence the use of the term 'vocational' – and concentrated on particular areas of the records management life cycle rather than looking at the subject as a whole. As the description suggests, vocational training benefits greatly by including mentors in the undertaking. The role of mentoring is discussed more fully below.

Vocational training will typically be modular. The following is a suggested framework:

- Understanding the principles and practices of records management: compliance and regulatory environment; principles of appraisal; and archives and permanent preservation (paper and electronic).
- Classifying and managing records: business requirements; records creation; electronic file plans; day-to-day management; and local information management roles.
- Records maintenance: production and retrieval; processing new records; storage and security; and preservation.
- Records appraisal: appraisal systems – paper and electronic; maintain and implement retention and disposal schedules; and deletion and destruction.
- Develop and maintain effective working relationships with customers.

At the time of writing The National Archives is developing a programme on these lines, aimed at central government but relevant to the wider public sector. The intention is that it will be delivered by records managers and will promote consistency in this area. The programme will not be formally accredited but will be supported and maintained by The National Archives.

In recent years there have been detailed vocational programmes promoted under the NVQ banner – one aimed at records managers and one aimed at archivists. Sadly these were abandoned when the government put forward its scheme of National Training Organisations (NTO). For a few years there was much work undertaken to introduce an Information Services NTO and then a Cultural Heritage NTO. Neither of these took off. The former is in the process of being absorbed by Lifelong Learning UK (LLUK); the latter has been completely wound up. There has, therefore, been something of a vacuum in this area of records and information management training and education.

ADVANCED

Advanced programmes of training and education in records and information management are aimed at those staff who make a career out of the subject. They are often – though not exclusively – linked to universities and therefore very academic in nature. As might be expected, the training examines areas of records and information management in great depth and often includes related areas such as business frameworks and management tools. In this respect they focus more on theory than practice.

Records and information managers who make a career out of the subject have access to several advanced programmes of training and education. In the United Kingdom there are five main programmes in this area: Liverpool University Centre for Archive Studies (LUCAS), www.liv.ac.uk/lucas, School of Library, Archive and Information Studies, University College London, www.ucl.ac.uk/slais, Department of Information Studies (DIS), University of Wales, Aberystwyth, www.dil.aber.ac.uk, Division of Information and Communication Studies, Northumbria University, http://online.northumbria.ac.uk/faculties/art/information_studies/index.htm, Dundee University, http://www.dundee.ac.uk/prospectus/distlearning2004/courseprofiles/armms.htm.

There are several other universities that, at the time of writing, provide courses on or related to information management. They include: City University, London, Thames Valley University, London, London Metropolitan University, University of Central England, Birmingham, University of Brighton, University of Bristol, Cranfield University, Leeds Metropolitan University, Liverpool John Moores University, Loughborough University, Manchester Metropolitan University, University of Sheffield, Queen's University, Belfast, University College Dublin, Robert Gordon University, Aberdeen, Queen Margaret University College, Edinburgh, and University of Strathclyde, Glasgow.

Table 9.1 Summary of the Aspects of Records and Information Management Training and Education

	Senior management	Operational staff	Records Liaison staff
Organisation wide	*Aim:* Awareness of current developments and understanding of major issues *Method:* Short presentation at governance meetings; invitations to RM events	*Aim:* Awareness of good record keeping practices *Method:* Newsletters, intranets and circulars; target line managers	*Aim:* Promote networking with records management staff; provide the skills to carry out duties *Method:* Half-day introduction; specialist courses; annual event

	Introductory	Vocational	Advanced
Records and information management staff	*For:* New staff in records management organisations *Content:* Basic records management principles and practices *Method:* Hands on training; directed reading; courses	*For:* Staff who have completed the introductory phase of their careers *Content:* Focussed on particular aspects; respond to developments in the profession *Method:* Courses and mentoring	*For:* Career records and information managers *Content:* In depth examination of subjects *Method:* University programmes

MENTORING

Mentoring happens when one person assists another to develop their potential, to acquire new skills and knowledge, and to grow into their chosen profession. The mentoring relationship is important in building confidence in the mentored person, helping them to take increasing responsibility for their own development. It is often hard to define because it overlaps with coaching and counselling. These two approaches can be seen as two ends of a scale, with mentoring in between:

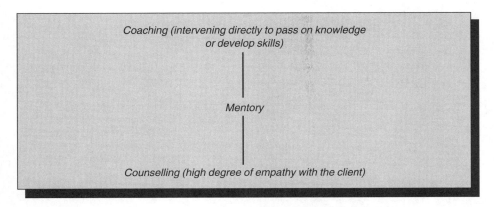

Figure 9.1 The Coaching – Mentoring – Counselling scale

Mentoring might move up and down this scale depending on the context. For example, concentrating on career mentoring will be closer to coaching; concentrating on social mentoring will be closer to counselling.

Mentors do not need to be qualified trainers and do not need to be highly skilled in the job that the mentored person undertakes. It is common to view the

211

mentored and mentor as equal partners in the relationship. What often distinguishes the mentor is their greater experience in the profession.

Mentoring involves a range of approaches, depending on the mentored person. These might be summarised as:

- Developing organisational skills;
- Developing job-related skills;
- Mentored person's personal development.

The mentor should set out specific aims at the beginning of the relationship, such as: What are my client's aims for learning and development? What can the mentor do to help them reach these aims? The achievement of these aims should be monitored on a regular basis until they can be said to have been completed and the mentoring processes can be drawn to a conclusion.

Among the best sources of information on mentoring are the *Mentors Forum* website at www.mentorsforum.co.uk and *The Coaching and Mentoring Network* at http://www.coachingnetwork.org.uk/.

10 The future: developing an integrated programme

AIMS

The world of information management is changing more rapidly than many of us expect or enjoy. One of the greatest challenges over the next decade or so is to manage those changes so that we are still able to deliver effective products to our users. This brief chapter covers change in two respects – business change and culture change, and makes some suggestions for integrated programming in that context. In a similar context it also looks at performance management – a key component of the management of change.

BUSINESS CHANGE

While the implementation of recent legislation and government policies like Freedom of Information is about good policies and procedures, and about staff training and awareness, it is also very much concerned with change – change in business processes and change in culture.

CHANGE PROGRAMME

Public sector organisations need to look at ways to handle these changes. A programme for this might have four focal points:

1 Leadership

Records management champions and senior managers in organisations should:

- make records and information management a priority;
- monitor compliance with legislation;
- resource new policies and procedures adequately;

- help resolve issues that may arise from the management of information (for example, not being able to find requested information, the application of FOI exemptions, etc.);
- ensure new staff understand how good records and information management procedures are part of the corporate responsibilities.

2 Communications and Involvement

Managers must create the right environment to ensure that new legislation and new records management practices are understood and can be followed as part of normal corporate working. This means involving as many people as possible in changes to policy and procedures, consulting users and ensuring that everyone knows about subsequent changes.

3 Learning

Since developments in records and information management increasingly affect everybody in the organisation, staff must have the appropriate knowledge and skills to discharge their duties effectively. This may mean acquiring new skills for some staff (such as those responsible for implementing an electronic records management system). In general all members of staff should have a good understanding of record keeping practices. The immediacy of access to information means that filing and retrieval of records and information becomes more important.

4 Measurement

Managers need to know that new initiatives are working properly and effectively. Accordingly they should be monitored and measured on a regular basis. They should include Records Management in performance assessments, recognise effectiveness of responses to requests for information, and ensure that the records management system is still delivering information to the correct place and in a timely fashion

CULTURE CHANGE

Public servants have deep-seated traditions on the way they handle and provide information. There are three areas where these traditions need to change, and these are detailed below.

SECRECY TO OPENNESS

In the United Kingdom, and many other countries, the presumption of new access to information regimes is that all information held by public authorities is made available to those who request it. There are, of course, exemptions, as there must be if public sectors are to operate effectively. This is a major change from earlier attitudes – which have varied slightly between different parts of the public sector. People often keep information to themselves (perhaps they feel more powerful if they do so). They query why anyone should need to know what they know.

This openness issue is nothing new in the UK. Those working in local authorities will be only too aware of the need to make available minutes of local council meetings, reports and papers (since 1985); and there has been access to various types of environmental information since 1988. There have also been codes of practice on openness in the public sector for several years – some will say they are among the best kept government secrets. The White Paper Open Government, CM2290 – published in July 1993 – set out proposals for new legislation and for a Code of Practice on Access to Government Information. In subsequent years similar codes of practice were introduced for the Welsh Assembly, Scottish Executive and the National Health Service. These codes of practice all had the same basic premise – that people have access to available information about services provided, the cost of those services, quality standards and performance against targets; they are provided with explanations about proposed changes and have an opportunity to influence decisions on such changes; and they know what information is available and where they can get it.

More and more governments are being pressed into greater transparency and greater accountability for the decisions and actions that they undertake. The change – and the challenge – is to recognise that we need to move away from the need to know towards the right to know.

INDIVIDUAL TO CORPORATE

Records management has long been considered a low priority for most organisations. Paradoxically, while the last decade or so has seen a greater emphasis on corporate planning and corporate targets, the supporting records and information sources have remained set along traditional lines. In a paper environment records were often centralised but managers and operational staff needed live records to hand and often needed them immediately. In addition the low grade staff manning the perceived low grade work in registries and record centres meant that many staff did not believe that they would ever see their files again if they put them away in the file store. When computers were introduced into the office environment those live records were increasingly stored on individual hard disks. When local area networks were introduced it seemed natural to maintain those folders that had been created, or at least duplicate them on the network. The concept of sharing information is struggling to emerge from these traditional attitudes. It is only in recent years, with the greater availability of systems designed specifically to manage records corporately, and – lest we forget – with the introduction of freedom of information legislation, that the change in culture is quickening.

The attitude of 'my records in my cabinet in my office' is no longer valid. Records and information created by individuals in the course of their official employment are corporate records and information and, with few exceptions, should be made available to the corporate body.

PAPER TO ELECTRONIC

New access to information legislation is linked inexorably with other developments in information management – most importantly with strategies for electronic government. The electronic delivery of services to business and the citizen will depend on good management of electronic records.

Up to now new information systems do not always generate electronic records that fall under any formal corporate control and management. Meeting government targets on modernisation means that we have to look carefully at the processes of managing information in this (and other) formats. We must:

- know what records are out there in the organisation;
- develop a policy for the effective management of the records;
- evaluate the records for retention;
- prepare sustainability strategies for maintaining access to, and reliability of, electronic documents identified as having continuing value.

There are still many people who do not trust electronic records – and this is not just something that will be overcome with the age generations; it has to be taken on board now if we are to meet our business targets and discharge our legal obligations. There are two examples that might illustrate these points.

With regard to the destruction of records, some organisations still insist on having written (and signed) certification when records are destroyed. Why was this laid down in the first place? – to prove that destruction had taken place and had been undertaken by an authorised person. An electronic communication, perhaps in the form of an email, will do just as well. Electronic audit systems can prove – probably more conclusively – that that email was sent and sent by the person it says sent it.

There is a common misconception that email messages are an ephemeral form of communication but they are increasingly becoming the primary business tool for both internal and external working. The types of email that might need to be managed as a record include discussions, information distributed to groups of people, agreement to proceed, and other exchanges relating to the discharge of business. Email messages can provide evidence about why a particular course of action was followed, which means that it is necessary not just to capture the email relating to the final decision but discussions that might indicate why one decision was made as opposed to another. This is certainly important in a business context but may also be vital in answering freedom of information requests. As soon as an email message needs to be forwarded for information purposes, it should be considered as a record. Furthermore, as soon as an email message has been identified as a record of a business transaction, it is important that the message is retained with other records relating to that particular business activity – this might be on an electronic records management system or another appropriate corporate system.

PERFORMANCE MANAGEMENT

It is all very well setting up a records management programme and integrating it into the culture of your organisation but the work (of course) does not stop there. You need to be sure that the systems are working effectively, that they are delivering their objectives and the perceived benefits are being realised. In short, there needs to be an element to the programme that can measure performance and make corrections as and when required.

Performance indicators should focus on end users to measure how effectively the system is being used and managed. They should include aspects such as placing electronic records in the relevant folder of the file plan, the accurate retrieval and production of records, the timely destruction of records in accordance with disposal policies and the control of access to sensitive material. However, record users cannot be expected to meet performance levels required of them unless they are made aware in the first place of what these requirements are. This sounds like stating the obvious but there is some evidence that this important element is sometimes overlooked. Managers have to educate and motivate staff to identify what information and records need to be created to reflect the true business process and to locate these into the corporate records management system established by the organisation. In this context users are often unclear, for example, about the status and importance of email communications. Email policies may be at a level that does not provide the detailed guidance that end users need.

The choice of performance indicators depends largely on the nature of the organisation, its corporate objectives and even its culture. The following are likely to feature in most organisations:

- quantity of records created and captured into the records management system;
- quantity of records appraised, selected and destroyed;
- quantity of records deposited in an archive;
- response times in retrieving records and information;
- user satisfaction;
- time spent on specific tasks;
- accessibility of records and information after filing or deposit;
- duplication of records;
- sharing of information about the records management system ('marketing');
- levels of awareness;
- costs; and
- realisation of benefits

As part of the development of the international standard on records management (ISO 15489), the British Standards Institute have produced BIP 0025-3 (2003) Effective records management: Performance management for ISO 15489 BS/. This contains detailed advice and guidance on the use of performance measurement that helps organisations comply with the standard.

Appendix 1:
Codes of Practice

LORD CHANCELLOR'S CODE OF PRACTICE ON THE MANAGEMENT OF RECORDS UNDER SECTION 46 OF THE FREEDOM OF INFORMATION ACT 2000 NOVEMBER 2002[1]

FOREWORD

General

(i) This Code of Practice (hereafter referred to as 'the Code') provides guidance to all public authorities as to the practice which it would, in the opinion of the Lord Chancellor, be desirable for them to follow in connection with the discharge of their functions under the Freedom of Information Act 2000 (FOIA). The Code applies also to other bodies that are subject to the Public Records Act 1958 and the Public Records Act (NI) 1923.

(ii) The Code fulfils the duty of the Lord Chancellor under section 46 of the FOIA.

(iii) Any freedom of information legislation is only as good as the quality of the records to which it provides access. Such rights are of little use if reliable records are not created in the first place, if they cannot be found when needed or if the arrangements for their eventual archiving or destruction are inadequate. Consequently, all public authorities are strongly encouraged to pay heed to the guidance in the Code.

---

[1] Note that the code refers to the 'Public Record Office', which after April 2003 became the National Archives.

(iv) The Code is a supplement to the provisions in the FOIA. But its adoption will help authorities to comply with their duties under that Act. It is not a substitute for legislation. Public authorities should seek legal advice as appropriate on general issues relating to the implementation of the FOIA, or its application to individual cases. The Code is complemented by the Code of Practice under section 45 of the FOIA and by Memoranda of Understanding setting out how the consultation requirements of section 66 of the FOIA will be put into effect.

(v) The Information Commissioner will promote the observance of the Code by public authorities, acting as required by the FOIA. If it appears to the Commissioner that the practice of an authority in relation to the exercise of its functions under the FOIA does not conform with that set out in the Code, he may issue a practice recommendation under section 48 of the Act. A practice recommendation must be in writing and must specify the provisions of the Code which have not been met and the steps which should, in his opinion, be taken to promote conformity with Code.

(vi) If the Commissioner reasonably requires any information for the purpose of determining whether the practice of a public authority in relation to the exercise of its functions under the FOIA conforms with that proposed in this Code, he may serve on the authority a notice (known as an 'information notice') under the provisions of section 51 of the Act. This requires it, within such time as is specified in the notice, to furnish the Commissioner, in such form as may be so specified, with such information relating to conformity with the Code of Practice as is so specified.

(vii) An information notice must contain a statement that the Commissioner regards the specified information as relevant for the purpose of deciding whether the practice of the authority conforms with that proposed in the Code of Practice and of his reasons for regarding that information as relevant for that purpose. It must also contain particulars of the rights of appeal conferred by section 57 of the FOIA.

(viii) Authorities should note that if they are failing to comply with the Code, they may also be failing to comply with the Public Records Acts 1958 and 1967, the Local Government (Records) Act 1962, the Local Government Act 1972, the Local Government (Access to Information) Act 1985 or other record-keeping or archives legislation, and they may consequently be in breach of their statutory obligations.

(ix) The Public Records Act (NI) 1923 sets out the duties of public record bodies in Northern Ireland in respect of the records they create and requires that records should be transferred to, and preserved by, the Public Record Office of Northern Ireland.

Main features of the FOIA

(x) The main features of the FOIA are:

1. A general right of access to recorded information held by a wide range of bodies across the public sector, subject to certain conditions and exemptions. The right includes provisions in respect of historical records which are more than 30 years old.

2. In relation to most exempt information, the information must nonetheless be disclosed unless the public interest in maintaining the exemption in question outweighs the public interest in disclosure.

3. A duty on every public authority to adopt and maintain a scheme which relates to the publication of information by the authority and is approved by the Information Commissioner. Authorities must publish information in accordance with their publication schemes. This scheme must specify:

- classes of information which the public authority publishes or intends to publish;
- the manner in which information of each class is, or is intended to be, published; and
- whether the material is, or is intended to be, available to the public free of charge, or on payment.

4. A new office of Information Commissioner and a new Information Tribunal, with wide powers to enforce the rights created and to promote good practice.

5. A duty on the Lord Chancellor to promulgate Codes of Practice for guidance on specific issues.

6. The amendment of the public records system to integrate it with the new right of access under the FOIA.

Training

(xi) All communications in writing (including by electronic means) to a public authority fall within the scope of the FOIA, if they seek information, and must be dealt with in accordance with the provisions of the Act. It is therefore essential that everyone working in a public authority is familiar with the provisions of the FOIA, the Codes of Practice issued under its provisions, any relevant Memoranda of Understanding, and any relevant guidance on good practice issued by the Commissioner. Authorities should ensure that proper training is provided.

(xii) In planning and delivering training, authorities should be aware of other provisions affecting the disclosure of information, such as the Environmental Information Regulations 1992 and their successors which, for example, do not require requests to be in writing.

Authorities subject to the Public Records Acts

(xiii) The guidance on records management and on the transfer of public records in the Code should be read in the context of existing legislation on record-keeping. In particular, the Public Records Act 1958 (as amended) gives duties to public record bodies in respect of the records they create. It also requires the Keeper of Public Records to supervise the discharge of those duties. Authorities that are subject to the Public Records Acts 1958 and 1967 should note that if they are failing to comply with the Code, they may also be failing to comply with those Acts.

(xiv) The Public Records Act (NI) 1923 sets out the duties of public record bodies in Northern Ireland in respect of the records they create and requires that records should be transferred to, and preserved by, the Public Record Office of Northern Ireland.

(xv) The Information Commissioner will promote the observance of the Code in consultation with the Keeper of Public Records when dealing with bodies which are subject to the Public Records Acts 1958 and 1967 and with the Deputy Keeper of the Records of Northern Ireland for bodies subject to the Public Records Act (NI) 1923.

(xvi) If it appears to the Commissioner that the practice of an authority in relation to the exercise of its functions under the FOIA does not conform with that set out in the Code, he may issue a practice recommendation under Section 48 of the Act. Before issuing such a recommendation to a body subject to the Public Records Acts 1958 and 1967 or the Public Records Act (NI) 1923, the Commissioner shall consult the Keeper of Public Records or the Deputy Keeper of the Records of Northern Ireland.

(xvii) The content of this Code has been agreed by the Deputy Keeper of Records of Northern Ireland. Part Two, in particular, describes the roles which public record bodies should perform to ensure the timely and effective review and transfer of public records to the Public Record Office or to places of deposit (as defined in Section 4 of the Public Records Act 1958) or to the Public Record Office of Northern Ireland (under the Public Records Act 1958 or the Public Records Act (NI) 1923). For the avoidance of doubt the term 'public records' includes Welsh public records as defined by Sections 116-118 of the Government of Wales Act 1998.

Role of the Lord Chancellor's Advisory Council on Public Records and of the Public Record Office

(xviii) To advise authorities on the review of public records, the Lord Chancellor, having received the advice of his Advisory Council on Public Records, (hereafter 'the Advisory Council') may prepare and issue guidance. This may include advice on the periods of time for which the Advisory Council considers it appropriate to withhold categories of sensitive records beyond the 30 year period. In Northern Ireland similar guidance shall be issued by the Deputy Keeper of the Records of Northern Ireland following consultation with the Departments responsible for the records affected by the guidance.

(xix) The Public Record Office will provide support as appropriate to the Advisory Council in its consideration of applications from authorities in respect of public records and in its preparation of guidance to authorities. In Northern Ireland the Public Record Office of Northern Ireland will provide similar support to the Sensitivity Review Group.

CODE OF PRACTICE
ON (1) THE MANAGEMENT OF RECORDS BY PUBLIC AUTHORITIES AND (2) THE TRANSFER AND REVIEW OF PUBLIC RECORDS UNDER THE FREEDOM OF INFORMATION ACT 2000

The Lord Chancellor, after consulting the Information Commissioner and the appropriate Northern Ireland Minister, issues the following Code of Practice pursuant to section 46 of the Freedom of Information Act.

Laid before Parliament on 20 November 2002 pursuant to section 46(6) of the Freedom of Information Act 2000.

INTRODUCTION

1. The aims of the Code are:

(1) to set out practices which public authorities, and bodies subject to the Public Records Act 1958 and the Public Records Act (NI) 1923, should follow in relation to the creation, keeping, management and destruction of their records (Part One of the Code), and

(2) to describe the arrangements which public record bodies should follow in reviewing public records and transferring them to the Public Record Office or to places of deposit or to the Public Record Office of Northern Ireland (Part Two of the Code).

2. This Code refers to records in all technical or physical formats.

3. Part One of the Code provides a framework for the management of records of public authorities and of bodies subject to the Public Records Act 1958 and the Public Records Act (NI) 1923, and Part Two deals with the review and transfer of public records. More detailed guidance on both themes may be obtained from published standards.

4. Words and expressions used in this Code have the same meaning as the same words and expressions used in the FOIA.

PART ONE: RECORDS MANAGEMENT

5. Functional Responsibility

5.1 The records management function should be recognised as a specific corporate programme within an authority and should receive the necessary levels of organisational support to ensure effectiveness. It should bring together responsibilities for records in all formats, including electronic records, throughout their life cycle, from planning and creation through to ultimate disposal. It should have clearly defined responsibilities and objectives, and the resources to achieve them. It is desirable that the person, or persons, responsible for the records management function should also have either direct responsibility or an organisational connection with the person or persons responsible for freedom of information, data protection and other information management issues.

6. Policy

6.1 An authority should have in place an overall policy statement, endorsed by top management and made readily available to staff at all levels of the organisation, on how it manages its records, including electronic records.

6.2 This policy statement should provide a mandate for the performance of all records and information management functions. In particular, it should set out an authority's commitment to create, keep and manage records which document its principal activities. The policy should also outline the role of records management and its relationship to the authority's overall strategy; define roles and responsibilities including the responsibility of individuals to document their actions and decisions in the authority's records, and to dispose of records; provide a framework for supporting standards, procedures and guidelines; and indicate the way in which compliance with the policy and its supporting standards, procedures and guidelines will be monitored.

6.3 The policy statement should be reviewed at regular intervals (at least once every three years) and, if appropriate, amended to maintain its relevance.

7. Human Resources

7.1 A designated member of staff of appropriate seniority should have lead

225

responsibility for records management within the authority. This lead role should be formally acknowledged and made known throughout the authority.

7.2 Staff responsible for records management should have the appropriate skills and knowledge needed to achieve the aims of the records management programme. Responsibility for all aspects of record keeping should be specifically defined and incorporated in the role descriptions or similar documents.

7.3 Human resource policies and practices in organisations should address the need to recruit and retain good quality staff and should accordingly support the records management function in the following areas:

- the provision of appropriate resources to enable the records management function to be maintained across all of its activities;
- the establishment and maintenance of a scheme, such as a competency framework, to identify the knowledge, skills and corporate competencies required in records and information management;
- the regular review of selection criteria for posts with records management duties to ensure currency and compliance with best practice;
- the regular analysis of training needs;
- the establishment of a professional development programme for staff with records management duties;
- the inclusion in induction training programmes for all new staff of an awareness of records issues and practices.

8. Active Records Management

Record Creation

8.1 Each operational/business unit of an authority should have in place an adequate system for documenting its activities. This system should take into account the legislative and regulatory environments in which the authority works.

8.2 Records of a business activity should be complete and accurate enough to allow employees and their successors to undertake appropriate actions in the context of their responsibilities, to

- facilitate an audit or examination of the business by anyone so authorised,
- protect the legal and other rights of the authority, its clients and any other person affected by its actions, and

226

- provide authenticity of the records so that the evidence derived from them is shown to be credible and authoritative.

8.3 Records created by the authority should be arranged in a record keeping system that will enable the authority to obtain the maximum benefit from the quick and easy retrieval of information.

Record Keeping

8.4 Installing and maintaining an effective records management programme depends on knowledge of what records are held, in what form they are made accessible, and their relationship to organisational functions. An information survey or record audit will meet this requirement, help to promote control over the records, and provide valuable data for developing records appraisal and disposal procedures.

8.5 Paper and electronic record keeping systems should contain metadata (descriptive and technical documentation) to enable the system and the records to be understood and to be operated efficiently, and to provide an administrative context for effective management of the records.

8.6 The record-keeping system, whether paper or electronic, should include a set of rules for referencing, titling, indexing and, if appropriate, security marking of records. These should be easily understood and should enable the efficient retrieval of information.

Record Maintenance

8.7 The movement and location of records should be controlled to ensure that a record can be easily retrieved at any time, that any outstanding issues can be dealt with, and that there is an auditable trail of record transactions.

8.8 Storage accommodation for current records should be clean and tidy, and it should prevent damage to the records. Equipment used for current records should provide storage which is safe from unauthorised access and which meets fire regulations, but which allows maximum accessibility to the information commensurate with its frequency of use. When records are no longer required for the conduct of current business, their placement in a designated records centre rather than in offices may be a more economical and efficient way to store them. Procedures for handling records should take full account of the need to preserve important information.

8.9 A contingency or business recovery plan should be in place to provide protection for records which are vital to the continued functioning of the authority.

9 Disposal Arrangements

9.1 It is particularly important under FOI that the disposal of records – which is here defined as the point in their lifecycle when they are either transferred to an archives or destroyed – is undertaken in accordance with clearly established policies which have been formally adopted by authorities and which are enforced by properly authorised staff.

Record Closure

9.2 Records should be closed as soon as they have ceased to be of active use other than for reference purposes. As a general rule, files should be closed after five years and, if action continues, a further file should be opened. An indication that a file of paper records or folder of electronic records has been closed should be shown on the record itself as well as noted in the index or database of the files/folders. Wherever possible, information on the intended disposal of electronic records should be included in the metadata when the record is created.

9.3 The storage of closed records awaiting disposal should follow accepted standards relating to environment, security and physical organisation.

Appraisal Planning and Documentation

9.4 In order to make their disposal policies work effectively and for those to which the FOIA applies to provide the information required under FOI legislation, authorities need to have in place systems for managing appraisal and for recording the disposal decisions made. An assessment of the volume and nature of records due for disposal, the time taken to appraise records, and the risks associated with destruction or delay in appraisal will provide information to support an authority's resource planning and workflow arrangements.

9.5 An appraisal documentation system will ensure consistency in records appraisal and disposal. It should show what records are designated for destruction, the authority under which they are to be destroyed and when they are to be destroyed. It should also provide background information on the records, such as legislative provisions, functional context and physical arrangement. This information will provide valuable data for placing records selected for

228

preservation into context and will enable future records managers to provide evidence of the operation of their selection policies.

Record Selection

9.6 Each authority should maintain a selection policy which states in broad terms the functions from which records are likely to be selected for permanent preservation and the periods for which other records should be retained. The policy should be supported by or linked to disposal schedules which should cover all records created, including electronic records. Schedules should be arranged on the basis of series or collection and should indicate the appropriate disposal action for all records (e.g. review after x years; destroy after y years).

9.7 Records selected for permanent preservation and no longer in regular use by the authority should be transferred as soon as possible to an archival institution that has adequate storage and public access facilities (see Part Two of this Code for arrangements for bodies subject to the Public Records Acts).

9.8 Records not selected for permanent preservation and which have reached the end of their administrative life should be destroyed in as secure a manner as is necessary for the level of confidentiality or security markings they bear. A record of the destruction of records, showing their reference, description and date of destruction should be maintained and preserved by the records manager. Disposal schedules would constitute the basis of such a record.

9.9 If a record due for destruction is known to be the subject of a request for information, destruction should be delayed until disclosure has taken place or, if the authority has decided not to disclose the information, until the complaint and appeal provisions of the FOIA have been exhausted.

10 Management of Electronic Records

10.1 The principal issues for the management of electronic records are the same as those for the management of any record. They include, for example the creation of authentic records, the tracking of records and disposal arrangements. However, the means by which these issues are addressed in the electronic environment will be different.

10.2 Effective electronic record keeping requires:

- a clear understanding of the nature of electronic records;
- the creation of records and metadata necessary to document business processes: this should be part of the systems which hold the records;
- the maintenance of a structure of folders to reflect logical groupings of records;
- the secure maintenance of the integrity of electronic records;
- the accessibility and use of electronic records for as long as required (which may include their migration across systems);
- the application of appropriate disposal procedures, including procedures for archiving; and
- the ability to cross reference electronic records to their paper counterparts in a mixed environment.

10.3 Generic requirements for electronic record management systems are set out in the 1999 Public Record Office statement *Functional Requirements and Testing of Electronic Records Management Systems*, (see http://www.pro. gov.uk/recordsmanagement/eros/invest/default.htm). Authorities are encouraged to use these, and any subsequent versions, as a model when developing their specifications for such systems.

10.4 Audit trails should be provided for all electronic information and documents. They should be kept securely and should be available for inspection by authorised personnel. The BSI document *Principles of Good Practice for Information Management (PD0010)* recommends audits at predetermined intervals for particular aspects of electronic records management.

10.5 Authorities should seek to conform to the provisions of BSI DISC PD0008 – *Code of Practice for Legal Admissibility and Evidential Weight of Information Stored Electronically (2nd edn)* – especially for those records likely to be required as evidence.

PART TWO: REVIEW AND TRANSFER OF PUBLIC RECORDS

11.1 This part of the Code relates to the arrangements which authorities should follow to ensure the timely and effective review and transfer of public records. Accordingly, it is relevant only to authorities which are subject to the Public Records Acts 1958 and 1967 or to the Public Records Act (NI) 1923. The general purpose of this part of the Code is to facilitate the performance by the Public Record Office, the Public Record Office of Northern Ireland and other public authorities of their functions under the Freedom of Information Act.

11.2 Under the Public Records Acts, records selected for preservation may be transferred either to the Public Record Office or to places of deposit appointed by the Lord Chancellor. This Code applies to all such transfers. For guidance on which records may be transferred to which institution, and on the disposition of UK public records relating to Northern Ireland, see the Public Record Office *Acquisition Policy* (1998) and the Public Record Office *Disposition Policy* (2000).

11.3 In reviewing records for public release, authorities should ensure that public records become available to the public at the earliest possible time in accordance with the FOIA.

11.4 Authorities which have created or are otherwise responsible for public records should ensure that they operate effective arrangements to determine:

a. which records should be selected for permanent preservation; and
b. which records should be released to the public.

These arrangements should be established and operated under the supervision of the Public Record Office or, in Northern Ireland, in conjunction with the Public Record Office of Northern Ireland. The objectives and arrangements for the review of records for release are described in greater detail below.

11.5 In carrying out their review of records for release to the public, authorities should observe the following points:
11.5.1 transfer to the Public Record Office must take place by the time the records are 30 years old, unless the Lord Chancellor gives authorisation for them to be retained for a longer period of time (see section 3 (4) of the Public Records Act 1958). By agreement with the Public Record Office, transfer and release may take place before 30 years;

11.5.2 review – for selection and release – should therefore take place before the records in question are 30 years old.

11.5.3 in Northern Ireland transfer under the Public Records Act (NI) 1923 to the Public Record Office of Northern Ireland is normally at 20 years.

11.6 In the case of records to be transferred to the Public Record Office or to a place of deposit appointed under section 4 of the Public Records Act 1958, or to the Public Record Office of Northern Ireland, the purpose of the review of records for release to the public is to:

- consider which information must be available to the public on transfer because no exemptions under the FOIA apply;
- consider which information must be available to the public at 30 years because relevant exemptions in the FOIA have ceased to apply;
- consider whether the information must be released in the public interest, notwithstanding the application of an exemption under the FOIA; and
- consider which information merits continued protection in accordance with the provisions of the FOIA.

11.7 If the review results in the identification of specified information which the authorities consider ought not to be released under the terms of the FOIA, the authorities should prepare a schedule identifying this information precisely, citing the relevant exemption(s), explaining why the information may not be released and identifying a date at which either release would be appropriate or a date at which the case for release should be reconsidered. Where the information is environmental information to which the exemption at Section 39 of the FOIA applies, the schedule should cite the appropriate exception in the Environmental Information Regulations. This schedule must be submitted to the Public Record Office or, in Northern Ireland, to the Public Record Office of Northern Ireland prior to transfer which must be before the records containing the information are 30 years old (in the case of the Public Record Office) or 20 years old (in the case of the Public Record Office of Northern Ireland). Authorities should consider whether parts of records might be released if the sensitive information were blanked out.

11.8 In the first instance, the schedule described in 11.7 is to be submitted to the Public Record Office for review and advice. The case in favour of withholding the records for a period longer than 30 years is then considered by the Advisory Council. The Advisory Council may respond as follows:

a. by accepting that the information may be withheld for longer than 30 years and earmarking the records for release or re-review at the date identified by the authority;
b. by accepting that the information may be withheld for longer than 30 years but asking the authority to reconsider the later date designated for release or re-review;
c. by questioning the basis on which it is deemed that the information may be withheld for longer than 30 years and asking the authority to reconsider the case;
d. by advising the Lord Chancellor if it is not satisfied with the responses it receives from authorities on particular cases;

e. by taking such other action as it deems appropriate within its role as defined in the Public Records Act.

In Northern Ireland there are separate administrative arrangements requiring that schedules are submitted to a Sensitivity Review Group consisting of representatives of different departments. The Sensitivity Review Group has the role of advising public authorities as to the appropriateness or otherwise of releasing records.

11.9 For the avoidance of doubt, none of the actions described in this Code affects the statutory rights of access established under the FOIA. Requests for information in public records transferred to the Public Record Office or to a place of deposit appointed under section 4 of the Public Records Act 1958 or to the Public Record Office of Northern Ireland will be dealt with on a case by case basis in accordance with the provisions of the FOIA.

11.10 Where records are transferred to the Public Record Office or a place of deposit before they are 30 years old, they should be designated by the transferring department or agency for immediate release unless an exemption applies: there will be no formal review of these designations.

11.11 When an exemption has ceased to apply under section 63 of the FOIA the records will become automatically available to members of the public on the day specified in the finalised schedule (i.e. the schedule after it has been reviewed by the Advisory Council). In other cases, if the authority concerned wishes further to extend the period during which the information is to be withheld in accordance with the FOIA, it should submit a further schedule explaining the sensitivity of the information. This is to be done before the expiry of the period stated in the earlier schedule. The Public Record Office and Advisory Council will then review the schedule in accordance with the process described in paragraph 11.8 above. In Northern Ireland, Ministerial approval is required for any further extension of the stated period.

11.12 In reviewing records an authority may identify those which are appropriate for retention within the department, after they are 30 years old, under section 3(4) of the Public Records Act 1958. Applications must be submitted to the Public Record Office for review and advice. The case in favour of retention beyond the 30 year period will then be considered by the Advisory Council. The Advisory Council will consider the case for retaining individual records unless there is already in place a standing authorisation by the Lord Chancellor for the retention of a whole category of records. It will consider such applications on the basis of the guidance in chapter 9 of the White Paper *Open Government* (Cm 2290, 1993) or subsequent revisions of government policy on retention.

ANNEX A
Standards Accepted in Records Management

British Standards (BSI)

BS 4783	Storage, transportation and maintenance of media for use in data processing and information storage
BS 7799	Code of practice for information security management
BS ISO 15489-1	Information and Documentation – Records Management – Part 1: General
PD 0008	Code of practice for legal admissibility and evidential weight of information stored on electronic document management systems
PD 0010	Principles of good practice for information management
PD 0012	Guide to the practical implications of the Data Protection Act 1998

Public Record Office standards for the management of public records

The Public Record Office publishes standards, guidance and toolkits on the management of public records, in whatever format, covering their entire life cycle. They are available on the Public Record Office website (http://www.pro.gov.uk/recordsmanagement).[2]

---

[2] See the updated website www.nationalarchives.gov.uk.

Appendix 2:
Model action plan

MODEL ACTION PLAN FOR DEVELOPING RECORDS MANAGEMENT COMPLIANT WITH THE LORD CHANCELLOR'S CODE OF PRACTICE UNDER SECTION 46 OF THE FREEDOM OF INFORMATION ACT 2000

[2]
Model Action Plan for
Local Government

August 2002

1   INTRODUCTION

1.1   The Lord Chancellor's *Code of Practice on the Management of Records under Freedom of Information* has been issued in accordance with the requirements of section 46 of the Freedom of Information Act 2000. It has been designed, in consultation with public authorities, to support the objectives of Freedom of Information (FOI) legislation by setting out the practices which public authorities should follow in relation to creating, keeping, managing and disposing of their records.

1.2   The report of the Advisory Group on Openness in the Public Sector (December 1999) recommended that all public authorities should develop records management action plans detailing the steps which they will take to reach the standards set out in the Code of Practice. To assist in this process the Public Record Office (PRO) undertook to produce model action plans for public authorities to use as the basis for their own action plans.

1.3   Different parts of the public sector have different requirements in this area. Although the main elements of a model action plan would be relevant to all, some minor issues might not be. Accordingly variations to the model plan are being developed aimed at different parts of the public sector. This version of the plan is aimed at local government authorities.

1.4   The model plan focuses on the actions required to prepare records management practices specifically for FOI. Many of the actions are similar to those required in preparing for electronic service delivery by 2005 – successful delivery of electronic services is underpinned by an effective infrastructure which includes the creation and management of records created in the course of service delivery. The plan is not suggesting that the two sets of actions need to be carried out separately for the different purposes, but rather provides a checklist of FOI requirements so that they can be built into existing activities wherever possible.

2   FOCUS

2.1   This action plan focuses on how information is acquired, and how it should be organised and retrieved, so that responses to FOI requests can be dealt with quickly and efficiently. The actions are first presented chronologically in the summary below in section 3 and are then presented thematically in greater detail, following the themes set out in the Code of Practice

3   ACTION POINTS: SUMMARY

While the timing of each action point is indicative, it is important to follow the sequence of steps in any authority action plan. The following table summarises the action points and provides a recommended timetable:

Completion by	Milestone (see related text in the model plan)	Code Ref
31 Jan 2003	1. Examine functional organisation to see whether responsibility for FOI implementation and departmental records can be placed in the same area *(4.1.1)*	5.1
	2. Ensure that all information functions are part of the same command or that there are close working relationships between them *(4.1.2)*	5.1
30 Apr 2003	1. Undertake an audit of records management to establish the need for action to reach compliance with the Code, and establish lines of communication with FOI champion/officer *(4.2.2)*	
	2. Analyse business activities in preparation for drafting an overall records management policy statement *(4.3.1)* and departmental statements *(4.3.2)*	6
30 June 2003	1. Ensure that adequate resources are in place to support the records management function *(4.1.3)*	7.3
	2. Establish a competency framework to identify skills and knowledge required by records management staff *(4.2.4)*	7.3
	3. Establish the need, or otherwise, for records management support staff *(4.2.3)*	7.3
	4. Make available the agreed records management policy statements *(4.3.3)*	6
	5. Draw up a programme on awareness of records management issues for inclusion in induction training *(4.4.1)*	7.3
30 September 2003	1. Recruit records management support staff, if required *(4.2.5)*	7.3
	2. Complete an information survey *(4.5.1)*	8.4
31 January 2004	1. Introduce a programme of professional training for records management staff *(4.4.2)*	7.3
	2. Design and implement a system to ensure that records are appraised in good time *(4.7.1)*	9.4
	3. Design and implement a system for documenting appraisal decisions *(4.7.2)*	9.5
	4. Design and implement a system for documenting disclosure and non-disclosure decisions *(4.8.1)*	8
30 June 2004	1. Ensure that record keeping systems are in place that meet operational needs and accord with the regulatory environment *(4.5.2)*	8.5 & 8.6

237

Completion by	Milestone (see related text in the model plan)	Code Ref
	2. Ensure that records maintenance procedures are in place that enable the quick and efficient location and retrieval of information *(4.6.2)*	8.7 & 8.8
	3. Ensure that a business recovery plan is in place *(4.6.1)*	8.9
1 January 2005	Establish a performance measurement scheme for the records management system *(4.9)*	6.2

4 ACTION POINTS: DESCRIPTION

4.1 The Records Management Function

Records management is a corporate function, in a similar way to human resources, finance and estates management. With other issues such as FOI and data protection it is a vital part of information management as a whole.

Objective: **To secure a co-ordinated approach to the management of information**

Steps:

4.1.1 Review the structure of the organisation to see what changes might be required to achieve this objective.

4.1.2 Ensure that all information functions are part of the same command or, alternatively, working arrangements for close liaison have been established.

4.1.3 Ensure that adequate resources to support the records management function are in place, working with those responsible for determining the level of resources and those responsible for assigning such resources.

The inclusion of information management functions within the same command will ensure co-ordinated and consistent progress towards the implementation of FOI and the achievement of other Government objectives under the *Modernising Local Government* agenda.

4.2 Roles and Responsibilities of Records Managers

Records management responsibilities must be clearly defined and assigned, and made known throughout the organisation.

Objective: **To ensure relevant staff understand their responsibilities and acquire the necessary skills**

Steps:

4.2.1 Ensure that a Records Manager is in place. The requirement will meet the provisions outlined in the International Standard ISO 15489, *Records Management*, and in Section 224 of the Local Government Act 1972.

4.2.2 Priorities for the Records Manager will be to conduct an audit of records management practices against the Code of Practice to establish whether action is needed to reach compliance and to liaise closely with the appointed FOI champion/officer.

4.2.3 Assess the need for records management support staff.

4.2.4 Establish a competency framework to identify the skills and knowledge required by records management staff. A model framework is set out in *Records Management: Human Resources* (PRO, 1999).

4.2.5 Where the need for additional resources has been identified, ensure that the records management support staff are in place.

4.2.6 Ensure that the responsibilities of each person undertaking records management roles are set out in a performance agreement, role description or similar document, within one month of appointment.

The identification of professional skills and knowledge will enable departments to recruit and train staff at a level which will ensure that the records management function acquires the appropriate professional standing.

4.3 Records Management Policy Statement

A policy statement on how the authority manages its records must be drawn up and made available to all staff.

Objective: **To ensure business information is managed effectively throughout the organisation by providing an authoritative statement on the management of records**

Steps:

4.3.1 Undertake an analysis of the organisation's business activities and the environment in which they take place. From this analysis draw up an overall records management policy statement. Its aim will be to provide a record keeping system, which will:

- meet the authority's business needs
- address the needs of the authority's stakeholders
- conform to relevant legislation, regulations and standards
- provide a basis for accountability
- identify in general terms responsibilities for records and in particular refer to the role of the Records Manager

See also action point 4.5.1

4.3.2 Supporting the overall policy statement there should be departmental records management policy statements agreed between the council departments and the Records Manager.

4.3.3 Make available the final records management policy statements to all staff, having secured the approval of the Chief Officers.

The records management policy statements provide a mandate for the performance of all records and information management functions.

4.4 Training and Awareness

Training in records management policies and procedures takes place at two levels:
- *professional development for records management staff*
- *awareness of records issues and practices by all members of staff*

240

Objective: **To ensure records staff are appropriately qualified, trained or experienced and that all staff understand the need for records management**

Steps:

4.4.1   Ensure that all induction training programmes, as well as FOI and other related training programmes, include awareness sessions on record keeping issues.

4.4.2   Draw up a programme of professional training for records staff. This will involve the Records Manager working with training and development staff. The programme should identify particular records management training needs in the light of the competency framework and arrange for those needs to be met, using internal and external training as appropriate. The programme should be ongoing.

The professional training of records staff and the awareness by all staff of records management issues will ensure that the records management function receives the appropriate quality of support.

4.5   Records Creation and Record Keeping

Each authority must have in place a record keeping system that documents its activities and provides for the quick and easy retrieval of information.

Objective: **To ensure information can be identified and retrieved when required by providing a well-structured record keeping system**

Steps:

4.5.1   The Records Manager will need to undertake an information survey. The basis for this will be the analysis undertaken at action point 4.3.1; this survey should determine whether:

● business areas of the authority are creating records that adequately document their activities
● records are linked with metadata which documents and provides for their business and other contexts

241

- records are arranged in a record keeping system that enables the authority to retrieve information quickly and efficiently and facilitates implementation of authorised disposal arrangements
- the record keeping system or associated procedures and guidelines includes guidance on referencing, titling, indexing and protective marking
- the record keeping system is adequately documented
- record keeping procedures and guidelines are established and methods for measuring compliance with them are in place

See also action point 4.6.

4.5.2 Where the above arrangements are not in place, Records Managers will need to prepare plans so that by full implementation of FOI authorities have in place record keeping systems that meet   their operational needs and accord with the regulatory environment.

The need to locate and retrieve information takes on added importance under FOI. The requirements of sections 1 and 16 of the FOI Act cannot be met unless adequate record keeping systems are in place.

4.6   Record Maintenance

The record keeping system must be maintained so that the records are properly stored and protected, and can easily be located and retrieved.

Objective: To ensure authentic records are maintained over time by providing appropriate protection of records throughout their life cycle

Steps:

4.6.1 The information survey described in action point 4.5 should also determine whether:

- adequate storage accommodation is provided for the records
- a tracking system is in place that controls the movement and location of records so that they can be easily retrieved
- access controls are in place
- a business recovery plan is in place that provides for the protection of vital records

242

4.6.2   Where the above arrangements are not in place, Records Managers will need to prepare plans so that by full implementation of FOI authorities have in place records maintenance procedures that enable them to locate and retrieve information quickly and efficiently.

The efficient maintenance of records will ensure that they receive adequate protection from fire, flood, theft, etc and can easily be located and retrieved when required.

4.7   Record Disposal

Authorities must have in place clearly defined arrangements for the appraisal and selection of records, and for documenting such work.

Objective: To ensure selection and disposal decisions can be explained by careful documentation of the appraisal and disposal of records

Steps:

4.7.1   Ensure that the authority has in place systems for records to be appraised in time for their archival preservation and availability for research in accordance with agreed procedures under section 224 of the Local Government Act 1972. These should comprise:

- a system to assess the amount of records due for review and disposal each year
- a programme to compile selection policies for each business unit of the authority
- a programme to prepare disposal schedules for records common to several business units schedules can be cost-effective if applied to some rather than all units
- a system to implement selection policies and disposal schedules for each year or cycle
- contingency planning to ensure that minimal risk is entailed in the event of delay in appraisal
- the transfer of records selected for permanent preservation to the local archives
- the timely destruction of records not selected for permanent preservation and no longer required for business purposes

4.7.2   Ensure that the authority has in place a system for documenting appraisal decisions. This should include information on records selected for permanent preservation, destroyed or retained by the authority. Disposal schedules may form part of this document-ation.

It is particularly important under FOI that there are clearly defined policies and procedures for disposing of records (either by destruction or transfer to an archives) and that these are well documented. This will provide appropriate evidence in the event of questions about the provision of information under FOI.

4.8 Access

Authorities must have in place clearly defined arrangements for documenting exemption and disclosure decisions.

Objective: To ensure access decisions are documented so that they are consistent, and can be explained and referred to

4.8.1   Authorities should have in place systems for recording when information has been disclosed and, if disclosure has been refused, the reasons for non-disclosure.

4.9 Performance Measurement

Objective: To identify whether information is being managed effectively through monitoring of compliance with records management policies and procedures

Steps:

4.9.1   Ensure that the authority has in place a scheme that will monitor the performance of the records management system. This should include performance indicators on:
   ● quantity of records created (for example, in linear metres or megabytes)
   ● response times in providing information from the records or retrieving the records themselves

- quantity of records appraised, selected and destroyed or transferred to the archives
- user satisfaction

Performance measurement is necessary to relate records activities to needs, to assess the efficiency or effectiveness of records activities, and to demonstrate value and accountability.

Appendix 3:
Acts and Regulations (UK)

The following list comprises provisions that may impact on records and information management. Organisations should obtain professional legal advice on the application of these provisions.

Access to Health Records Act 1990
Access to Medical Reports Act 1988
Census (Confidentiality) Act 1991
Civil Evidence Act 1995
Computer Misuse Act 1990
Consumer Protection Act 1987
Control of Substances Hazardous to Health Regulations 2002 (COSHH)
Copyright, Designs and Patents Act 1990
Crime and Disorder Act 1998
Data Protection Act 1998
Electronic Communications Act 2000
Environmental Information Regulations 2004
Freedom of Information Act 2000
Health and Safety at Work Act 1974
Health and Social Care Act 2001
Human Rights Act 1998
Limitation Act 1980
Police and Criminal Evidence Act 1984 (PACE)
Privacy and Electronic Communications Regulations 2003
Public Interest Disclosure Act 1998
Public Records Acts 1958 and 1967
Radioactive Substances Act 1993
Re-use of Public Sector Information Regulations 2005

Appendix 4: Bibliography and other Sources

Access to Health Records Act 1990

Access to Medical Reports Act 1988

Access to Personal Files Act 1987

Australian Standard AS 4390–1996, Records Management

British Standards Institute *Effective Records Management: Management Guide to the Value of BS/ISO 15489* (ref: BIP 0025–1)

British Standards Institute *Effective Records Management: Practical Implementation of BS/ISO 15489* (ref: BIP 0025–2)

British Standards Institute *Effective Records Management: Performance Management of BS/ISO 15489* (ref: BIP 0025–3)

British Standards Institute *BIP 0008 Legal Admissibility and Evidential Weight of Information Stored Electronically*

British Standards Institute *PD 0010 Principles of Good Practice for Information Management*

British Standards Institute *BS 7799–1 Code of practice for information security management*

British Standards Institute *Code of Practice for Legal Admissibility and Evidential Weight of Information Stored Electronically, PD0008* (2006)

British Standards Institute *Principles of Good Practice for Information Management* , PD 0010 (1996)

Brown, A *Archiving Websites: a practical guide for information management professionals* (2006)

BS 1153: *Processing and storage of silver-gelatin type microfilm* (1992)

BS 4737: *Intruder alarms systems*

BS 4783: *Storage, transportation and maintenance of media for use in data processing and information storage* (1988)

BS 5454: *Recommendations for the storage and exhibition of archival documents* (2000)

BS 5588: *Fire precautions in the design, construction and use of buildings*

BS 5839: *Fire detection and alarm systems in buildings*

BS 5979: *Code of Practice for remote centres for alarm systems*

BS 7042: *Specification for high security intruder alarm systems in buildings*

BS 7799: *Code of practice for information security management*

BS/ISO 15489: *Information and documentation – records management Part1, General* (2001)

Code of Practice Access to Government Information (April 1994)

Code of Practice for Information Security Management (BSI, BS 7799)

Code of Practice for Legal Admissibility and Evidential Weight of Information Stored Electronically (BSI, PD 0008)

Code of Practice on Access to Government Information, published 4 April 1994, second edition 1997

Code of Practice on Public Access to Information (National Assembly for Wales), third edition, December 2004

Code of Practice on the Management of Records under Section 46 of the Freedom of Information Act 2000 (Nov 2002)

Code of Practice on Openness in the NHS (1995)

Committee on Departmental Records: report (Grigg Report) (Cmd 9163) (1954)

Couture, C and Rousseau, -Y *The Life of a Document* (1987)

Data Protection Act 1998

Department of Health *Records Management: NHS Code of Practice*

Dublin Core metadata scheme www.dublincore.org

E-Government Policy Framework for Electronic Records Management (Public Records Office, July 2001)

Emmerson, P (ed) *How to manage your records; a guide to effective practice* (1989)

Encoded Archival Description (EAD) http://lcweb.loc.gov/ead/

Environmental Information Regulations 1992, 1998, 2004

Environmental protection Act 1990

Environmental and Safety Information Act 1988

Erlandsson, A *Electronic records management: a literature review* (ICA, 1996)

For the Record (HSC 1999/053), Department of Health, 1999

Fire Precaution Act 1971

Fire Precaution (Workplace) Regulations 1997

Freedom of Information Act 2000

Freedom of Information (Scotland) Act 2002

Hamer, A C *The ICSA Guide to Document Retention* (2004)

Hare, Catherine and McLeod, Julie *Developing a records management programme* (1997)

Health & Safety at Work Act 1974

Human Rights Act 1998

International Council of Archives (ICA) Study No 10, *Electronic Records Management: A Literature Review*, 1997, Summary, p. 7

ISAD(G): General International Standard Archival Description, second edition 1999 (International Council on Archives)

ISO 19005, Document management – Electronic document file format for long-term preservation – Part 1: Use of PDF 1.4 (PDF/A–I)

Jenkinson, H *Manual of Archive Administration* (1966)

Kennedy, J and Schauder, C *Records management: a guide to corporate record keeping* (1998)

Knightbridge, A A H *Archive legislation in the United Kingdom* (1985)

Land Registry Act 1988

Limitation Act 1980

Local Authorities (Executive Arrangements) (Access to Information) (England) Regulations 2000

Local Government Act 1972 (s224)

Local Government Act 2000

Local Government (Access to Information) Act 1985

Local Government (Records) Act 1962

Local Government (Scotland) Act 1973

Lord Chancellor's Department *Government Policy on Archives* (1999)

The Manorial Documents Rules 1959 and 1967

McKemmish, S and Piggott, M *The records continuum* (1994)

Modernising Government (Cmnd. 4310)

Moreq, Model requirements for the management of electronic records (2001); see www.cornwell.co.uk/moreq

National Archives and Records Administration (USA), *A Modern Archives Reader* (1984)

The National Archives – Business Classification Scheme Design (2003)

The National Archives – Records Management Standards and Guidance (1999–2005), see www.nationalarchives.gov.uk/recordsmanagement/

National Archives of Australia DIRKS: a strategic approach to managing business information (2001); see www.naa.gov.au/recordkeeping/dirks/

National Archives of Scotland www.nas.gov.uk

National Heritage (Scotland) Act 1985

Open Goverment, Cm 2290, July 1993

Parker, E *Managing your organisation's records* (1999)

Parochial Registers and records Measure 1978 and 1993

PRINCE 2, Introduction to PRINCE 2: management overview (2001); see www.ogc.gov.uk/prince/

Procter, M and Cook, M *Manual of Archival Description* (2000)

Public Interest Disclosure Act 1998

Public Record Office [now The National Archives] Model Action Plans for developing records management compliant with the Lord Chancellor's Code of Practice under section 46 of the Freedom of Information Act 2000; see http://www.nationalarchives.gov.uk/recordsmanagement/code/model_action_plans.htm

Public Record Office *Acquisition Policy* 1998

Public Record Office *Disposition Policy* 2000

Public Records Act (Northern Ireland) 1923

Public Records Acts 1958 and 1967

Public Records (Scotland) Act 1937

Public Registers and Records (Scotland) Act 1948

Records Management: NHS Code of Practice (Department of Health), April 2006

Rehabilitation of Offenders Act 1972

Royal Commission on Historical Manuscripts *A standard for record repositories* (1990)

Schellenberg, T R *Modern archives: principles and techniques* (1956)

Study of the Records Life Cycle (JISC – www.jisc.ac.uk)

Tithe Rules 1960 and 1963

Wilson Committee Report, *Modern Public Records, Selection and Access* 1981, Cmnd 8204

Index